Praise for *Schmoozing*

"A book about how Jews talk by a philosopher who knows how Jews think—what a delightful and perfect combination."

> —Joseph Telushkin, author
> of *Biblical Literacy* and
> *Words That Hurt, Words
> That Heal*

"This is a brave and exciting book. Even better, there is truth on every page, expressed with charm, verve, humor, and compassion."

> —Neil Postman, author of
> *Amusing Ourselves to
> Death*

"This fascinating study of the American Jewish personality lifts the veil on matters discussed only in private. Honesty and self-recognition break forth on every page. It makes one think that Jews have a special prayer thanking God for being so complicated. There is plenty of grist here for further reflection and *schmoozing*."

> —George P. Fletcher,
> Cardozo Professor of
> Jurisprudence, Columbia
> University School of Law

schmoozing

The Private Conversations
of American Jews

Joshua Halberstam, Ph.D.

A Perigee Book

A Perigee Book
Published by The Berkley Publishing Group
A member of Penguin Putnam Inc.
200 Madison Avenue
New York, NY 10016

First edition: October 1997

Published simultaneously in Canada.

The Putnam Berkley World Wide Web site address is
http://www.berkley.com

Library of Congress Cataloging-in-Publication Data

Halberstam, Joshua, 1946–
    Schmoozing : the private conversations of American Jews / Joshua
    Halberstam.
        p.   cm.
    ISBN 0-399-52157-7
    1. Jews—United States—Attitudes.   2. Jews—United States—
Interviews.   3. United States—Ethnic relations.   I. Title.
E184.J5H256   1997
305.892'4073—dc21   97-3530
                                                            CIP

Printed in the United States of America

10   9   8   7   6   5   4   3   2   1

For my children, Ariana and Amitai,
with love and admiration.

Contents

Acknowledgments

I am asked repeatedly, "Why write a book on the private conversations of American Jews? Do you think Jews are so secure that they can risk washing their laundry in public? Why parade before the world these discussions about Jews and money, Jewish intelligence, Jews and their attitudes toward fellow Jews and non-Jews—Why ask for trouble?" I point out that the book portrays the successes of American Jews at least as much as their failures, but this hardly calms the worries. "Why flaunt our triumphs? All you generate is envy and anger."

These are serious concerns. Anyone writing a book of this kind can't be flippant about communal obligations, especially when the community has a history as fragile as that of the Jews. I am convinced, however, that this is the right and needed thing to do. Right, because if this blood-soaked century has taught Jews anything, it is the folly of believing that what they say or do is the cause of their enemies' animosity. Needed, because this is a critical period in the history of American Judaism, and American Jews need to hear each other's ideas, and read each other's hearts. Honest self-reflection is a healing process and an enobling one too. This is true not just for American Jews but for all Americans.

Acknowledgments

If we are ever to manage our ethnic divisions with intelligence and dignity, we need to ratchet up our tolerance levels and really listen to what Americans say when they drop the posturing and express their genuine beliefs within their own diverse communities.

Given these concerns, my thanks to all those who encouraged this project is all the more heartfelt. The conversations in this book emerge from the thousands of discussions I had with individuals across the American Jewish spectrum, and from dozens of in-depth interviews. Some of these people appear in the book by name and in their own words. In other instances, a reticence to be publicly identified required a change in name; I can assure the reader, however, that the relevant characteristics of these individuals and the content of their remarks are genuine. Quoted or not, my thanks to them all.

And now some special thank-yous. These individuals read earlier versions of the book and provided gracious and perspicacious comments (apologies if I forgot anyone—the book has been a long time in arriving): Gina Biegeleisen, Rabbi Irwin Kula, Dr. Larry Lowenthal, Shimon Neustein, Seth Siegel, Peter Silverman, and Rabbi Moshe Waldoks (an outstanding schmoozer who also suggested the title of the book). And my wife, Yocheved Cohen, for doing it all, yet again, but of course. The book was brought to Perigee by Julie Merberg, held to the highest editorial standards by John Duff and then—lucky me—turned over to Suzanne Bober, whose outstanding editorial skills, intelligence, and sensitivity helped so much in the formation of this book. Suzanne, thank you. And thanks to my agent, Agnes Birnbaum.

The book is dedicated to my wonderful children, Ariana and Amitai. Keep the conversation going, guys.

schmoozing

The Private Conversations
of American Jews

Introduction

Fingerprints will get you every time. So this clever thief decides to have his fingerprints surgically removed, figuring that this way he will become anonymous and avoid apprehension. But of course when the police come upon a robbery with no telltale fingerprints, they immediately trace the crime to him—he is the only one in town without fingerprints.

There are no generic individuals. As the philosopher George Santayana noted, "It is no more possible to be a human being in general than it is to speak a language in general." This is why all great narratives are about lives lived in the concrete. Homer tells stories about the specific battles of specific Greeks, Dostoevski writes about the inner turmoil of particular nineteenth-century Russians, Cervantes narrates the dreams of one romantic Spaniard, and Faulkner describes the tribulations of individuals in the poor American South. World literature, the literature that speaks to everyone, is always the literature of someone.

There are no generic communities either. Each has its own legacy of pride and despair. Each has its own unique fingerprints. This particularism is the central universal truth of all communi-

1

ties. It is the lesson America must take to heart as it becomes home to more and more groups who insist on maintaining their own heritage and interests. If you want to know how communities work, don't theorize. Look. And listen. Surveys can provide mounds of helpful data, but that information, in itself, is cold and bloodless. To discover genuine concerns and convictions, the actual hostilities and hopes of a community, you need to hear the talk behind closed doors.

This book listens in on one of those communal discussions—the private conversations of American Jews.

Both by choice and by force of circumstance, American Jews have managed to maintain a remarkable array of communal structures. It hasn't been easy—a barbarous century attests to that. But now the very openness of American society confronts American Jews with a threat of disintegration in many ways more dangerous than any they have previously faced. How they grapple with the challenge of continuity will be immensely illuminating to other groups who already do or will soon face similar challenges. This "illumination by example" is indeed an essential feature of the Jewish people.

For millennia Jews have called on themselves to fulfill the biblical injunction to be "a light unto nations." Many have interpreted this phrase as an exhortation to teach ethics or justice or piety to people all over the world. For both philosophical reasons and Jewish reasons, I am unhappy with this standard interpretation and suggest a different reading, a more literal reading of the phrase "a light unto nations" (*ohr l'amim* in Hebrew): The Jewish nation is told to be a light, not to individuals, but to other nations. By dint of their biblical covenant and long, complex experience, a history that, alas, also includes disastrous internal bickering and catastrophic miscalculation, the Jews have learned important lessons about building and sustaining community. These are lessons they desperately need to review themselves and can profitably share with others.

Which American Jews are we talking about? The religious or the secular? The conservatives or the liberals? The alienated or the committed? This book steadfastly tries to include the discussions of them all, for any comprehensive overview of the American Jewish community must encompass everyone, from the extreme ultra-Orthodox Jew to the confirmed atheist Jew. Indeed, one motive for writing this book is to remind American Jews of all persuasions just how much they have in common.

My personal history allows me to be privy to conversations that span the range of American Judaism, and I'm constantly struck by the similarities in attitudes that I hear when schmoozing in Yiddish with my Chassidic family in Brooklyn and when schmoozing with my totally secular Jewish friends ''out in the world.'' Individuals on both ends of the spectrum would be startled to learn how similar they are when it comes to issues of self-image and their core concerns as Jews.

Which conversations are included here? Despite my claims for comprehensive inclusion, some discussions are pointedly excluded. You won't find, for example, separate entries for religion and politics. Some may find the omission of these topics glaring, so let me explain their absence.

Countless books, and a few excellent ones among them, survey the religious landscape of Jewish America. You can find books documenting the state of religious belief of American Jews, the theological differences among the various denominations, and more than a few devoted to reinvigorating Jewish spirituality.

There is no need to duplicate that material here. Moreover, while American Jews do often talk about their religious beliefs, or lack thereof, rarely does that conversation move across the theological divides. If you ask a series of questions about the nature of God, the coming of the Messiah, afterlife, evolution, the election of Israel, and the inerrancy of the Bible, you would find that the beliefs of most Reform Jews are closer to those of Unitarian Christians than to those of Orthodox Jews. Orthodox Jews, for their part, share more beliefs with fundamentalist Christians than with theologically liberal Jews. Nonetheless, when it comes to key issues of community and communal self-definition—the topics discussed in this book—Jews across the religious span speak a common language. The Jewish theologian Richard Rubenstein was on target when he concluded that "far more Jews today accept the unity of Jewish destiny than the unity of Jewish belief."

For much the same reason, there is little emphasis here on the political differences that now rage within the American Jewish community. A significant proportion of American Jews is shifting to a conservative politics while the majority of Jews continue to espouse, and vote, the liberal point of view. A parallel hard-line/soft-line dispute among American Jews proceeds with regard to Israel's policies. Although these debates are more about personal politics than Judaism, each side is busy stamping its views with the imprimatur of "true to Jewish tradition"—in other words, these arguments are characterized by a whole lot of apologetic justification. Political polemics (and religious concerns too, for that matter) appear in various guises throughout the conversations chronicled in this book—how could they not? But they are not given center stage. First, journals of opinion devoted to these issues already abound; second, because those discussions

4

typically address the day's hot news and not the underlying, long-term concerns of the American Jewish community, they are best left analyzed elsewhere.

Which conversations are explored here? Those that are directed to the self-image and core values of the American Jews—how they perceive their intelligence, their bodies, their money, their personalities, their future in the United States, as well as how they perceive their enemies, other ethnic groups, and non-Jews in general. And there is more: What do American Jews find funny and what do they deem threatening? Who are their heroes and who are their traitors?

American Judaism is at a pivotal stage in its development, and these private conversations reflect both the anxiety and the promise of the moment. As never before, the destiny of American Jewry is in its own hands. The No Admittance signs have largely vanished, and an overt Jewish identity is rarely an impediment to higher office in government, the professions, or the corporation. American Jews can assimilate as much as they please—America will accept them, and the Jewish community can't stop them. No Jewish community in the Diaspora has ever enjoyed such freedom, so there are no precedents to rely on for guidance.

As the American Jewish community gears itself for the century ahead, it looks back to a century during which it has dramatically transformed its self-image. This has been, after all, a remarkable period in Jewish history and a breathless roller coaster for American Jews in particular. As are Jews everywhere, American Jews, if only subliminally, are still shell-shocked from the worst trauma of their national history.

As Winston Churchill said, the Holocaust was "probably the greatest and most horrible crime ever committed in the whole history of the world,'' and it happened not a thousand years ago, but just a half century ago, not to just anyone, but to the families of American Jews. The implications of this horror and the possibility of future similar horrors are ever-present backdrops to every Jewish conversation. This century has also seen the creation of Israel. The majority of American Jews have grown up with the reality of a flourishing Jewish state, a permanent haven but one under constant siege. The identity of American Jewry has become intimately informed by its relationship with Israel, and this connection will continue in the years ahead.

The immediate attention of American Jews, however, is directed not at recent European history, or the Middle East, but at their own astonishing development in the United States. The attrition rate has been high, as Jews increasingly desert the Jewish community. More and more Jews have fewer and fewer children. Jews are, on average, older than any other ethnic group in the country. Judaic illiteracy is widespread. But on other measures, Jews are thriving—so much that sociologists consider American Jews the most successful immigrant group of the past hundred years. For example, American Jews are the richest group in the United States. They are also the best educated. American Jews occupy positions of power and influence in nearly every facet of American business. And while anti-Semitism is a constant threat, it is rarely a tangible threat. The contrast between the triumphs of contemporary American Judaism and the struggles at the beginning of the century is truly startling.

The changes have been dramatic, but they are just beginning. Eavesdropping on the private conversations of American Jews—as this book does—reveals again and again that contemporary American Judaism is in its earliest stages of formation. Although Jews have been in this country from its incipiency, and although the United States has been home to the largest Jewish population in the world for more than a half century, until recently American Jews have lived off the cultural baggage brought over by their European parents and grandparents. But now 85 percent of American Jews were born in the United States, and a majority are at least third-generation Americans. Even those American Jews who steadfastly retain the religious faith and rituals of their ancestors are shedding the European cultural habits of their forebears. With few exceptions, American Jews no longer have their own language—the American Jewish press, the lingua franca of the Jewish street, and even much of contemporary sacred writing are in English. Jewish foods survive only in the tired humor of tired comedians; American Jews are more familiar with sushi than gefilte fish. Jewish mothers and their sexually clumsy sons are fading figures in the quarter-of-a-century-old pages of *Portnoy's Complaint*. American Jews work and play like everyone else, and with regard to most cultural markers, they are indistinguishable from their Christian neighbors.

It is a mixed blessing. American Jews are happy to leave many of their ethnic trappings behind them, but many balk at the head-long rush to embrace the pervasive purposelessness of the contemporary "American" ethos (an ethos to which American Jews themselves have contributed so much). At the same time, American Jews are fully committed to the modern values of individualism, egalitarianism, and tolerance. But how do they preserve a communal heritage without lapsing into chauvinism? How do they teach group identity to their children while preaching the equality of all? These are not impossible goals, of course, but no one should assume they can be achieved without strain. Undoubtedly, this dilemma is endemic to the conversations of all communities in open societies; they certainly punctuate the private conversations of American Jews.

This is a book about talk, but there is an unspoken theme that suffuses this book. In his best-selling book *Chutzpah,* Alan Dershowitz argues that American Jews are unnecessarily diffident about their status in the United States. It still hasn't sunk into their heads that they are not just visitors at the beneficence of the non-Jewish "real" Americans. He writes: "Notwithstanding the stereotype, we are not pushy or assertive enough for our own good or for the good of our more vulnerable brothers and sisters in other parts of the world. . . . We don't appreciate how much we have contributed to the greatness of this country and don't accept that we are entitled to first-class status in this diverse and heterogeneous democracy." I think he is right, but more follows. It isn't enough for American Jews to applaud their achievements. They also owe it to themselves and to other Americans to better understand the ingredients that gave rise to this success.

American Jews have not succeeded by accident; they have succeeded because of their values. They do no one a favor by being coy about this. But, as these conversations demonstrate, American Jews also continue to be hampered by self-doubt, internal division, and charred self-esteem. They certainly cannot afford to be coy about these flaws either. The conversations explore these pockets of pride and defeat. As they enter the next century, American Jews need to ask themselves which values have sustained them in the past and which values they want to sustain in the century ahead. We need to talk about this.

CHAPTER ONE

Jews Talk About Money

What is the object of the Jew's worship in this world? Usury. What is his god? Money. Money is the zealous God of Israel beside which no other God may stand. The bill of exchange is the Jew's real God.   Karl Marx

Know that wherever there is money, there is the Jew.
                                        Charles Montesquieu

Bargain like a Jew but pay like a Christian.
                                        Polish proverb

A real Jew will get gold out of straw.
                                        Spanish proverb

With money in your pocket, not only are you wise and handsome, but you sing well too.
                                        Yiddish proverb

A Chassidic rebbe said that wisdom and wealth were both virtues but wisdom the greater. Someone asked him, "Why, then, do the wise wait upon the rich, and not the rich upon the wise?"
    The rebbe answered, "Because the wise, being wise, appreciate the value of wealth, but the wealthy, being only wealthy, don't understand the value of wisdom."

Part I. Money: Getting It

I don't know this man. He's a friend of the friend who invited me to this civilized, high-minded dinner party. He seems pleasant enough, intelligent and open-minded. He says to me, "My mother used to tell me that I must have Jewish blood because I've always had a knack for business." I must have seemed taken aback because he quickly added, "You aren't offended, are you? I meant it as a compliment."

I'm sure he did. And I don't think I was offended. Uneasy maybe, a feeling hovering between disappointment and bemusement. I've yet to figure out how to balance my checkbook, and the supposition that as a Jew I have some natural ability with money always strikes me as comical. But his remark certainly didn't surprise me; the bit about Jewish business acumen is something Jews hear all the time from their non-Jewish friends, their non-Jewish enemies, and at least as often from their fellow Jews.

Jews and money—there are so many variations on this constant theme. Jews love money, extraordinarily so. Jews are good at making money, exceptionally so. Jews are outstanding entrepreneurs. Jews are in league to control international finance. Jews are cheap. Jews are cheaters. From Buenos Aires to Baghdad, from the days of ancient Rome to the present, the world talks about Jews and their special relationship with wealth. This well-worn topic punctuates the proverbs of civilized and uncivilized nations alike, their jokes and their curses. The Jewish affinity for the dollar is surely the most famous—or infamous—Jewish attribute of all.

The really peculiar part of all these slogans about Jews and money, however, is the equivocation with which Jews react to the charges. Especially American Jews. Proud of their financial achievements, American Jews often congratulate themselves on their success, but when a non-Jew points to the same Jewish affluence, American Jews become extremely nervous and suspect lurking anti-Semitism. A long, painful Jewish history underwrites the anxiety. But what, then, is the reasonable response? How guarded, how coy, should this community be about its economic prosperity? In Jewish living rooms across the country, different generations, geographies, and personal experiences figure into a varying spectrum of opinion. Here, as so often in the private discourse of American Jewry, the immediate concern only masks a deeper worry: How secure, finally, is American Jewry in the United States?

This much is clear: Secure or not, American Jews have managed a stunning set of financial triumphs in this century, achieving a level of wealth without parallel in Jewish history. American Jews have a higher average income than any other religious denomination in the country. We should hasten to add that large numbers of American Jews are far from prosperous and some are desperately poor. But Jews, in general, thrive economically in the United States. According to current estimates the average income of Jews is nearly twice that of non-Jews. In terms of average income, the religious group that follows the Jews is the Unitarians, followed, in turn, by agnostics—and Jews constitute a significant number of both these categories. Altogether, not too bad for a community, most of whose members had great-grandparents who arrived in this country at the beginning of the century with a mean sum of nine dollars, even less than the average of fifteen dollars for other immigrants.

Each year *Forbes* magazine publishes a list of the four hundred richest Americans. There are only a handful of Italians, blacks, Hispanics, and Eastern European gentiles on this list. Based on their percentage of the national population, there should be eight Jews on the chart. But there are well over a hundred. Of the top forty names, nearly 40 percent are Jews. Billionaires? Nearly 30 percent are Jews. Or, to put this another way; there are more Jewish billionaires in the United States than the total number of billionaires in France and England combined. The high percentage of Jewish mega-rich is not restricted to the United States. Among Canada's most prominent families of wealth, for example, are the Belzbergs of Vancouver, the Bronfmans of Montreal, and the Reichmans of Toronto.

Furthermore, the Jewish presence in America's upper corridors of "new money" is increasing. In a 1994 special report on "The New Establishment" in *Vanity Fair,* writer Elise O'Shaughnessy argued, as do many, that the collective clout of the computer, entertainment, and communications industries now eclipses both Washington and Wall Street. The article profiled eighteen leaders, the power elite of this "new boys' network." Ten were Jewish. This exclusive club of media luminaries consisted of Bill Gates (Microsoft), John Malone (TCI), David Geffen (David Geffen Company), Michael Eisner (Walt Disney), Ray Smith (Bell Atlantic), Edgar Bronfman, Jr. (Seagram), Robert Allen (AT&T), Michael Ovitz (Creative Artists Agency), Sumner Redstone (Viacom), Gerald Levin (Time Warner), Craig McCaw (MCI), Barbra Streisand (Barwood Films Ltd.), Barry Diller (QVC), Ronald Perelman (MacAndrews & Forbes Holdings, Inc.), Oprah Winfrey (Harpo Productions), Ted Turner (Turner Broadcasting), Steven Spielberg (Amblin Entertainment), and Rupert Murdoch (The News Corporation). For those keeping score: No, Oprah Winfrey is not Jewish, but yes, Sumner Redstone is.

Who is counting? Jews and anti-Semites.

It is no surprise that anti-Semites compile such lists, but why should Jews? That's what many American Jews ponder.

"To what end?" asks Mrs. Stepha Goldreich. The Goldreichs have been living in the same well-appointed but moderate home in Fair Lawn, New Jersey, for the past thirty years. Mrs. Goldreich's earlier life was hardly as calm; a roller-coaster ride of comfort and destitution is a more accurate description. She grew up in middle-class surroundings in Vienna, spent two years in a German labor camp during the war, and in the early 1950s came to the United States with her husband, Bernard. With the help of a relative, Bernard Goldreich went into the real estate business, and, as they say, "he did all right for himself." Mrs. Goldreich is nonetheless offended by the display of Jewish wealth by American Jews. "There were a few well-known rich Jews back in the old country, but who was so brazen about it as the Jews are here in the United States? This showing-off is ugly and stupid. Why stick your success in everyone's face? Why ask for the envy? Jews should show more self-control."

Mrs. Goldreich's husband, Bernard, is equally upset by blatant displays of Jewish wealth. "American Jews are incredibly naive. Don't they know anything about history? These people coast along, ostentatious like it's nobody's business, oblivious to the hostility they generate. Don't they realize how easy it is to make the leap from the fact that many Jews are wealthy to the conclusion that there exists a vast Jewish conspiracy to control the economy? All it takes is a few visible millionaires, a few garish mansions, several key executive jobs, and people see a vast Jewish takeover of the country. Believe me, and unfortunately, I know this too well, plenty of non-Jews are ready to see Jews that way."

Does Jewish wealth engender hatred? Those who think it does point to prewar Germany for corroboration, suggesting eerie parallels to the situation of contemporary American Judaism. Despite representing less than 1 percent of Germany's population in the years 1819 to 1935, Jews controlled 20 percent of the country's commercial activity. In 1911 eleven of Prussia's twenty-five richest individuals and 27 percent of the country's two hundred wealthiest people were Jews. In the years right before World War II, Jews controlled 25 percent of retail sales. The most glaring overrepresentation of Jews in German commerce was in the entertainment sector. For example, in 1930, 80 percent of Berlin's theater directors were Jewish and 75 percent of the plays produced were written by Jews. The Nazis made a big deal of these numbers, proclaiming that the Jews had taken over the economy of the true Germans. Many Americans entertain a similar fantasy about Jewish control of the economy. A recent study by Daniel Yankelovich and his staff reveals that 25 percent of Americans believe that Jews have too much power in American business.

But others, also with an eye on Jewish history, insist that the economic condition of the Jews has little bearing on how much they are disliked. The Japanese may not know a Jew from a Bantu, but their best-seller lists regularly feature books "exposing" the clandestine schemes of international Jewish financiers. And even when Jews were starving, non-Jewish populations believed that the Jews controlled their country's economy. For much of their history in Eastern Europe, Jews barely eked out a living, yet were attacked as money-grubbing, conniving merchants; still today, along the roadsides in contemporary Jewless Poland, you can buy figurines of a bearded Jew carrying a pouch filled with gold, a magical talisman to help one's fortune. In any case, the ending was the same for both the rich and the poor Jewish communities of Europe—the wealthy Jews of Frankfurt were gassed together with their impoverished cousins from Lvov.

The Goldreichs' son, Michael, is visiting his parents and

thinks all these historical comparisons are useless. An endocrinologist with a thriving practice in Denver, Michael is perfectly at ease with his wealth and doesn't see why other American Jews shouldn't be as well. "It's paranoia . . . understandable, but paranoia nevertheless," he says. "My parents' apprehension of lurking anti-Semitism is a reflection of their hapless Jewish experience in Europe. The dread of having others notice one's assets seems to be bred in the Diaspora Jew's bones, a cowering so deep it's automatic. You know the joke, no?

" 'An immigrant Jew is hit by a car in Brooklyn. A policeman covers him with a blanket and asks if he's comfortable.

" 'Comfortable?' he answers. 'I make a living.'

"But look, searching for historical precedents is a red herring. American Jews must come to terms with the realization that this is America, not Rumania, not the Ukraine. It's time to get real— Jewish wealth isn't going to trigger pogroms in this country. Centuries ago, de Tocqueville described his wonder at how much Americans honor wealth. They still do. Here it's okay to have a fat wallet, especially if you worked for your money. If you got it fair and square, if you're entitled, then no matter who you are, nobody minds. On the contrary."

Many American Jews, and perhaps most younger American Jews, share Michael Goldreich's ease with Jewish displays of luxury. They are only mildly worried, if at all, that Jewish affluence will awaken dormant anti-Semitism, and many will tell you that the economic accomplishments of American Jews are at least as much admired as resented by the non-Jewish population. The attitude one often hears expressed is "Why should we hide behind the rags in the attic? Since anti-Semites don't like poor Jews any more than they like rich Jews, we might as well be rich and enjoy it.'' Moreover, they say, most Americans don't really care about balancing Jewish checkbooks—Jewish money isn't a problem for them. Yet what about that Yankelovich study indicating that a quarter of non-Jews think American Jews have too much economic power? The same study also found that three-quarters of American Jews incorrectly thought that most non-Jews believe that Jews have too much economic power; Jews assume non-Jewish ill will toward them, even when it isn't there. Suspicions of anti-Semitism are grounded in a sordid reality, but, along with Michael Goldreich, the younger generation of American Jews seems to believe that ''we debase ourselves when we hide our achievements out of fear of what the *goyim* will think.'' Michael looks at his parents, then at me, and says, ''It's the old story. As Abba Eban said, 'Jews are a people who won't take yes for an answer.' ''

The Holocaust made it painfully clear that anti-Semitism depends on the fact that Jews *are,* not on what Jews in fact *do.* Here was the most brutal equal-opportunity hatred, directed against religious Jews and atheist Jews, political radicals and political reactionaries, educated and ignorant, and rich and poor alike—the differences didn't make a difference. This experience, combined with faith in American ''fair play'' and the empowering exhibition of Israeli fortitude, has made American Jews less concerned with how they appear to non-Jews than, perhaps, any other Diaspora Jewish population in history.

But this is not a comfort that has—as yet—deep roots. The fragility of this confidence was starkly revealed when the insider-trading scandals hit the news in the 1980s. Many of those involved in the financial shenanigans were Jewish—Michael Milken, Ivan Boesky, and Dennis Levine among the more famous. American Jews took note of the last names of those implicated and were ashamed. Prominent Jewish leaders feared that these individuals would reinforce the stereotype of Jews as profiteers and financial exploiters. The esteemed international lawyer Sol Linowitz gathered a group including Felix Rohatyn and Laurence Tisch to discuss the possible anti-Jewish backlash. Rabbis referred to the scandals as a call for more reflection; Rabbi David Gordis, a prominent Conservative clergyman, said that in response to these misdeeds, "as a people we must look more deeply into the recesses of our tradition, our experiences and our values." One Jewish writer concluded that "if the American Jewish community, qua community, takes pride in the successes of its sons and daughters, it must also assume regret for the transgressions of its other members." The sentiment was, however, far from unanimous. Many Jews countered that such displays of public chagrin were not only inappropriate but also undignified. "Why," they asked, "should Jews adopt collective responsibility for the sins of the few? Isn't this just accepting the arguments of one's enemies?"

Vicki Hollander, a junior at the University of Michigan, believes that this Jewish discomfort with the financial transgressions of well-known Jews splits along a generational divide. "Young Jews, at least the ones I know," she says, "just don't have the same hang-ups as their parents do about being Jewish and visible. We don't walk around worrying about 'what the *goyim* will say,' not when it comes to money or the supposed Jewish influence in the country. My class was studying about the Nixon era the other week and we read that excerpt in the Haldeman diary where Nixon talks about the danger of the 'Jewish domination of the media.' For goodness' sake, this is the president of the United

States talking! Yet everyone in the class, both Jews and non-Jews, saw this as another example of Nixon's paranoia, not as a signal for Jews to worry about Jew-hatred in this country. I thought that was a pretty instructive example about the comfort level among college-age Jews.''

The analogy between Jewish economic clout and Jewish media prowess is often recognized, but the larger parallel worth noting is the irrelevance of the number of Jews in positions of influence. The percentage of influential Jews in the media is certainly conspicuously disproportionate to their numbers in the population—as is the unusually high percentage of Jews on the Forbes 400 list. What follows from this abundant Jewish presence? Much for social history, precious little for policy. A quick survey is instructive; let's have a look.

The two most distinguished newspapers in the country are the *New York Times* and the *Washington Post*. Both are owned by Jewish families; the *Times* by the Ochs/Sulzberger clan and the *Post* by Katharine Graham, who inherited the paper from her father, Colonel Eugene Meyer, a prominent Jewish entrepreneur. Are these, then, Jewish papers? Hardly. Graham, like her mother, is a practicing Lutheran (her husband's cousin is that other famous Graham, Billy). The Jewishness of the *New York Times* is equally invisible. For every reader who believes the *Times* has a pro-Jewish, pro-Israel slant, another believes the opposite. Many in the *Times* family converted to Christianity long ago, and those that didn't made sure to avoid the slightest suspicion of their Hebraic ties. When, in 1937, the late Arthur Krock aspired to an editorship at the paper, the publisher, Arthur Hays Sulzberger, told him straight out, ''We never put a Jew in the showcase.'' These days Jews are very much showcased on the paper's editorial page. "Well, that explains the *New York Times'* conservative cast," one liberal complains to me. "Look who writes there—Jewish conservatives like A. M. Rosenthal and William Safire." But a conservative friend has the very opposite complaint: "The *Times* is a Jewish liberal mouthpiece, and, indeed, look at the Jewish liberals who write there, Anthony Lewis, Thomas Friedman, and Frank Rich."

The same ideological range of Jews can be found throughout the media. The *Wall Street Journal* is no one's idea of a pinko paper, and it has been under the editorial control of Jews for years (Warren Phillips was the CEO of Dow Jones, the company that owns the *Journal,* and the paper's former editor in chief is Norman Pearlstine, who is now editor in chief of *Time*); while Jews reign at the helm of the *Village Voice,* the *Nation,* and other liberal publications.

This political spectrum in the media "controlled" by Jews is as wide when it comes to specifically Jewish issues as it is with respect to American concerns. What, for example, is the position of the supposedly Jewish-dominated media on the peace process in Israel, affirmative action, or black-Jewish relationships? That depends on which Jewish-run magazine or journal you pick up—the left-wing magazines *Tikkun* and *Dissent* or the conservative *Commentary,* the *Public Interest,* or *U.S. News & World Report.* Average out these journals of opinion and you get something close to the centrist position of the *New Republic,* another magazine owned by a Jew. Publishing mogul S.I. Newhouse owns more magazines than anyone else in the country, in addition to owning the nation's third largest newspaper chain and Random House. There's nothing even remotely Jewish about any of his publications.

Many American Jews have money—lots of it—but some perspective is in order. Episcopalians and Presbyterians are smaller denominations than the Jews, each with less than 2 percent of the population, but 70 percent of the nation's CEOs belong to one of these two Protestant groups. One-fifth of United States senators, the most exclusive club in America, are Episcopalians, ten times their proportion of the general population. Nonetheless, as we've seen, many American Jews are convinced that Jewish financial success reads differently in a Christian country and that publicizing that success is self-destructive; other American Jews do not share these worries. This is part of the private conversation about money among American Jews, but only one part. There is another, even more intense aspect of this discussion that is directed not to how Jewish wealth is perceived in America, but what Jewish wealth is doing to the Jews themselves.

Is the acquisition of material holdings causing American Jews to lose their souls? Are the widespread habits of consumption, the braggadocio, the pandering to the rich, scraping away at the tendons that hold the Jewish people together? Is this just rhetoric or a genuine concern?

Sandra Levy is an executive at a Jewish philanthropic organization and relies on the beneficence of the wealthy to do her job. She is quick to tell you that many big givers take their charitable work seriously, that they are truly motivated by their causes, not the limelight of applause. But Levy is also resentful of the deference extended to philanthropists. ''Let's not kid ourselves. Who are the Jews that get respect in this country? Survey the roster of national Jewish leaders, examine the names of the honorees of Jewish associations and synagogues, and what do you find? The learned? The pious? The do-gooders? No, you find money. This is true across the denominational divide: from the directors of Jewish cultural organizations to the fellow that gets the prestigious *aliyah,* the call to the Torah, in Orthodox shuls.'' I asked her why she picks on the Jews in this regard. Aren't rich people everywhere honored? The United States Senate, too, is a millionaires' club. Does she really believe that lusting after lucre is a peculiarly Jewish trait?

"Not at all," says Levy, "and that is precisely the problem. We live in a country that glorifies capital, so we parade our treasures to show how we've made it, and then, believing our own press, pay our own tribute to the shekel. The whole pattern is demoralizing . . . and dangerous. We are destroying our Jewish spirit in the process.'' The influence of money in public Jewish life is, indeed, a secret all over the block. A survey of community organizations would suggest that Levy is right in claiming that wealth has "bought" positions of power in American Jewish institutions. Learning and commitment to Judaism count for less. But not everyone agrees that this somehow indicates an inordinate worship of wealth on the part of American Jews or a prognosis of "demoralization."

My old friend Andrew Pinsker is one of many American Jews who adamantly deny that there is substance to this concern. Andy, the owner of a wholesale business that sells sundries to retail outlets, reacts strongly when I restate to him Sandra Levy's views. "Halberstam, grow up," he says impatiently. "I'm sick and tired of this exercise in American Jewish self-flagellation. A whole lot of people in the world are enchanted with money and a whole lot of people aren't. Guess what? That's true of Jews too—some are devoted to it, some aren't. Do you really think American Jews as a group pursue money more avidly than others, or more than Jews elsewhere, or more than Jews in the past? It just looks that way because, for a change, many of us are winning at this game. Who says this harms our spirit—whatever you mean by that? What I want to know is why Jews are so driven to judge themselves as venal and greedy. When Jews don't make money they complain. When Jews do make money they still complain. Enough already with this gelt guilt.''

Without doubt, large segments of American Jewry have a long-standing discomfort with their wealth. Read a magisterial tome like Irving Howe's *World of our Fathers* and you'll learn all about how Jews toiled in the sweatshops, how the great labor leaders rose from the tenements of New York's Lower East Side, but you will learn nothing about the Jews who became millionaires, about Jews like David Sarnoff who sprang from the same East Side slums and ended up owning RCA. Michael Gold's book *Jews Without Money,* published in 1930, went into fifteen printings. Sure, early immigrant Jews were horrendously poor, but the larger point is that those meager beginnings were the springboards to an inspiring, magnificent story of achievement.

While Judaism, like every other religious and moral system, condemns avarice, it nonetheless considers the accumulation of wealth a perfectly acceptable pursuit. But Judaism also requires—both in theory and in practice—that the personal quest for fortune proceed within the context of communal life. This notion isn't as commonplace as it might seem. Many communities are uneasy around those individuals who have gone on to attain large fortunes. They are no longer equals, and, not surprisingly, the rich move away physically and emotionally. In the traditional Jewish community, however, one's economic fortunes are accounted as another asset to enjoy and share: You have a melodious voice, then sing for us; you have a sense of humor, then make us laugh; you have wisdom, then teach us; and so, too, you enjoy affluence, then let others enjoy the benefit of your bounty. It is not so much the community that gains from this acceptance as the wealthy individual himself; he or she keeps the rewards of communal belonging. Jewish historians point to the relative lack of class struggle within the Jewish communities of prewar Europe. Despite the significant economic stratification, both the rich and the poor shared the same fears, and this solidified their commonality and created mutual responsibilities. That, so far, has largely been true of the American Jewish community as well.

Two pieces of data are crucial in understanding the relationship between money and Jews in the United States: One, American Jews are the nation's richest ethnic group, and two, American Jews are the most philanthropic group in the country. These are not unrelated phenomena. The traditional Jewish emphasis on charity is a critical factor in Jewish financial success. To better understand this connection, to see the bigger picture, to apprehend the context in which American Jews now talk when they talk about money, and to better appreciate why the twenty-first century poses dramatic new possibilities and new dangers to the economic status of American Jewry, we need to revisit the conspicuous role of money in Jewish history.

If I Were a Rich Man . . .

Orthodox Jews have a reputation as shrewd, eager, and sometimes overreaching businesspeople. Some are incredibly rich— until several years ago, the Reichmans of Toronto were on top of the heap with reported assets exceeding $9 billion. Yet if Paul

Reichman or any other observant Jew, rich or poor, took a quiet walk on a Saturday afternoon and came upon a hundred thousand dollars in cash lying on the ground, he would not pick it up. Money is *muktzah,* among a class of items that may not be handled on the Sabbath or holidays; currency, even talk of business, violates the sanctity of the day. With the arrival of three stars in the night sky heralding the end of the Sabbath, these same Jews return to their business affairs with relish. Motivational theorists have a lot to learn from their example. Observant Jews who chain-smoke all week won't touch a cigarette from sundown Friday until sundown Saturday. They easily repeat this pattern every week.

Judaism is a this-world-oriented religion, and making money is considered a natural human endeavor. Unlike Christianity, Judaism never considered poverty a virtue; the idea that the meek shall inherit the earth is a New Testament doctrine, not a Jewish one. Nor do Jews believe in the related Gospel warning that it is easier for a camel to pass through the eye of a needle than for a rich man to enter heaven. The Jewish patriarchs, Abraham, Isaac, and Jacob, were blessed with cattle and land in abundance; asceticism and self-denial are not Jewish ideals. In traditional Jewish stories, indigence is never a spiritual flaw, but it brings no glory. "Where there is no flour, there is no Torah," the Mishna says, suggesting that an adequate income is a prerequisite for a flourishing spiritual life. The danger of material accumulation is that the individual who is esteemed for his fortune will overestimate his true worth, but this is a challenge that can be overcome. Whether one may risk the seductions of wealth was a recurring issue in Jewish teaching—it was, for example, the subject of the most bitter internal battle in the history of Chassidism. To the consternation of some of his colleagues, a major eighteenth-century Chassidic leader, the Ruzhiner Rebbe, believed that as the leader of his flock he should preside over a court of splendor and, accordingly, lived and traveled in sumptuous luxury. According to legend, he wore gold slippers. Those slippers, however, had no soles. "For my Chassidim," the Rebbe explained, "I must appear elegant, but for myself I require humility."

History, not theology, dictated the Jewish attitude toward money. For the Jews in Diaspora, cash, jewelry, movable goods became the currency of survival. With money you managed to live at the edge of extinction; without it you went over the edge. (One of the innovations of the Nazi horror that caught Jews so off guard was that for the first time in their exile they could not purchase their lives. The Germans took all their belongings and murdered them anyway.) Daily life was subjected to a barrage of special taxes that Jews paid not as citizens, but as Jews: a tax on the right to travel, to pray with others, to marry, to have children, to bury a corpse in the cemetery. Jews were excluded from landownership and the guilds, and as a result were effectively forced to live on the margins in dire penury so that for long stretches an estimated one-third of Jews lived on charity. As recently as the beginning of the nineteenth century, the average Jewish income in Europe was lower than that of the poor peasantry.

Jewish earnings began to rise only when Jews became urbanized. The move to the city also ushered in new professions. For example, in Galicia, Poland, after World War I, the Jews were 10 percent of the population, but 40 percent of the shoemakers, half the merchants, and 80 percent of the tailors. In Cracow, the region's largest city, Jews were 60 percent of the doctors and lawyers. Similarly, 46 percent of the Jews of Germany were self-employed, three times the national average, and in Hungary in the 1930s Jews constituted less than 5 percent of the population but owned 36 percent of the retail stores and warehouses. The European experience repeatedly taught Jews the value of owning transportable assets and transportable expertise. They learned their lesson well: By the turn of the century, 75 percent of the newcomers to the United States from Poland and southern Italy were farmers or manual laborers, but two-thirds of the Jews were skilled workers. However, they didn't remain workers for long. The Jews brought to America an ingrained understanding that money too often meant not only the good life but life itself. They were determined to manage their own fortunes, and the key to their economic ascent was to become entrepreneurs.

Have I Got a Business for You

For years now, Americans have been flocking to courses on how to manage their own businesses, and a steady stream of mass-market books, videos, and audiotapes flows forth to help these eager entrepreneurs. The promise of independent wealth has taken hold in the nation's psyche: 16 percent of the men and women in America are now entrepreneurs. Jeffrey Langsam is the owner of a chain of copy stores in New York City, Long Island, and Philadelphia, with more outlets slated to open in Boston. He got the entrepreneurial bug along with millions of other Americans in the 1980s.

Langsam will tell you that his business interests had always been latent, waiting for direction. He will also tell you that his

Jewish upbringing has much to do with this inclination. Recent studies support his intuition. Noting the national rise in entrepreneurship, economists Robert Farlie of the University of California at Santa Cruz and Bruce Meyer of Northwestern set out to learn which cultural groups were most disposed to entrepreneurship. They undertook a study of sixty-two of the nation's ethnic groups. The results indicate that entrepreneurial rates vary widely. On the low end of the spectrum for men, only 4 percent of Laotians and Puerto Ricans were entrepreneurs. At the top of the chart were Koreans and Israelis, with entrepreneurial rates approaching 30 percent. American Jews altogether have nearly twice the self-employment rate of other ethnic groups in the United States, a ratio repeated in Great Britain and the European Continent.

"My parents expected me to be a lawyer," says Langsam. "They say the definition of a lawyer is a Jewish kid who doesn't like the sight of blood, but it soon became clear to me that I disliked filing briefs as much as I disliked taking blood samples. So it was the business life for me and that was all right too. For my parents and probably for all of my Jewish friends' parents, any line of work was acceptable—law, medicine, accounting, professing, or business—as long as it didn't involve physical labor. Working with your hands is not a Jewish vocation." Again, the data corroborates Langsam's generalization. Sociologists characterize the Jews as the first ethnic group for which physical work is thoroughly absent. By 1970 a scant one-third of 1 percent of American Jews were manual laborers.

"The other widespread Jewish notion that influenced me," says Langsam, "is that if you go into business, you need to work for yourself. You know that Jackie Mason routine on how no Jew can stomach the idea of working for someone else, a boss who, of course, always turns out to be an utter jackass. 'A gentile works so that he can get the key to the men's room; a Jew works to get the key to the vault.' The Jew works for the business only if he thinks someday he'll own it. I think Mason is right. I think this is the prevailing mind-set of the American Jew.''

What in the Jewish experience gives rise to this entrepreneurial predilection?

I posed that question to Rachel Gurevitz, the founder and owner of a successful clothing store in Atlanta. ''An appreciation of patience certainly has to be on the list,'' she answered. ''Entrepreneurs need to bide their time and Jews are taught early on the value of delayed gratification: defer pleasure, work hard now, go to school, learn a trade, and you'll get your reward later. You can categorize the entire Jewish national experience in exile as an exercise in delayed redemption.'' She also mentions another commonly cited factor: the Jew as ''outsider.'' ''Running your own business is an appealing option to people who need to control their own destinies and don't want to depend on the whims—and bigotry—of employers.'' A willingness to take risks is certainly another important entrepreneurial trait that Jews historically possessed. Excluded from the established patterns of most enterprises, Jews were less invested, psychologically and materially, in seeing those patterns continue. They had less to lose, so they could afford to tread where others dared not.

In one of those ironic paradoxes of history, Jews became leading entrepreneurs in part because of the bigotry against them. Already in the early Middle Ages, they found themselves locked out of most avenues of commerce and so turned to the one venue they were permitted—the businesses of trading and lending. Continuous expulsions scattered Jews all over the world but, at the same time, placed them in an admirable geographical position to exploit the mercantilism of the expanding international markets. When the new economics emerged, the Jews were ready. They had the experience and connections. As Joel Kotkin explains in his provocative book *Tribes: How Race, Religion and Identity Determine Success in the New Global Economy:* "For a long-dispersed people working largely as money brokers, artisans and traders, the growth of capitalism was a boon of enormous proportions, playing directly to their skills in finance, cross-border commerce and arbitrage."

Jews, we need to remember, have been an international community for thousands of years; in fact, Jews have had a longer historical experience outside their homeland than within. Barely four centuries after the Jews established their first kingdoms in Palestine, conquering armies sprinkled the defeated Jews all over foreign territories; many were sent to Mesopotamia (Iraq), where they remained even after the restoration of the Israelite kingdom. By the time of the destruction of the Second Temple in A.D. 70, an estimated two-thirds of the Jews lived outside of Palestine. Fluent in many languages, the Jews forged international links early on, serving as financiers and traders for the Romans and later for the Byzantine Arabs, addressing each other in Hebrew and sealing their deals with a handshake. These international networks were an enormous asset as the Western world increasingly closed in on itself in the Middle Ages and remained closed for centuries.

By the nineteenth century, Jews had established trading outlets all over the world. Colonies of Iraqi Jews led by the Sassoon and Kadoorie families operated in regions as far-flung as Calcutta, Hong Kong, Shanghai, and Singapore. An uprooted people, the Jews ventured into new areas, both physically and commercially, continually identifying lucrative emerging markets and industries.

And so with the coming of the twentieth century, they came to the United States, poor, overwhelmed, but with their entrepreneurial skills well honed. These are the grandparents and great-grandparents of most contemporary American Jews, and their experiences—and their successes—are now part of the Jewish communal family history. In the private conversations of American Jews, one hears personal family sagas of ancestors who came to the States with nothing but desire, found the doors of industry locked, so opened their own businesses. That conversation is ineluctably followed by broader musings about the state of Jews in American commerce, and the dramatic changes of the past decades.

As recently as 1936, *Fortune* magazine conducted a survey of Jewish money and couldn't find Jews of any consequence in most major industries, including coal, rubber, chemicals, shipping, shipbuilding, railroads, aviation, automobile distribution, lumber, dairy, and heavy machinery. Forget about Wall Street, commercial and investment banking, and insurance—those businesses were beyond consideration. If the Jews were going to make it in the playing fields of capitalism, they'd have to form their own teams. And so they did. They were also lucky. The timing for astute self-employment was propitious as the American economy was in motion and needed entrepreneurial sweat to help it grow. Too poor to supply the bucks, these immigrant Jews gladly provided the entrepreneurial sweat. The trick was to find industries where heavy capital investment wouldn't be essential and where they could benefit from their connections with their cousins overseas.

The garment industry fit the bill nicely. Here was a decentralized agglomeration of small, specialized outlets that didn't require huge capital resources and where instant instincts and an international perspective were highly advantageous. Jews soon had the apparel business sewn up. Of the 241 clothing factories in the United States in 1885, 234 were owned by Jews; by 1915 one of every ten Jews was employed in the needle trades. Jews dominated the industry throughout the twentieth century, and although they have recently ceded the manufacturing phase to more recent immigrants, Jews continue to flourish in all sectors of the fashion industry. Back to the day of Levi's, for example, the jeans business has been a Jewish affair: Guess? jeans is owned by Algerian Jews, Gitano and Jordache by Syrian Jews, and Calvin Klein by Calvin Klein. Interestingly, textiles were also Israel's first competitive mass-production industry and still is second in size only to electronics.

The Jewish entrepreneurial spirit thrived. As they did in Europe, Jews turned to retailing. But this was America and here they could think big and innovative. The result was department stores, and the list is long: Macy's, Gimbels, Bloomingdale's, Neiman-Marcus, Kaufmann's, Sears, Roebuck, Abraham & Straus, B. Altman, Saks, and Loehmann's. Over the years the Jews would establish other retail beachheads—in supermarkets (Stop & Shop, Waldbaum's, Shop-Rite), in toys (Toys ''R'' Us), and in electronics (Nobody Beats the Wiz). Real estate would prove to be a treasure trove for even more American Jews. Jews cared less about land than they did about land values—they were, after all, history's wandering people. When the unwilling banks refused them loans, their families kicked in. But no business succeeds without *mazel,* lady luck, as a partner, and that's especially true in real estate; lots of Jews were in the right place at the right time. Ten percent of the Forbes 400 made their fortunes in real estate, and a high proportion of those fiefdoms are controlled by Jews.

To see firsthand the advantages of international connections in global businesses, take a stroll down New York City's 47th Street diamond district. Diamonds may be a girl's best friend, but for centuries they have certainly been friendly to Jews, bringing sustenance to thousands of families and extraordinary wealth to the most successful among them. The diamond business was international from its inception and therefore especially attractive to the far-flung Jewish community. And we do mean far-flung— by 1770 some twenty-eight Jewish houses accounted for nearly four-fifths of all diamonds exported out of India. Jews maintained leading positions in De Beers, which still controls four-fifths of the world's output of unpolished diamonds. Israeli Jews, like their cousins in New York and Antwerp, Belgium, quickly carved out a leading position in the diamond industry; Israel continues to be among the world's leaders in diamond cutting and trading, and the diamond business furnishes a third of the country's earnings from exports.

The chronicle continues. As the century progressed, so did the Jewish entrepreneurial reach. Jews established businesses in every sector of the economy. Here's a sampling: whiskey (Bronfman of Seagram), birdseed (Stern of Hartz Mountain), lipstick (Revson of Revlon), grain trade (Fribourg of Continental Grain), floor coverings (Lerner of GAF), dress patterns (Schapiro of Simplicity Patterns), photocopying (Palevsky of Xerox), computer software (Lautenberg of Automatic Data Processing), cheesecake (Cummings of Consolidated Foods), and art (Janis of Janis Gallery).

"Consider, will you, the range of these Jewish enterprises," says entrepreneur Rachel Gurevich. "One immediate lesson is that business acumen is fungible, able to sprout anywhere when the conditions permit. This variation also explodes the myth that a history of exclusion from the centers of industry forced Jews to become specialists only in moneylending and trading. Clearly, given the opportunity, they did a lot more. But for an even more telling counterexample to the stereotype of the Jewish middleman just look at Israel. Look at the industries in which the Jews of that country have excelled these past decades: arms manufacturing, security services, agriculture, building construction, and most recently, computer technology. These are not exactly the professions Jews learned in their villages in Czechoslovakia or Yemen, are they?"

The irony is that for all the caricatures of the Jew as the supreme money trader, the banking industry was most impenetrable for Jews throughout the centuries. No wonder Jews become irate when they hear, as they so often do, that they own their country's banks. The central charge of the Protocols of the Elders of Zion, the infamous Czarist forgery of 1903, is that Jewish bankers are joined in an international financial conspiracy, and this charge has been a persistent slogan of anti-Semitism everywhere for centuries. In fact, banking establishments systematically and vigorously excluded Jews not only in Europe but in the United States. In 1974 United States Senator William Proxmire declared: "There is probably no industry in this country that has more consistently and cruelly rejected Jews from positions of power and influence than the commercial banking industry."

True to form, Jews responded by becoming banking entrepreneurs. Modern banking, according to many economic historians, actually began in the nineteenth century with the rise of the House of Rothschild. Other Jewish banking houses followed suit: Bleichroder in Berlin, Warburg in Hamburg, Oppenheim in Cologne, Speyer in Frankfurt, the Sassoons in Bombay, and Haym Salomon of American Revolutionary War fame. These Jewish banking enterprises pioneered the idea of floating state loans to finance emerging industries and railroads. They did well, very well. But Jewish banks never acquired the clout of the major bank organizations, the United States fortresses, say, of the Harrimans, Fisks, Morgans, and Goulds.

In the 1960s, however, American Jews were once again in the vanguard of a new kind of entrepreneurial banking. They helped introduce the conglomerate, a multipurpose holding company with synergistic disparate profit centers and new investment banking establishments: Lehman Brothers, Lazard Frères, Loeb Rhoades, Goldman Sachs, Salomon Brothers, and their associated financial cowboys, including Saul Steinberg, Laurence Tisch, and Meshulam Riklis. Those who didn't play inside the dens of the investment banking offices played on Wall Street and made their fame and fortune there. Among the stellar cast: George Soros, Asher Edelman, Carl Icahn, Irwin Jacobs, Morton Davis, Michael Steinhardt, and Michael Milken. For these American Jews, money trading had become a dazzling quick ride to success.

American Jews, Money, and the Future

Will American Jews continue their outstanding record of financial achievement and professional success in the century ahead? Of the current millionaires in the United States, 80 percent are self-made, and innovation is critical not only to making money but to maintaining it as well. Willie Rosenberg has worked for forty years in that old Jewish standby, the garment business, and understands firsthand the dangers of coasting. He is convinced, in fact, that the experimental quality that drove American Jewish business in the past will be more difficult to sustain now that American Jews are no longer outsiders. "You can tell a great deal by the nicknames used for the textile industry. The '*shmata* business' we used to call it—it was, after all, a Jewish industry. People who worked in the trade were called *garmentos,* in recognition of the Italian factor. All that's changing. The manufacturers, the wholesalers, retailers, all are being taken over by the next wave of immigrants. You see more and more Indians and Pakistanis and they, no doubt, have their own nicknames for the business. But I'll tell you something else. These new immigrants are hungrier than we are now, more willing to take risks. It's sometimes difficult to accept the new reality, but we American Jews have become part of the establishment, and these days, being establishment in business is not an advantage. That's true in the garment business and I'm sure it's true in many other industries as well. You know, it's that old truth about the price of success. You hear that Jews are losing their edge in the smarts department—well, the same seems to be true in the business world. Jewish kids don't have the same drive to

35

achieve as their parents, who knew they had to work hard to make it. These young Jews aren't the only whiz kids in town anymore and I doubt, too, that they'll be the next generation's business stars.''

It would be a mistake, however, to conclude that American Jews have already become part of America's premier business establishments across the board. Indeed, it is in the boardrooms of the major corporations that Jews are noticeable by their absence. As one business professor who has researched the participation of Jews in corporate America concludes, although Jews have made enormous strides in the developing communications businesses, and have become movers and shakers in the entertainment and computer industries, they are still foreigners in the upper echelons of the old-line industries, like insurance and automobile manufacturing. ''More importantly, American Jews continue to feel like outsiders, and it's perception, not reality, that counts here. Even in a changing America, it takes more than one generation to dust off a couple of thousand years of outsider status.''

Other financial analysts are more optimistic about the future of Jewish businesses. The interesting news is that whether as insiders or outsiders, American Jews may have timing on their side again. Global economics is increasingly the name of the financial game, and Jews, as noted, have long been at home in the international arena. Their comfort with the global perspective will be especially beneficial in the emerging new world of cyberspace.

Simon Aldtstein, the owner of a cutting-edge telecommunications company, has given much thought to the role Jews might play in the new world of communications. ''My company is making headway by flying beneath the radar of the big conglomerates. This is where you find the most innovative thinking in the industry. The information highway is uncharted territory, where old boys' networks count for little and innovation counts for much; restlessness, curiosity, and an eye for developing markets—traits Jewish businesses have cultivated for centuries—are essential for success here. American Jews stand to make important inroads in this terrain. They have already."

Jews do have a head start in exploring this new marketplace. Communities in cyberspace, channeled through the meeting places of newsgroups and forums, are based on shared interest, not geographical proximity. For millennia the Jews have also been a community based on shared interest, not physical propinquity; though strewn across the globe, the Jews successfully maintained their communal ties. Here, too, in the United States, American Jews have nurtured the delicate balance of integrating local concerns with global obligations. This, in essence, is how the locally based but internationally embracing in scope "information communities" will operate. The advantages in this positioning for international business are immediate and significant.

And Now for the Real Challenge

Not willing to rely on hearsay about how well American Jews were faring financially, I sat down with several issues of the annual Forbes 400 and counted Jews. How does one count Jews? One sure way is to note when the bio reports "donates to Jewish philanthropies," as it does in most cases of Jewish millionaires. That one can determine who is Jewish by their philanthropic generosity is a striking quality of the American Jewish community.

It also points to a growing concern among Jews: It is not the endurance of the Jewish business drive that is in danger, but the endurance of the Jewish values that propel that drive. In particular, the commitment to community has eroded. Capitalism works well for most Americans and it has worked remarkably well for American Jews; the community was well primed for the workings of the competitive marketplace and the ethos of individualism that drives that marketplace. Until now, however, most Jews have tempered that individualism with a strong sense of communal belonging and responsibility, but many fear that communal tie is becoming increasingly frayed. The consequences of acquiring wealth work in both directions: Not only does getting make it possible to give but giving makes it possible to get.

Part II. Money: Giving It Away

The command to give charity weighs as much as all the other commandments put together ... he who gives alms in secret is greater than Moses.

Talmud

Hunger overtakes the world when mercy is not found in justice.
Zohar

A Protestant and a Jew are shipwrecked on a deserted island somewhere in the Pacific. The Protestant is understandably anxious about their safety, while the Jew is completely relaxed. The perturbed man asks the other, "How can you be so serene when we are lost on this forsaken island?"
The Jewish fellow tells him, "Relax, this is December, the month for the United Jewish Appeal drive in my community. Don't worry, they'll find me."

They come trooping in daily—Japanese, Germans, Dutch, French, all clutching their newspaper advertisements, all knowing precisely what they want and where to get it. Year after year, they arrive at 47th St. Photo, a de rigueur shopping stop on many New York City tourists' itinerary. They come for the bargains, not the pleasantries.

And a good thing too, because pleasantries are decidedly not the house specialty. Forget the polite chitchat and get right down to making your best deal on that mega-screen television. Expect the salesperson to tell you with absolute confidence which brand to buy and which, despite the hype, is second-rate junk. But don't bother asking which television set the salesperson has at home. He doesn't. Few of the employees at the store own television sets.

47th St. Photo is owned by Shia Yankel Goldstein, a Satmar Chassid, a member of the strictest sect in the ultrastrict world of Chassidim. Most of Goldstein's employees also belong to the Satmar group. Goldstein has done well in this business, but he also did good with his business. He is known in the vernacular Yiddish as a *groiser ba'al tzedakah,* an expansive giver of charity. The salaries of his employees at 47th St. Photo are based on the size of their family; with each new child an employee gets a raise. On the holiday of Purim, in the prosperous years, Goldstein would sit at his desk in the morning with a stack of thousands of dollars before him. The pile decreased steadily throughout the day as Goldstein dispensed the money to impoverished individuals and representatives of needy institutions who flocked to his door. Goldstein, however, is just one of many who are called upon to donate charity each Purim—and each day of the year. He is a ''giver,'' as he is ex-

39

pected to be. He will be the first to tell you that giving is his obligation as a Jew.

The obligatory nature of charity is at the heart of Jewish philanthropy. The contrast with Christianity is instructive. The word "charity" comes from the Latin *caritas,* meaning "love." Similarly, the word "philanthropy" derives from the Greek *philia,* which also means "love," in this case the love of humanity. In this tradition, then, one gives to the needy out of love and compassion. The Jewish word for "charity" is *tzedakah,* which derives from the word *zedek,* or "justice." The original source for the principle of *tzedakah* is the Bible itself. The book of Leviticus, for example, mandates that "you are forbidden to reap the whole harvest; a remnant in a corner must be left for the poor," and that sheaves or additional fruits left or forgotten in the fields automatically become available to the destitute and the owner may not return to gather them. The rabbis translated these precepts into practical legislation, delineating the obligations and rights of both the field owners and the poverty-stricken. In the nonagricultural realm, the Talmud provides detailed rulings on the minimum percentage of one's assets one must set aside for charity.

Most American Jews do not feel beholden to Jewish law, and indeed, most have only minimal knowledge of those laws. Nonetheless, if one Jewish tradition has maintained itself in modern Jewish America, it is the commitment to philanthropy. Jews may be making money as never before, but they are giving it away as they always did. About $150 billion was donated annually to charity in the mid-1990s in the United States, 80 percent of which came from individuals (the remainder from foundations and corporations). Americans contribute, on average, 2 percent of their disposable income to charitable causes. American Jews, in comparison, donate, on average, more than twice that amount. Over the past decade, the United Jewish Appeal (UJA), the largest Jewish charitable organization in the United States, has had an average annual campaign of nearly $1 billion—this from a community that comprises 2 percent of the country's population. Compare this with the $1.5 billion received by the United Way, the country's largest charity, which receives donations from 32 million Americans. *Money* magazine has rated the UJA as the nation's best-run charity organization, spending less than 5 percent of its income on operating costs. The UJA is but one of the thousands of organizations to which individual Jews contribute millions of dollars each year. On the organizational level, researchers have found that Jews are twenty-three times as likely to establish foundations for Jewish causes than Catholics are for Catholic causes or Protestants for Protestant causes. Jews, in short, donate inordinately large sums to charity.

The religious aspect of charity is certainly compelling, but the point of charity in Judaism—again, in contrast to other religious traditions—is not the spiritual benefits and salvation that redound to the donor, but the plight of the needy. And what counts as need is a subjective evaluation, not a matter of objective circumstance. Thus the Talmud recounts that the illustrious Hillel worked as a footman for some rich fellow who subsequently lost his fortune. Hillel believed he must give charity to this man to bring him up to, or near, the quality of life to which he was previously accustomed. In Judaism poverty is a human condition that can be altered by human intervention, not, as Calvinists maintain, a fixed condition reflecting Divine design. No one has to be poor; everyone has to help those who are.

Beyond the individual's obligation to provide for the needy, Judaism also demands that the community at large care for the needy. The Talmud says, for example, that a righteous scholar may not live in a town that does not possess a fund for charity. Maimonides prescribes that "in every city in which they live, Jews are obligated to appoint officials who are well known and trustworthy, who will go among the people during the weekdays and collect from each what is appropriate and what has been assessed of him by the officials of the community. Then they will distribute a weekly ration of food." These were not mere theoretical edicts but applied communal practices. Throughout the Middle Ages, Jewish communities everywhere established distribution channels for the delivery of food and clothes to the poor, set up hostels for travelers, provided dowries for brides, money for widows and orphans, and burial plots for the dead. This practice of routine communal charity continues to flourish in the traditional communities of contemporary Judaism.

Gita Eisen, a longtime Brooklyn resident, describes the operation Tomchei Shabbos, a collective fund to feed the poor in her Borough Park, Brooklyn, neighborhood. Her pride in this organization is palpable. "The key is to maintain anonymity. As you know, the highest form of charity is when both the giver and the receiver do not know each other's identity. So each Friday, parcels are delivered to the door of the needy family. The driver rings the bell, then quickly leaves before the door is opened so that the recipient is spared having to face anyone. Women in this community, in total privacy, without any recognition or applause, regularly cook for women who can't. The food—together with wine, chicken, challah, and other necessities—is brought to a central location every Thursday night where it is picked up by anyone who needs it. In fact, we have an entire communal welfare system in place here. We provide food, lodging, expert medical care, funds to marry off a daughter or care for a sick parent, and numerous free loan societies. And let me assure you that while people talk about the wealth of the Orthodox community here, there are many, many needy families among us who depend on these services.''

Perhaps the best-kept secret of the Orthodox Jewish community (well, maybe not the best-kept secret any longer) is its emergency medical service, Hatzalah. Chassidic young men and black-hat yeshiva boys trained in CPR first aid wear beepers to the synagogue even on Yom Kippur, and are ready to sprint to their ambulances if called upon in an emergency; in Jewish law, saving a life takes priority over the prohibition of violating even this holiest day in the calendar. Hatzalah is widely recognized as far more efficient than any other ambulance service in the city and is a paradigm for how communities can fund and manage their own basic needs.

American Jews, in fact, have exercised a communal responsibility from the moment they arrived on these shores in 1654 (mostly as displaced persons from Brazil, captured by pirates and finally released in New Amsterdam). They had little choice— Peter Stuyvesant refused to allow any Jews into the colony until the Jews promised to care for their own indigent and infirm. American Jews have maintained self-help institutions ever since.

This is the bright side. A potentially more ominous picture belongs to the future. American Jews are of two minds—at least two—on the prospects for Jewish philanthropy in the years ahead.

Some Jewish communal activists fear that the traditional Jewish commitment to charity is withering. Forty-six percent of all charitable giving in this country goes to religious targets. That spells danger for Jewish philanthropy. "It's all very nice to point out how charity is so integral to Jewish law," says Michael Blumberg, a full-time fund-raiser for the Jewish Federation in Baltimore. "It's nice to recall how in years gone by philanthropy was so diligently practiced in Jewish communities throughout the world, including here in America. But that pattern of giving is dissipating. Sure, these small Orthodox communities still exercise self-support systems, but nearly all of their money and effort stays within the Orthodox community and is earmarked only for Orthodox institutions. Most Jews, though, more than 90 percent, aren't Orthodox. I hear lots of talk about the importance of communal obligation, endless speeches about caring and social justice, but all those slogans don't translate into checks. Nearly all the Jews I talk to tell me that their grandmother had a *pushka* in her home, a can set aside for charity, and if not their grandmother then certainly their great-grandmother. How many American Jews now have a *pushka* on the windowsill? The fact is, a smaller percentage of American Jews, in general, and younger American Jews in particular, give to charity now than they did a generation ago."

Why are American Jews donating less? One theory repeated regularly by fund-raisers is the dwindling of religious commitment. American Jews are increasingly estranged from the traditional sources that put such a premium on charity; you give less regularly when giving is optional, and you give more regularly when it is a *mitzvah,* a commandment you must fulfill. Synagogue attendance is one telltale variable. "The reasons for this are hardly surprising,'' explains David Schnall, professor of management at Yeshiva University. ''Those who are close to the synagogue have a disposition to charity. It is a part of their religious world-view, as much a *mitzvah* as prayer and study. The synagogue helps mold and shape this impulse, providing focus and fostering its religious valence, along with such rituals as Shabbat and kash-rut.'' Most Jews, however, don't belong to synagogues. Even in New York City, proportionally the most observant Jewish city, only 45 percent are members of a synagogue; nationally, among Jews under forty, only 25 percent are members of a synagogue (that is the lowest percentage of any faith community).

Assimilation has also funneled the Jewish charitable dollar in diffuse directions. As the American Jew becomes secularized, so does his philanthropy. In the 1970s two-thirds of Jewish philanthropy went to Jewish causes. By the 1980s only half was targeted to Jewish causes; the other half went to the general American pie. That trend has continued. In 1994, 6 percent of American Jews contributed $1,000 or more per year to Jewish causes; the same percentage of American Jews contributed $1,000 or more to non-Jewish causes.

Marsha Glickman is not upset by these figures. Marsha is an active member of a *chavurah*, an alternative prayer group in San Francisco, and volunteers her time for a number of causes, both Jewish and non-Jewish. ''Jews have retained their sense of obligation to others. A survey by the *L.A. Times* in 1989 reported that half the Jews polled locally cited 'a commitment to social equality' as the chief characteristic of their Jewish identity as against only 17 percent who chose religious observance and about the same number who cited support for Israel. Sure, religious commitment has diminished among American Jews, but other

Jewish allegiances have taken its place. The research shows, for example, that American Jews who visit Israel return with heightened Jewish identity and are more likely to give money to Jewish causes. I'm convinced that Jews will continue to provide for their fellow Jews especially when the need is clear. Let me remind you, for example, that in 1973, within one week of the Yom Kippur War, the UJA collected $100 million in cash. And, more recently, when Americans were asked to help in transporting Ethiopian Jews to Israel, they brought in the dollars. In the meantime, lots of other people, non-Jews, have dire needs. So what's wrong with putting our money there? Charity begins at home, but it shouldn't end there.''

But as communal ties fray, many Jewish millionaires feel no need to affiliate with the Jewish community or any other. Rabbi Zevulon Meltzer is the spiritual leader of an affluent congregation in Cleveland and sees this development firsthand. ''Yes, I'm worried,'' he tells me. ''I think we will increasingly see many rich but communally untethered Jews in the future. But here is the paradox, if you will. I believe that if this trend continues, the percentage of the Jewish rich will decrease to more nearly reflect the Jewish proportion of the general American population. After all, it is not an accident that 20 percent of the richest Americans are Jews, that American Jews are the wealthiest group in the country. Many factors contributed to this success—high levels of education, raw brainpower, and motivation among them. But a key factor has been the ongoing sense of participation in a distinct community that wealthy American Jews have enjoyed through the years. They have shared their fortunes in direct, meaningful ways, and that has made their financial success more palatable and more rewarding for themselves. Jews with money but without community reap the dividends of their capital but lose their connection with people. . . . And that, one must conclude, finally and truly and without cynicism, is insufficient for most of us.''

The relationship between American Jews and money has come to a crossroads and there is palpable uncertainty about the future. As we've seen, this community is proud of how well it has done financially in the space of just a few generations, but continues to be extremely sensitive to public comments about that success; the connection between Jews and money in the rhetoric of anti-Semitism still resonates too loudly. American Jews are secure, but not *that* secure. Is it time to get over this insecurity? Of course, say some; how naive, say others. American Jews are also justly proud of their exemplary record of philanthropy, but will they sustain this achievement? Not without the communal values that drive that philanthropic impulse, say the pessimists, adding that the necessary bounds of community among American Jews are fraying. Philanthropy will thrive, counter the optimists, arguing that charity is part of the Jewish heritage, a heritage that will continue despite assimilation.

Earlier in this chapter someone suggested that the key to financial success of American Jews is not their communal ties, but their native intelligence, a confirmation of sorts of the old query, ''If you're so smart, how come you aren't rich?'' But if American Jewish financial clout results from Jewish cerebral prowess, then the future of American Jewish wealth is not promising. As we shall see in our next chapter, according to some researchers, changes in American Jewish demography and values are leading to a decline of American Jewish intelligence.

47

CHAPTER TWO

Jews Talk About Smarts

The Jews have the best average brain of any people in the world. The Jews are the only race who work wholly with their brains and never with their hands. . . . They are peculiarly and conspicuously the world's intellectual aristocracy.
Mark Twain

So this Martian lands in Washington and after graciously submitting to a battery of measurements by curious scientists holds a press conference.

"Why do you have six arms?" he's asked.

"To move the many rocks that are strewn all over the Martian surface," he answers.

"You are only four feet tall. Why is that?"

"The atmosphere above five feet is dangerous for us," he explains.

"You were given an IQ test and scored over 250. Is that true of all Martians?"

"Not the goyim.*"*

For it is not enough to have a good mind; the main thing is to use it well.
René Descartes

At this very moment, a miserable old Nazi lies in his bed in Munich dying of cancer as a result of his and his colleagues' murder of Jews more than half a century ago. The justice in this is minor, the price infinitely too high. Millions of innocent people die every week because of his dirty work.

It is likely that were it not for Auschwitz we would now have a cure for cancer. Brilliant, accomplished Jewish scientists were gassed to death by the thousands and young, promising scientists by the tens of thousands. Some of the most important medical research of the past decades has come from the pitifully few survivors and their offspring—another 6 million Jews and their children would have made a massive difference to science, scholarship, and the arts. The moral magnitude of this catastrophe is awesome, but rarely do we hear about the incalculable misfortune for all humanity.

The disregard is not surprising. Who is going to call attention to this global loss? Jews can't—it's unseemly to broadcast your group's intellectual contributions. It is far easier to talk about your suffering.

American Jews, perhaps more so than most other Jews, are uncomfortable calling attention to their cerebral strengths. They are certainly well aware of Jewish achievements, taking note of the names of this year's prize winners—score another point for the tribe. But American Jews also extol egalitarianism, and the idea that any one people is intrinsically superior grates on their democratic sensibilities. After all, who in this century has suffered more from the creed of racial superiority than the Jews? And yet, it sure does seem as if the Jews are a brainy community.

Dan Harris, a single, twenty-eight-year-old investment banker, doesn't belong to a synagogue, doesn't participate in any Jewish organizational life, hasn't visited Israel, can't read Hebrew, and, by his own admission, knows little of Jewish tradition. But he is proud of his Jewish roots and thinks American Jews are far too reticent about their intellectual achievements. ''The same Jews who have no problem beating their breasts in public about their shortcomings, who have no problem making sweeping and snide assertions about Jewish guilt, or Jewish stinginess, or Jewish neurosis, slap aside any mention of Jewish smarts as unacceptable chauvinism. Why can't Jews proudly point to their positive qualities? Brains are one of them. I mean, who is kidding whom here?'' He has no doubts that ''anyone who isn't thoroughly numbed by political correctness recognizes that American Jews are right up there among the country's intellectual elite.''

Listen in as American Jews express their genuine feelings on this issue and you will hear Harris's viewpoint repeated often, though not immediately. You are first likely to be told about the speaker's uneasiness with genetic explanations for intelligence. If Jews are intelligent, you are assured it must be for other reasons. Next, you will be reminded that Jews aren't the only smart folk in the world—those superachieving Asians are up there too. But, finally, the acknowledgment is sure to come: American Jews have done remarkably well in a remarkably wide range of fields, from the sciences to the humanities. Jews clearly have something going in the smarts department.

Why, then, the reticence to say this aloud? Indeed, why in general is so much more attention paid to the supposed substandard intellectual performance of some groups than to the above-standard performance of other groups, such as American Jews? Humility in this case, some argue, is counterproductive. If intelligence is not predominantly hereditary, but environmental, is that not all the more reason to explore the cultural ingredients that impel some groups to excel? We need to get beyond catchphrases about the Jewish appreciation of learning; the contributing factors are a lot more complicated. Yet, this inquiry is rarely pursued, and the topic never seriously discussed—not by Jews, not by non-Jews.

''Hold on,'' some Jews say. ''There are excellent reasons not to discuss Jewish intelligence.'' I get an earful on the subject from Lucy Weinstein, a Washington labor lawyer.

"What's to talk about? Many Jews perform well on IQ tests. So what? What does this imply? That the next Jew you meet is a luminous genius? No, nor that the next non-Jew you meet is dim-witted. The taller candidate usually wins in presidential elections, from which follows . . . absolutely nothing. And so, too, nothing follows from generalizations about higher or lower IQs of ethnic groups—the whole notion of group intelligence is useless, stupid, and offensive. Besides, it's obnoxious to toot your own horn and no better to brag about the qualities of your ethnic community. I want to get credited for my accomplishments and blamed for my failures because of what *I* do, because of *my* efforts, not because I'm identified with some group of higher or lower capacities." For Weinstein, boasting about Jewish intellectual achievement isn't good for humanity, America, or the Jews.

In fact, Jews themselves were sometimes thought culturally and mentally inferior to the Christians among whom they lived. Throughout much of the nineteenth century and the first half of this century, noted intellectuals promoted the idea that Jews were incapable of producing transcendental works of art; Wagner was the most famous of the lot, but certainly not alone in deeming Jewish aesthetic output as hopelessly derivative. How did they explain the numerous instances of Jewish artistic genius? They were reinterpreted as the by-product of Jewish mental instability and melancholia. Jews, they insisted, contribute little of substance to a society's cultural life. As recently as 1950, the eminent historian Henry Steele Commager published a book about the making of the American mind in which not one figure discussed was Jewish (or Catholic or black for that matter).

Even in the realm of pure intelligence, respected experts suggested that Jews were a slow-witted people. In 1912, in perhaps

the most famous example of the "scientific" basis for this judgment, Henry Goddard, a leading expert in intelligence testing,
administered a battery of tests to large groups of immigrants at
Ellis Island and determined that 83 percent of Jews were "fee-
bleminded." (Goddard later admitted that his tests were seriously
flawed. A statue of the man stands in front of the headquarters
of the renowned Educational Testing Service in Princeton.) This
was, however, by no means the dominant view; many European
researchers noted that Jews performed exceptionally well on intelligence measures and sometimes excluded them from their national studies so as not to skew their findings. Anti-Jewish social
scientists, however, recast this demonstrable intellectual ability as
pernicious. Francis Galton, for example, argued that Jews had
developed into a parasite race which used its superior intelligence
to prey on gentiles. A more frequent tack was to reinterpret this
obstinate Jewish intelligence as something else entirely. For example, writing in the first half of the twentieth century, Chief
Justice Harlan Stone, appalled by the influx of Jews into the legal
profession, complained that "they exhibit social tendencies toward study by memorization. . . . and display a mind almost
Oriental in its fidelity to the minutiae of the subject without regard to any controlling rule or reason."

I mentioned Harlan Stone's comment to Reuven Lasker, an
articulate, twenty-six-year-old yeshiva student. Lasker just
laughed. Immigrant Jews suffered from a host of inferiority com-
plexes, but the idea that they were cerebrally inferior to non-Jews
was an absurdity to them. "Maybe Justice Stone thought Jews
got by on 'memorization,' " Lasker suggested, "but that's because he never worked his way through the labyrinth of a page

of Talmud." As do most students of Talmud, Reuven Lasker will often spend a week on a single page of text, but finds the criticism about attention to minutiae particularly galling. "I notice this phrase 'Talmudic thinking' seeping into the English language. It's supposed to suggest some sort of tricky cleverness as opposed to clear thinking. But hardly anyone who uses that phrase has a clue about how one thinks when one studies Talmud. Attacking our attention to fine-tuned distinctions, to the 'minutiae,' is the typical complaint of those who can't keep up with the rigors of a complex argument."

Lasker would have us recognize, too, that aspersions about the lack of genuine Jewish intellectual achievement never much bothered Jews, who always had ample evidence of their abilities. "You need to remember," he points out, "that much of this evidence is internal to the community. For almost two thousand years our best minds were engaged in writing glosses on the holy texts in a language foreign to everyone else. Some of our best and brightest are unknown to the world even today. Some of them are right here in this study hall, toiling within the four cubits of Torah."

Most Jews today live outside those four cubits. Most Jews, in fact, for most of Jewish history had at least one foot in the secular world. Even during the Middle Ages, Jewish scholars strolled the intellectual corridors of the scientific establishments and were internationally recognized for their contributions to secular learning. George Sarton, in his five-volume history of science, examined the state of science during the 150-year period between 1150 and 1300. The number of Jews in the world during this period was about 1.5 million while the world population was estimated at around 300 million—Jews were half of 1 percent of the world's inhabitants. Sarton located 626 outstanding scientists in the entire world (including Asia), of which 95, 15 percent of the total, were Jewish. In the year 1300, Jews were 2.7 percent of the population of Spain and 41 percent of the country's scientists; in France, Jews were .7 percent of the population and 24 percent of its scientists, and so on for the rest of Europe.

Whatever their comfort level in discussing this data in public, American Jews are well aware of their outstanding performance on just about every available measure of intelligence testing. When the controversial book *The Bell Curve* appeared in 1995, American Jews were quick to locate the two key sentences that referred to them: "Jews—specifically, Ashkenazi Jews of European origin—test higher than any other ethnic group. A fair estimate seems to be that Jews in America and Britain have an overall mean IQ somewhat between a half and a full standard deviation above the mean, with the source of the difference concentrated in the verbal component." Jews are quick to notice the confirmation of superior Jewish mental ability that comes from many quarters: Jews do significantly better than the rest of the population on SAT tests, achievement tests, and a battery of other examinations designed to measure intelligence and aptitude; Jews, on average, get higher grades in college than others; 70 percent of the world's best chess players are Jews. Whether the Stanford-Binet gauges actual intelligence, whether, indeed, there is such an animal as "actual intelligence," are cans of swarming worms best left unopened here, but no one doubts that this and similar measurements correlate highly with actual accomplishment. Jews around the world certainly make note of those accomplishments. Pointing to the high proportion of Jewish Nobel laureates, for example, is a custom practiced around Jewish tables everywhere. Swaggering aside, the numbers are genuinely extraordinary. Jews, now less than half of 1 percent of the world population, constitute about 20 percent of the Nobel Prize winners and an even higher percentage if you don't count political awards such as the Peace Prize (for example, Jews constitute more than 40 percent of the Nobel Prizes won by Americans in science and economics). No other ethnic group comes even remotely close to these percentages. That's Nobel Prizes—don't even ask about violin virtuosos.

Jews may delight in reviewing these statistics in private, but what do they really suggest? In fact, a great deal.

That Jews on average do well on cognitive tests has little bearing on social policy inasmuch as the mass of human beings, Jews, non-Jews, Caucasians, Asians, blacks, all score largely within the same range. On the other hand, if intelligence, however calibrated, is, as many social theorists believe, the single best predictor of success in school and in many professional pursuits, this might explain why Jews, on average, do well in an open and fair market. Take business, for example. On this account, to understand the triumph of so many Jews in the world of finance, don't focus on the importance of money for Jews, their particular ethnic incentive to prosper, or their social values (though certainly all these count); focus rather on intelligence: Jews succeed in business not because they are more motivated than people of other ethnic backgrounds, but primarily because they are smarter and better educated, and smarts and education are significant advantages in the world of commerce. Assuming an equal degree of motivation and a level playing field, then, we should also expect the Asians to do well financially—as increasingly is the case.

Similarly, high intelligence, not just incentive, is a key component in understanding why Jews excel in chess, comedy, theoretical physics—and stock fraud.

This is only part of the story. Intelligence surely helps when added to motivation, but the motivation to be intelligent is itself a self-fulfilling prophecy. Jews, as a people, may be inordinately smart but they certainly inordinately value smarts.

According to Sharon Teitlebaum, a teacher at a Solomon Schechter school in Los Angeles (a Jewish day school network affiliated with Conservative Judaism), that priority has changed little over the years. Back in Europe the highest accolade a young man could garner was to be deemed an *illuy,* a prodigy in Talmud, the one subject that mattered. Nowadays Jewish parents are as likely to gloat when their child is a computer whiz. "It's a modern subject but old-fashioned pride," says Ms. Teitlebaum. "Having a 'good head' remains the grandest praise a Jewish parent can attribute to a child. And conversely," she adds, "no matter what other qualities a child might have, a dull child is an ongoing burden in this community. Our staff is forever thankful to the new array of psychological labels. No Jews now have dumb children, not even average children . . . Jews only have children with 'learning disabilities.' "

Teitlebaum says that you can tell just how highly intelligence is valued by the way Jews express comradeship with Asians. "Many Japanese and Indian families live around here, and their children increasingly share with the Jews scholarships for the best high schools and colleges. The disappointment is palpable when Jews talk about how they have been nudged from their perch and are no longer the only cream of the crop. But you also hear the respect for the Asian youth who have taken their place. I can't tell you how many times I've heard Jews comment: 'Remember how all the prize winners were Jewish, how the esteemed Bronx High School of Science was a Jewish school? And now? Mostly Asian. Well, good for them.' ''

Asians, however, are something of a non-Jewish exception in the traditional Jewish mind-set. Although the Talmud expressly admonishes Jews to recognize that other nations possess learning and to defer to them in scientific debates when the evidence is convincing, the respect for non-Jewish cognitive skills gradually diminished. Yiddish folk idiom percolates with disparaging phrases about sluggish gentile intelligence, contrasting Jewish mental gifts with the feckless reasoning of the peasants with whom they lived. Obviously, Jews recognized the outstanding counterexamples, but the general idea was that "to think like a gentile" was to drop a notch on the scale of human intelligence. (Hence the most famous Jewish joke on this subject: Myron converts to Christianity. Next morning he gets up, dons his prayer shawl and phylacteries, and begins to recite the traditional morning prayers. His baffled wife reminds him, "Myron, what are you doing? Don't you remember that last night you converted to Christianity?" Myron slaps his forehead in dismay, *"Goyishe kop."*)

This attitude is fast fading. Contemporary American Jews interact too closely with the non-Jewish world and know too many non-Jews intimately to feel comfortable with this traditional intellectual chauvinism. The world has entered even into the most cloistered segments of American Judaism. One former yeshiva student, now in his third year at Columbia Law School, recounts the surprise that awaited him in his first term at the law school. "Yes, I knew in a general way that there were smart non-Jews.

Obviously. But legal analysis? That I thought was our domain. And here was this Irish professor making the sort of subtle distinctions and rigorous legal arguments that were as sharp as any I had ever heard. I must admit, I was blown away, the smugness knocked right out of me. The real kicker? The professor was a woman.''

Notice, though, how intelligence still ranks at the top of these Jews' hierarchy, even if they are now willing to share their capacities with non-Jews. Many American Jews, however, think this devotion to scholarship is bought at the expense of other important qualities—and the price isn't worth it. They believe Jews need to reconsider their priorities.

Janna Moscowitz is a thirty-year-old graphics designer in New Orleans. She is still upset about her parents' disapproval of her decision not to go to medical school and instead pursue a career in commercial art. ''I think the Jews overdo the brain bit. You know how some think of dark or curly hair as essential Jewish attributes? Well, for my parents, education was part of their definition of Jewishness. I'm not belittling the importance of learning and scholarship. But there's a trade-off here. Other values get smothered in this headlong pursuit, values like dignity, courage, physicality, sexuality, style, the ability to laugh freely, dance, even spiritual calmness . . . it's a long list. And in my case, I would add aesthetics. I'm not saying Jews don't care about those other qualities, but I am saying that they don't rank them as highly as academic brilliance. For me, intellectual achievement isn't everything, or even the most important thing.''

The complaint that Jews emphasize book learning to the detriment of other qualities is a constant refrain, particularly among younger Jews. But the most bitter complaint I heard in this regard came from an old man. Bernard Hymowitz, now in his late eighties and a resident of Miami, spent three years during World War II hiding in an attic in Lodz, Poland. He says to me, his voice rueful but strong, "You ask me whether I think Jews are a smart people? Let me tell you, a smart people doesn't have nearly all its children gassed to death. Look how pitifully few in number the Jews are still—what's so brilliant about managing to get wiped out? Yes, of course, it's not their fault, but maybe the Jews would have done better if they occasionally took their heads out of their books and looked around at what their enemies were up to. Maybe they would have gained a few minutes to make their escape. I would trade a few pages less of study for a little more political common sense. For a smart people, we're pretty stupid."

And so goes the continuing debate among American Jews over the emphasis on intellectual success. Many believe that Jews need to become "well rounded" and less obsessed with educational and professional achievement. Other American Jews worry that this deemphasis on education is already in progress and dangerously so. As one Jewish educator warns, the indifference toward the pursuits of the mind reflects a lingering dedication to become just like everyone else. "In aping the culture around them—a culture that does not particularly esteem intellectual achievement, to put it mildly—American Jews stand to forfeit one of their most important and distinctive characteristics . . . their ability to think well. The result can only be a terrible disappointment. A terrible loss for everyone, Jews and the country."

Is this worry warranted? Are Jews really in danger of losing their mental edge? That worry comes at the end of the conversation. Before that, and right after their intellectual prowess has been adequately reviewed, the bulk of the private conversations of American Jews on this topic addresses another big question: Just why are Jews smart?

Why Are Jews Smart?

Why, indeed? Social scientists and New York City taxi drivers have been hurling conjectures for years. Jews propel their favorite theories incessantly. The hypotheses cluster around the hoary nature-nurture debate.

Environment or genes? Every few years this eternal debate does another pirouette and the public is treated to the latest controversial findings. The dinner table discussion inevitably ends with someone somberly offering the banal insight that both environment and heredity contribute to who we are and what we do: our physical and mental diseases, our sexual orientations, why we stutter, cry easily, diet badly, or perform well in geometry. Of course, both genes and environment play a role in our development—that's obvious. The difficult issue is allocations, the *degree* to which each factor informs any particular behavior or disposition. Appropriate allocation is also the sticky part of the dispute over the determinants of human intelligence, and it is this puzzle that also confounds conversations about Jewish intelligence. Of the two critical factors, heredity and heritage, which leads and which follows?

Genetic Arguments for Jewish Intelligence

> For a learned man to marry the daughter of an ignoramus is like planting a vine tree among the thorns.
>
> Talmud Pesachim

In this view, intelligence is primarily an inherited trait manifested in both individuals and groups. More than other ethnic groups, Ashkenazic Jews are more likely to carry Tay-Sachs disease. So, too, they are more likely to carry genes that lead to above-average intelligence.

But how did the Jews come by these smart chromosomes? Many theorists like this hypothesis: For centuries, well-to-do, established Jews chose the most astute young men to be their sons-in-law, and these couples and their children were the best protected and most esteemed families in the community. Over on the Christian side of the tracks, a different pattern evolved. A significant portion of their best and brightest went into the priesthood, didn't marry, and didn't have children.

Indeed, for centuries, European scholars worried about the effects of celibacy on the intellectual life of the Western world, and in more recent times, scholars argued that those worries were well founded. Charles Darwin, for example, attributed the decline of the Spanish civilization to the rise of celibacy: "Almost all the men of a gentle nature, those given to meditation or culture of the mind, had no refuge except in the bosom of a church which demanded celibacy; and this could hardly fail to have had a deteriorating influence on each successive generation." The noted twentieth-century mathematical geneticist J. B. S. Haldane similarly observed: "Fellows of Colleges at Oxford and Cambridge lost their jobs on marriage up till the late nineteenth century, and the tradition of celibacy still persists. One result of this has been a lesser fertility of the educated." For this reason, concludes the great mathematical genius Norbert Wiener, "The biological habits of the Christians tended to breed out of the race whatever hereditary qualities make for learning, whereas the biological habits of the Jew tended to breed these qualities in." In other words, the Jews bred for smarts and the non-Jews did not.

These discussions usually include another less speculative and, many would add, less convoluted evolutionary explanation for Jewish intelligence. "Why are Jews smart?" The answer, in this view, is quite simple: The smart ones survived. As one advocate put it, "Intelligence is an especially valuable commodity when you belong to a persecuted minority, when danger lurks everywhere and to get by you need all the cunning you can muster. Over the generations, the Jews that survived tended to be the sharpest ones in the group, and their genes have been passed along in the Jewish hereditary pool."

Both genetic conjectures are intriguing theories with proponents among serious scholars, but both hypotheses are also difficult to sustain. With regard to the first idea, although many texts recommend that one marry off one's daughter to a scholar, there is considerable evidence that this was not the general practice during the past several centuries, the years in question. Moreover, the time frame for this supposed breeding of intelligence seems improbably brief. Nor is there compelling evidence that the brightest Christians did in fact join monasteries. And what of all those non-Christian faiths whose clergy do not practice celibacy, but whose population scores no better than average on intelligence tests?

The second evolutionary argument for Jewish intelligence raises its own set of problems. It may sound plausible that the smartest Jews were the most likely to survive persecution, but the actual historical evidence provides scant support for the assumption. In his assessment of the relevant material, sociologist Louis S. Feuer concludes the very opposite: "The likelihood is that in the massacres, progroms and legal measures directed against the Jews, it was the intellectual class which sustained disproportionate loss of numbers.'' Moreover, not all persecuted minorities demonstrate above-average intelligence, and conversely, nonpersecuted groups, like the Japanese, also perform above the norm on cognitive tests.

Social Theories

> To other people I'm a professional radical; but to my mother the important thing is that I'm a professional.
> Saul Alinsky

Because hereditary explanations of intelligence strike many Jews and non-Jews alike as thoroughly unappetizing, even dangerous, many gravitate to environmental explanations for Jewish cognitive strengths. Within this rubric, the suggestions cluster around two approaches: One focuses on the internal value placed on learning, the other focuses on external social pressures.

The Internal Social Theory

It's all about motivation, according to this view. Jews are intelligent because intelligence matters so much to them. If you undertook a survey of competing explanations for Jewish smarts, this approach would undoubtedly win as the most popular of all.

We should note at the outset that Jews didn't always glorify intelligence as they do now. Back in the ancient days, Jews demonstrated an advanced religious sensitivity, but not necessarily advanced intellectual capability. Learning Torah was always im-

portant, but mental agility in itself was secondary to other qualities, such as virtue and piety. The Bible doesn't praise the
intelligence of Abraham, Moses, or David, but their courage,
leadership, and service. The prophets were venerated not for their
flights of mental dexterity, but for their flights of religious insight.
The contrast with the philosophical achievements of the ancient
Greeks, contemporaries of these prophets, is instructive. According to social theorists, the comparison confirms, that values determine ability—the ancient Greeks deeply esteemed intelligence
and one would be hard-pressed to claim that the Hebrews, or any
other contemporary tribe for that matter, were more intellectually
advanced than the ancient Greeks at the time of Aristophanes,
Plato, and Aristotle.

Later in their exile, the Jews established learning as a central
value, and their abilities followed in tow. Before, during, and for
centuries after the Middle Ages, when the mass of human beings
on the planet were illiterate, most Jews could read their Hebrew
prayer book. Educational excellence became and has remained a
Jewish ideal throughout the ages—and one tends to excel at what
one values.

Sarah Goren, a New York child psychologist, believes that
the family culture is the decisive factor in Jewish mental ability. "Take any child of normal intelligence, raise him in an average Jewish home, and you are likely to have a child that will
be smarter than the norm. It isn't Jewish genes that matter, it's
Jewish values. It is the books, the learning opportunities, the
role-modeling, parents scrutinizing report cards, tutors hired for
enrichment, trips to the museums and concert halls. Think of
the behavior that gets reinforced in your typical Jewish house-

hold: play that Beethoven sonata for your Aunt Mindy, show Uncle Hal how you solved that calculus problem, analyze a page of Talmud for Rabbi Zelig. Just listen to how Jewish grandparents brag about their granddaughter's latest *chochma,* her latest display of cleverness. Grow up in a home like this— it doesn't have to be Jewish—and you are more likely to shoot for acceptance into Harvard than shoot for the college basketball team.''

The traditional Jewish concentration on education became— and is—even more intense in America, where higher education was—and is—the prime ticket to success. Jewish parents rarely discuss whether their child will go to college, but only *where* they will go. Young Jews head to college in record numbers. A 1990 study found that 87 percent of Jewish males between thirty and thirty-nine had some college education, as compared with 52 percent of whites in general; 69 percent graduated, as compared with 31 percent of the general white population; and 37 percent did some graduate work, as compared with 13 percent of the white population. Jewish women also attend college in higher proportions than women of any other ethnic group in the country. In fact, Jews have been the best-educated ethnic group in the country for decades. Already by 1970 they attended college in significantly higher percentages than any other group and were doing better once they got there; the percentage of Jews in Phi Beta Kappa is twice that of non-Jews.

American Jews have turned the Ivy League into the Oy Vay League and note the development with palpable pride, a pride made all the sweeter by the earlier decades of frustration. For the first half of the century, the Jews were frozen out of the best universities, but now no one squints in surprise when they see a student stroll across the campus of Yale University wearing a yarmulke. Jews now make up nearly 25 percent of that school's population, and the numbers are comparable at Harvard and other premier universities. In many departments at these top institutions the Jewish faculty representation is even higher. A dramatic change? In 1940 only 2 percent of American professors were Jewish; by 1970 the figure was up to 10 percent, and now, at some of the elite schools, the figure is as high as 35 percent. And even more startling, by 1987 Jews had served as presidents of nearly all the major universities in the United States, including Columbia, MIT, Penn, Chicago, and even Princeton, hitherto perhaps the most Waspish of all the Ivy Leagues. (In a first for a Jew, Henry Rosovsky, an esteemed dean at Harvard, turned down an offer to be president of Yale.)

Those who see the veneration of learning at the heart of Jewish intellectual achievement claim that this value cuts clear across the Jewish population, from rabbinical families to blue-collar workers. I hear an interesting version of this phenomenon from Sidney Zion, the outspoken writer and newspaper columnist. Zion has a long-standing interest in Jewish gangsters. He tells me about one particular encounter he had with an old Jewish mobster. ''I asked him what it was like to work for the Italians. The fellow glared at me and walked away. I went after him, apologized, and asked him what I said that so offended him. 'Listen,' the man said, staring me right in the eyes, 'get this straight. We Jews were as tough, as ruthless a bunch of sons of bitches as anyone. You wanna know what distinguished the Jewish gangsters from the Italians? I'll tell you. The Italian sons were raised by their fathers and became the next generation of mafiosi. Not the Jews. For us this was a one-generation effort to get us out of the ghetto. We promised to let our wives raise our children. They did, and the kids went to medical schools and law schools. That's why you see so many mobsters represented by Jewish lawyers.' ''

Cultural explanations are persuasive—if you make a big deal about academic achievement, people will put an effort in their schooling. But is this enough to explain Jewish intellectual achievement? Surely other groups of people have an attachment to education yet do not perform as well as Jews. And isn't this assumption about the critical role of environment begging the question in the other direction—perhaps Jews so value intelligence because they have a natural inclination for it?

The External Social Argument

What makes Jews smart? The answer, for advocates of this second environmental approach, is, in a word, anti-Semitism. According to this thesis, while genes might be a factor, and the emphasis on education is certainly an essential ingredient, the main catalyst for the development of Jewish cognitive ability is their status as outsiders. Living on the edge has given Jews a perspective unavailable to those on the inside, along with the creative freedom to explore where others dare not tread. As outsiders, Jews could—and do—question the foundations of society and offer fresh, provocative alternatives. This is what makes for their intellectual achievements.

Yulina Varer came to the United States fifteen years ago from Kiev and has no doubts that her being Jewish was instrumental in her becoming a successful engineer. ''It went without saying that if you were Jewish, you had to do better. You couldn't compete on equal terms with the non-Jews. If you wanted to get into a good medical school, engineering school, any career really, you had to make much better scores than non-Jews. And even then they'd discriminate against you. So we all worked harder, got the best grades. The hard work, the good brains, that was the only way we Jews could hope to get anywhere in the Soviet Union. That may not be the case here in America, but I bet it's still that way back there.''

The social theorist Thorstein Veblen adopted this hypothesis as his explanation for what he called the ''intellectual pre-eminence of Jews in modern Europe.'' Being forced to exist on the margins of society provided the Jew with the ''keen perspective of the outsider, unlike that of the safe and sane European.'' Intellectuals enamored of this explanation invariably point to major Jewish thinkers who are not only outsiders to European tradition but outsiders to their Jewish tradition as well. Veblen again: ''This renegade Jew who works outside the province of Jewish scholarship is homeless—exiled from both his Jewish and Gentile homes—so he is in a position to take intellectual risks.'' This is also the approach taken by Isaac Deutscher, who was brought up in a Chassidic family in Poland and became the renowned Marxist biographer of Stalin and Trotsky. The view expressed in his book *The Self-Hating Jew* is echoed so often that it deserves to be quoted at length:

> I do not believe in the exclusive genius of any race. Yet I
> think that in some way they (Spinoza, Trotsky, Rosa Lux-
> embourg, Marx, Heine, Freud) were very Jewish indeed.
> They had in themselves something of the quintessence of

Jewish life and Jewish intellect. They were *a priori* exceptional in that as Jews they dwelt on the borderlines of various civilizations, religions and national cultures. They were born and brought up on the thinking of various epochs. Their mind matured where the most diverse cultural influences crossed and fertilized each other. They lived on the margins or in the nooks and crannies of their respective nations. Each of them was in society yet not in it, yet not of it. It was this that enabled them to rise in thought above their societies, above their nations, above their times and generations, and to strike out mentally into wide new horizons and far into the future.

This is romantic stuff. The Jewish outcast from society works away in his poor man's café or atelier, and from this lonely outpost, living on the margins, he shakes the very pillars of established society. Arlene Mandel, a vice-president of a film distribution company in Los Angeles, objects to the description of this theory as "romantic." "I think the idea makes a lot of sense and, in fact, I think it explains the Jewish creative genius here in the United States. Take my industry—media. Let's face it, Jews have long been and continue to be leaders in creating the images that describe America. I don't think you can be deep within the culture and do that effectively. You need distance, and despite all their success, Jews have that distance. And that's why they're so good at depicting the spirit, the ethos, of the country."

Unfortunately, tracing Jewish intellectual ability to their status as outsiders raises recalcitrant objections. First, it is historically untenable to identify the intelligent Jew as the "secular" Jew who is outside not only gentile culture but his own. The outstanding rabbis in Jewish history did not feel marginal and were not motivated by the rebellious impulse, yet their intellectual achievements were no less inspiring, although less known to the outside world. (One interesting exception is the eighteenth-century Talmudic scholar the Vilna Gaon, whose remarkable feats of brilliance are included in *Ripley's Believe It or Not*.) Alienation hardly seemed a necessary condition for extraordinary Jewish scholarship throughout the ages. And what of all the great revolutionary thinkers who were not Jews—Aristotle, Darwin, Newton, and Kant, to name a few? Their intellectual accomplishments were clearly not hampered by their attachment to the society they lived in. Finally, how does this theory explain contemporary American Jews, who, for the most part, and contrary to Mandel's assumptions to the contrary, do not feel detached from the social milieu in which they live and work yet continue to make important intellectual contributions?

Which explanation for Jewish cognitive capacity is the most persuasive? None seems sufficiently compelling on its own. And so Jews continue to argue, mixing and matching various theories and notions. But some researchers are telling us that if the present trend continues within the Jewish community, this conversation may soon come to an end, for there may not be anything to talk about. American Jews, they worry, are losing their intellectual edge.

Are Jews Becoming Less Smart?

We do, indeed, have anecdotal data suggesting a decline in the IQ scores of American Jews. Given the possible explanations for higher Jewish IQs which we have explored, this slide is not surprising. Consider this: If Jews are smarter because of their genetic inbreeding, then their IQs will drop as intermarriage rates climb (although we should also note that Jews who intermarry tend to marry educated non-Jews who are their intellectual equals). The other genetic argument—that Jews became smart because they bred for survival in a hostile environment—also points to a diminished intelligence in the years ahead, since America poses no apparent physical danger to its Jewish citizens.

Those who favor the nurture side of the debate can't be any more optimistic about the future. As Jews become "more American," they will adopt the pervasive cultural attitude that demotes learning and promotes consumption, immediate hedonism, entertainment, and all the rest of the common demons of modern American life. American Jews, some predict, will "dumb down" as a result. Finally, with regard to the last of the hypotheses considered above, as American Jews increasingly become cultural insiders, they will lose the intellectual edge they presumably enjoyed as outsiders; having already made it, they will lose the incentive to pioneer new intellectual frontiers.

"It's not easy to quantify a slippage in intellectual ability," acknowledges Allen Lukas, a science teacher at one of New York City's prestigious private high schools, "but I have no doubt that this has been happening to the Jewish community. This is just my experience, so take it for what it's worth, but I can tell you that things have changed since I started teaching here seventeen years ago. Back then, the Wasp kids got into the school because they had adequate academic ability but lots of money, while the Jews had adequate money but lots of intellectual ability. These days, the Jewish kids are fine, but not particularly exceptional in the smarts department—in quite a few instances, it's their deep pockets that wins them admission. Nobody says it aloud, but it used to be that if you had a student named Schwartz or Goldberg, you expected superior intellectual performance. No longer.'' Lukas assures me that this isn't just his own perception. ''I think most of my colleagues here and in other schools will tell you, if they're candid, that the high academic expectations have shifted from the Jews to the Asians.''

Rabbi Hirsch Lindenbaum, the assistant high school principal at a Jewish day school in Silver Spring, Maryland, isn't ready to accede the point to Lukas. ''It's an old story—I've been hearing it for years: The Jews aren't as smart as they used to be, we're becoming like everyone else, and all the rest. Well, I don't buy it. Look at our kids here at this school. They all manage a double curriculum of Jewish and secular studies, they put in ten-hour or more days and they do great. This isn't just because they're religiously motivated—a fair number of these students come from nonobservant homes—but because they're intellectually motivated. Sure, the Jewish emphasis on learning and education can use strengthening, but it's very much alive. You can't extinguish centuries of values in a decade or two. I have no doubt that American Jews will continue to be among the country's intellectual elite.''

Rabbi Lindenbaum's optimism notwithstanding, the seeds of doubt have entered the American Jewish conversation. Jews continue to count their Nobel Prize awards and add up the Jewish names of this year's Merit scholarships, but they now do so with a hint of concern that their children will have far fewer numbers to count.

CHAPTER THREE

Jews Talk About Their Bodies

The foreign born, especially the Jews, are more apt to malinger than the native born.

> United States World
> War I Medical Advisory Board Manual

There are more misconceptions in circulation about the Jews than any other people. And our age old sufferings have made us so depressed and so discouraged that we ourselves parrot and believe these canards.

> Theodore Herzl

We Jews have been accused of many crimes. Yet our one indictable crime in history has been the crime of weakness. Be assured that we shall never be guilty of that crime again.

> David Ben-Gurion

"Er kikt ois vee a shaigitzel. Tahke, a good-lookin' boychik."

Most people wouldn't immediately notice the child's graceful smile, his dancing blue eyes, an already well-formed chin promising that uncommon facial blend of delicacy and character. They would fixate first on his *payes,* the long side curls that drape the sides of his crew cut head. They'd notice his odd black cap called a *cashketle,* worn by Chassidic Jews back in Poland and resurrected—in an extraordinarily complex piece of sociology—here in Brooklyn. Then, perhaps, they would notice the young boy's outstanding good looks.

I'm sitting at the table in the *shtieble,* the small two-room synagogue where my grandfather was the rebbe, thinking about how my friends from the outside world would see this young child, thinking about Indian ragas, and thinking about the prin-

ciple that associates the two thoughts, namely: One only observes
subtle distinctions from the inside. To my mother, all rock and
roll is the same obnoxious noise. Alas, many of my college students can't tell the difference between Mozart and Mahler—as
far as they are concerned, all that dreary classical music is alike.
And I can't discriminate between the intricacies of an Indian
morning raga and an evening raga, though knowledgeable Hindus
do so with ease. We focus naturally, unwittingly, on the big picture and miss the nuances of individual variations. To me, raised
in his world, the child looks adorable; to nearly everyone else he
looks like a Chassid.

By nearly everyone I mean most other Jews as well. That's
hardly surprising—after all, Chassidim dress centuries apart from
the rest of the modern world, and it's in the modern world that
most Jews live. What would surprise both old-world Chassidim
and their mainstream Jewish counterparts is the degree to which
they share aesthetic judgments about physical beauty.

All of which is the long way to the central point: Jews don't
consider themselves good looking.

"He looks like a young gentile" is how the man sitting next
to me prefaced his remarks about the handsome child. The Yiddish phrase he used is laden with the semantic baggage of a
troubled history; nonetheless, alluding to the boy's non-Jewish
looks was certainly not meant to be disparaging—quite the contrary. (This contrasts starkly with other attributions of non-Jews;
in traditional idiom, at least, it would have been an insult to
suggest that the boy had a gentile's mental acumen or moral
temperament.)

When you ask Jews whether they believe that Jews are worse
looking than anyone else, they abruptly reject the very question.

"What do you mean by 'Jewish looking'?" they ask. "There's no such thing. Eastern European Jews look like Eastern Europeans, Jews from Arab countries look like Arabs, Indian Jews look Indian. Do Ethiopian Jews look as if they just got off the train from Odessa?"

A seemingly sensible response: It does seem that wherever Jews live they most closely resemble their neighbors. This poses an ancient puzzle: How did European Jews get to look like Europeans? After all, Abraham, Isaac, and Jacob were of Mediterranean stock, not Slavic or Scandinavian; Moses and Aaron were hardly Anglo-Saxons. The standard explanation is that the blond hair and blue eyes you find among Ashkenazic Jews are the result of centuries of rape, intermarriage, and conversion. Studies of single gene markers seem to confirm this theory of ethnic interchange. For instance, a genetically controlled enzyme deficiency, G6PD, is rare among both Ashkenazic Jews and Eastern European non-Jews but common among both Mediterranean Jews and Mediterranean non-Jews. Nor do Jews appear related by blood. Blood types are variably distributed around the world, and here again Jews most closely resemble their host populations: Yemenite Jews share a low 8 percent frequency of type O blood with non-Jewish Yemenites, European Jews show a middle percentage of this blood type along with other Europeans, and 20 percent of Jews from Bombay have type O blood, as do 20 percent of other Indians. It appears, therefore, that European Jews and their descendants (and that includes most American Jews) are indigenous to the European continent, not Asia.

As usual, the evidence gets complicated when we turn to the other side of the coin. Given the tendencies of genetic drift, we would expect Jews to resemble their host populations to some extent. Nevertheless, the opposing evidence for the genetic communality of Jews is equally persuasive. When it comes to such identity tags as fingerprints, Rhesus blood frequencies, and other enzyme markers, European Jews more closely resemble Mediterranean Jews and Mediterranean non-Jews, such as Egyptian Copts and Palestinian Arabs, than non-Jewish Europeans. Dermatoglyphic data and dental morphology also indicate that Eastern European Jews are far more similar to North African and Middle Eastern Jews than to non-Jewish Eastern Europeans.

One leading researcher, Batsheva Bonne-Tamir, concludes from her studies that "not much admixture has taken place between Ashkenazi Jews and their Gentile neighbors during the last 700 years or so." There are also significant differences between Sephardic Jews and the non-Jewish population with whom they live. All told, many experts in the field agree that despite their wide dispersion for centuries in different parts of the world, Jews everywhere, in Europe, North America, and the Middle East, show clear signs of sharing an original Mediterranean gene pool.

How do we explain the discrepancy between the genetic similarities and the genetic differences of Jews around the world? A number of biologists propose the controversial solution that some genes are more disposed to alteration by environment than other genes. Because certain blood types fight malaria, for example, they are more likely to change in a population as that disease dies out. Fingerprints, on the other hand, don't seem to have any survival differentiation so remain intact. For these evolutionary theorists, the fact that Jews share many basic genetic traits with each other but other genetic traits with their neighboring non-Jews suggests the possibility that human evolution is more recent and more rapid than we previously thought.

Most American Jews aren't aware of these genetic studies and evolutionary theories, but they have no problem with the notion of "looking Jewish." Barbra Streisand looks Jewish; Sharon Stone does not. If you are casting for a "typical"-looking Jew, you search for someone with curly hair, large nose, dark complexion, and dark eyes, not the fellow with the straight blond hair and tiny bobbed nose. Caricature? Of course, but caricatures always define type, and ethnic stereotyping is precisely the nub around which group self-image rotates. We generalize this way all the time, judging Swedish women as uncommonly pretty, the Japanese as excelling at spatial relations, northern Italians as having superb style, and the French as enjoying great cooking. Anthropologists make their living generalizing about peoples. Jews have outstanding qualities, and good looks aren't assumed to be among them. Few Jews, be they Chassidic Jews in Williamsburg or assimilated Jews in Wilmington, construe it as a compliment when told they look Jewish.

Alina Weinstock wouldn't express herself quite that way: It's not that she minds looking Jewish, but that she isn't enamored of the way Jews look. Alina is nineteen now, had a nose job on her seventeenth birthday, and is perfectly at ease talking about the procedure. "I suppose lots of Jews have long noses, but it's not that I worried about looking Jewish. Absolutely not. I'm proud to be Jewish. What I minded was having a long nose. Yes, I know, I live on Long Island, your typical Jewish American Princess having her nose job and all that, and for a while I was embarrassed about having had the operation. Like most of my friends, I invented a story to explain the nose job—in my case, it was some supposed blockage obstructing my breathing. But I'm not self-conscious anymore about having had the operation.

The fact is that my nose is a lot nicer now than it was before, so why not? What's wrong with doing what you can to look better? No one is ashamed about wearing braces on their teeth. What's the difference?''

We would expect Jews to think they were less beautiful than others—the psychology literature teems with descriptions of how minority groups adopt the beauty paradigms of the dominant culture. The psychological process is hardly subtle. From early on we all share in the national image of the beautiful, observe the same portrayals of glamour in our advertisements, stare at the same depiction of sexual allure on our billboards, and thrill to the same romantic leads in our movies. Back in the 1950s the research of Dr. Kenneth Clark dramatically demonstrated just how profoundly and collectively we internalize dominant aesthetic preferences. In his seminal study, young black children consistently chose white dolls over black ones, deeming them prettier—a finding that helped prompt the ''black is beautiful'' campaign a decade later. The problem for ethnic outsiders hasn't disappeared. To be sure, we've come some distance, and now diverse racial and ethnic types grace our commercials and Hollywood productions. Media marketing staffs not only became more socially sensitive but learned how to read the profile of America's new demographic complexion. All the same, the central emblems of beauty remain intact. Exotic exceptions aside, our national supermodels continue to represent the classical Wasp looks of the past. They don't look classically Peruvian, Arabic, Cambodian—or Jewish.

On the face of it, this self-denigration would be neither problematic nor uncommon if, indeed, it were relegated just to the face of it. ''But it doesn't stop there—so many Jews don't like

79

their bodies either,'' says Mark Galinsky, a karate teacher in Kew Gardens, Queens. ''When Jewish parents bring in their children, they tell me how they think it's especially important for their children, as Jews, to develop their bodies. Even those Jews who are perfectly secure with their own individual physical capabilities, people in terrific shape, repeat clichés about the physically deficient Jew.''

Galinsky points to an age-old issue in the Jew's conception of his body. As always, you can find the telltale signs of a culture's self-image strewn about the lattices of its folk language, and Yiddish idiom is replete with references to interactions between the frail Jew and the *gezunta goy,* the healthy, strong gentile. Classic Jewish literature abounds with stories about the Jewish *schlemiel* in all his self-mocking infirmity. This contrasting image of the rugged gentile and the slight Jew is also the stock-in-trade of Jewish humor. Galinsky asked if I knew the classic joke about the Jewish lumberjack. I said no, knowing he would tell it to me no matter what I answered.

Rabinowitz, a diminutive, seemingly fragile Jewish man, applies for a job as a lumberjack. The hulking foreman has one look at the applicant and can hardly restrain his mirth at the man's presumption.

''Are you serious?'' he asks. ''You want a job chopping down trees? Look at you. I could eat you for breakfast.''

The Jew is persistent and the foreman finally agrees to let him prove his ability. ''All right, then, chop down that stripling.'' In a matter of seconds, Rabinowitz completes the task. ''Not bad,'' says the impressed foreman, ''not bad at all. Now try that middle-sized tree.'' Again, he completes the job in a flash. ''Remarkable,'' admits the foreman. ''How about that giant red-

wood?'' In no time, Rabinowitz chops down the enormous tree. The foreman is stunned. "That is absolutely incredible. Where did you learn how to do that?''

"In the Sahara forest," says Rabinowitz.

"Forest?" the foreman corrects him. "You mean desert."

"Heh, now!" says Rabinowitz.

"You know," says Galinsky, making sure I get the point, "the quip wouldn't work as well if the guy's name was Kilpatrick."

When it comes to body image, Jews differ from other ethnic groups in the United States: the Poles, the Irish, African Americans manage to feel secure about their physical abilities even if they suffer inferior feelings about their appearance. Not so the Jews. Jews have a lingering image of themselves as a people lacking both in looks and in body. Well, what if that's true? Is this a problem worth combating?

Tom Ungerer thinks this is all a lot of noise about nothing. "The only problem I see with Jewish physicality is the idea that there is a problem." Vice-president of communications at a leading investment firm in Minneapolis, Tom puts in a solid thirty minutes four days a week on the company's executive treadmill. He vehemently rejects the notion that American Jews are physically different from other Americans. "Enough already. Enough of the tired image of the *schlemiel,* the bungling, nerdy Jew you always run into in literature, film, and stand-up comedy . . . usually brought to you, I might add, by Jews. I'm sick of this caricature and I think most American Jews are too. Jews were physically underdeveloped in Eastern Europe, a consequence of their undernourishment, and we still play off that experience— and pay for it. Here in the United States the problem exists only in the Jewish mind, not in reality." I asked him to explain the scant number of professional Jewish athletes in the country. Jews aren't on the cover of *Sports Illustrated* very often, to say the least. "Big deal," he answers. "How many Italian American forwards are there in the NBA, Korean American wide receivers in the NFL, or Mexican American goalies in hockey? Listen, Sandy Koufax did his job for American Jewry. It's done, finished. It's time we got over the implicit inferiority complex of those Great Jews in Sports books we give as bar mitzvah presents." What does Ungerer propose American Jews do about this self-deprecation? "That's easy," he answers, "stop self-deprecating."

Ungerer is convinced that eventually this insecurity will die of its own accord, in any case. "The whole bit has grown thin and no longer resonates within the modern American Jewish community, and it will soon disappear together with the borscht belt culture to which it belongs." But he doesn't see why Jews should wait that long. "We need to be out front on this. We should complain loudly every time that insulting stereotype of the weak Jew flashes across the cultural screen."

Marsha Gordon, a dentist in Skokie, the "Jewish suburb" of Chicago, also finds manifestations of Jewish physical insecurity in the way Jews talk and behave. "Think of the way Jews are thrilled to discover that some actor or actress is Jewish," she suggests by way of example. "The older generation of American Jews would sit in the living room after dinner and remind each other ad nauseam that Tony Curtis's real name was Bernie Schwartz, Lauren Bacall was Betty Joan Perske, Kirk Douglas was born Issur Danielovitch, Larry King was originally Larry Zeiger, and so on down the list of Jewish celebrities. Leslie Howard and Cary Grant were Jewish, as were Judy Holliday, Paulette Goddard, and Barbara Stanwyck. Now the next generation marvels to discover that Winona Ryder's real name is Horowitz, that Alicia Silverstone went to a yeshiva, that stars with at least one Jewish parent include Paul Newman, Harrison Ford, Paula Abdul, Jamie Lee Curtis, Michael Landon, River Phoenix, Geraldo Rivera, and Daniel Day-Lewis. We play 'Guess Who's Jewish' partly out of pride but that's not the whole story—the game hides the same old insecurity about Jewish looks. I doubt that Presbyterians sit around discussing which actors are Presbyterians. It's time we Jews got over this.''

But other American Jews think they have good reason to be concerned with their body image.

New Age health centers may not be as popular in New York City as in Boulder, Santa Fe, and other western cities, but you'd never know it by judging the flow of clients that streams into Anya Eli-Dan's office. Eli-Dan teaches the Alexander technique, a practice that aims to realign the contortion in people's bodies. Actors and musicians make up the bulk of her clientele, but individuals from all walks come to her for therapy. She claims to find a decided physical difference between the Jews and non-Jews on whom she works. ''As a Jew interested in Judaism and a physical therapist interested in bodies, I pay close attention to this subject and I must say that I think Jews are more alienated from their bodies than other people—obviously not all Jews, but too many. There's a physical rigidity in so many of the Jews I work on. I see it in their mannerisms, in their physical discomfort, in their breathing.''

Does she have a theory to explain this supposed strained attitude toward the body? ''Yes, strained attitude is a good way to describe it," says Eli-Dan. "It's not a hereditary problem, it's attitudinal. All those years in the Diaspora, Jews valued mind over matter and it shows. I also think all these years of fear have worked their way into the Jewish anatomy. You can see a difference in the way Israelis, especially younger Israelis, move, in their posture, in their physical assurance. If American Jews are to reclaim their bodies, they need to get rid of this persistent, subliminal fear. Mind you, I believe the whole culture needs to learn how to be more at home with the body, but the need is especially acute for Jews."

Jessica Kay, a member of the tennis team at the University of Pennsylvania, expresses a similar view. "I'm not into all this Eastern meditation, breathing, and natural health stuff, but I do think it's fair to say that the Jewish kids here at school tend to be more alienated from their physical selves than others. I don't know the specific numbers, but you could tell that they do not participate in athletics to the same degree as non-Jews. I'm sure it's a matter of traditional values, but if that's what it is, then those values need to be changed. So I do agree that we Jews need to get more comfortable with our bodies."

For still other Jews, however, this whole discussion misses the point. To the question "Are Jews less physically endowed than others?" they answer, "Yes, but who cares?" This whole focus on the prowess of the body is "un-Jewish" at its core, they say. "Jews have always been more concerned with the strength in the forehead than the strength of the forearm."

All this "body talk" irritates Professor Wilhelm Blecher. Blecher's college office is appointed with the typical academic fixtures of books and neatly stacked academic papers, but he himself presents a barrage of mixed personal cues: He wears a wedding ring, the mark of a "modern" Jew, but his large black yarmulke places him within the observant community; the hair swept on the side can be read either as cosmopolitan stylish or as potential *payes,* the side curls worn by Chassidim; he spent many years studying in a traditional yeshiva in Israel and holds a rabbinical degree from the Conservative Jewish Theological Seminary and a Ph.D. in social psychology, the subject he now teaches. What is not equivocal about Blecher is the confidence with which he talks about the role of the body in contemporary American Jewish thinking. He thinks that American Jews—"both in the intellectual and personal domains"—are moving in the wrong direction with this "recent focus on the body."

"I study social behavior, that's what I do for a living. I am an observant Jew, that's what I do with my life. Both perspectives tell me that Jews need to stop being defensive about their physicality, not because they are excellent physical specimens, but because it's just not that important to who Jews are as a people. To tell you the truth, I don't think Jews are a particularly good-looking people. But what of it? Their strengths lie elsewhere." Blecher thinks the emphasis on the aesthetics and accomplishments of the body has gone way overboard and Jews should be fighting the current, not swimming with it. "We live in a country where physical talent has long garnered the garland, but of late the adulation of athletes and models has reached new heights—or depths, I'd say. We keep saying it, but it is no less startling for the repetition, that ours is a society where the ability to throw a baseball ninety-five miles per hour brings you national acclaim and an income of millions, while the ability to investigate cancer cell cultures in a university laboratory brings you anonymity and a fraction of the athlete's salary. The national press fete high school football players as heroes, while Westinghouse scholarship winners sometimes manage to get a photograph in the *New York Times* before being hurled back to oblivion; athletes are 'all-American,' while scholars are nerds. Presidents hone their old-boy images by playing touch football, golfing, or shooting ducks, not by reading literature. America's notorious anti-intellectualism is an old story, but its potentially dire consequences are in the nation's immediate future.''

This raises an important challenge for American Jews, Blecher concludes. ''Which side are we on? Do we become like the rest of the country? Obviously, we shouldn't neglect the physical side of our lives, but it's a question of priorities. Let me tell you my view: The idolization of the body is and should be alien to Jewish values. I don't know if this sounds reactionary, but for me, the intellectual and spiritual pursuits trump the physical.''

These surface differences about skin and muscle veil a serious dispute both about how Jews should perceive themselves and about how they should present themselves to the world. The debate strikes at fundamental aspirations: Who will be the Jewish role models in the years ahead? Which legends will be recited and which forgotten?

The debate turns on the role of Jewish might in the Jewish self-definition. Historically, Jewish empowerment was never entirely absent, not in biblical times, nor even during the Diaspora (contrary to the widespread assumption that Jews spent all of their Diaspora unable and unwilling to defend themselves from attack, prior to the thirteenth century many Jewish communities were armed). Nevertheless, Jews did perceive themselves as a non-military people. More important, not only was physical heroism absent from their lives, so, too, was it absent from their values.

Consequently, Jewish children listened to very different bedtime stories than did the non-Jewish children across the road. The Jewish child did not hear about the daring of King Arthur and Richard the Lion-Heart, nor did he or she quicken to the gallantry of Tristan and Isolde, nor receive moral instruction through the legends of hard-back heroes like Paul Bunyan and Daniel Boone. Tales told to Jewish children were not of bravery and strength, but of cleverness and piety. In traditional Jewish families, children were recounted the wisdom of Maimonides, the mysteries of the holy sage of Prague, the spiritual heights of the Baal Shem Tov, the kindly piety of the Chofetz Chaim. Jewish children in secular homes learned of the scientific brilliance of Albert Einstein, the narrative talents of Sholem Aleichem, and the sublime music of Jascha Heifetz. Not for them were the adventures of warriors.

Jewish history was not the history of military achievement. Non-Jews thought so too. Jean-Paul Sartre, for example, though later a staunch critic of Israel's military posture, described the Jews as ''the mildest of men, passionately hostile to violence. That obstinate sweetness which they conserve in the midst of the most atrocious persecution . . . is perhaps the best part of the message they bring to us and the true mark of their greatness.'' Many Jews agreed: Jewish glory doesn't come at the point of a sword, but from its spiritual and intellectual excellence. Two subgroups of American Jews who adhere most vociferously to this self-image are the unlikely coupling of ultraorthodox Jews and Jews on the political left.

But the Jews at Galinsky's karate club with whom I discussed Jewish physicality believe this way of thinking about Jews and Judaism is nothing short of appalling. Sartre's reference to Jewish "obstinate sweetness" and their status as "the mildest of men" has been, they say, an invitation for persecution, and if Jews are truly of this nature, it is time for a radical overhaul, complete with the need for new stories and new champions. Indeed, this commitment to the body became an essential feature in the ethos that created the State of Israel. In a deliberate effort to replace the perceived Diaspora acceptance of weakness with a culture that glorified strength, Zionist leaders resurrected the neglected military feats of biblical conquerors such as Joshua, David, Samson, and Gideon, and modern Israel's commanders have generated their own contemporary legends. In the United States many Jews evince the same determination. Miriam, one of the mothers at the karate club, spoke with the assuredness of the black belts practicing on the mat: "Understand, I'm no JDL-nik or Kahana supporter. I don't advocate violence. But I think it's a good idea to have every Jewish kid trained in the martial arts. No one ever again should think he can kick us with impunity. Everyone needs to know that from now on we, too, kick ass. That's the only way to stay out of the ovens."

New role models emerged in the United States as a result of this emergent emphasis on physical courage. One indication of this development is the elevation of Chanukah from the relatively minor holiday it was in Europe to the major Jewish holiday it is in the United States today (the Talmud devotes a scant two pages to Chanukah while dedicating an entire volume to Purim). The holiday's popularity is due primarily to the need for a Jewish winter gift-giving festival that parallels Christmas, but Chanukah's allure also lies in its story of Jewish military power in the face of oppression. The adventures of the Maccabees have a special appeal to a generation still faint from the trauma of Jewish frailty in World War II.

The destruction of European Jewry looms as a constant backdrop to all current conversations about might and weakness among American Jews. Here's a telling example. Though you won't hear these concerns voiced too often in public, many American Jews are ambivalent about the proliferation of Holocaust museums, memorials, and movies. No one questions the need to teach future generations about the atrocities of those hellish years, but some worry about the long-term effects of these institutional displays. One widespread apprehension, again usually expressed in private, concerns the wisdom of depicting the Jew as victim. To some, these museums are temples to Jewish impotency, projections of a demeaning and dangerous image of cowering Jews. Certainly, this was a powerless, emaciated, and murdered population, but some wonder about the merit of focusing on this weakness. Leon Weiseltier, literary editor of the *New Republic,* provides exquisite expression of the opposing tugs of this debate: ''. . . In the memory of oppression, oppression outlives itself. The scar does the work of the wound. It is a posthumous victory for the oppressors when pain becomes a tradition. And yet the atrocities of the past must never be forgotten. That is the unfairly difficult dilemma of the newly emancipated and the newly enfranchised: an honorable life is not possible if they remember too little and a normal life is not possible if they remember too much.''

American Jews constantly debate their looks, their strength, and their heroes, and so many other disputes that do not seem related to their physical self-image quickly trace to these concerns as well. These conversations are not new and do not occur in a vacuum. To better understand what drives these discussions, we need to step back and examine the place of physicality in Jewish history and Jewish thinking. The chronicle of the Jewish body makes for an intricate narrative indeed.

The Background

> The claim of our flesh is great. We require a healthy body. We have greatly occupied ourselves with the soul and have forsaken the holiness of the body. We have neglected health and physical prowess, forgetting that our flesh is as sacred as our spirit.
>
> Rabbi Abraham Isaac Kook
> Chief Rabbi of
> Palestine, 1919–35

You can change your noses but not your Moses.

Where do Jews get this notion that they are physically less well developed than non-Jews?

The degradation of the Jewish body is part of the larger annals of the degradation of the Jew. As Sandor Gilman, a contemporary scholar of body image, concludes, "The construction of the Jewish body in the West is absolutely linked to the underlying ideology of anti-Semitism, to the view that the Jew is inherently different."

Although they are called "people of the book," a phrase that originates in the Koran, Jews have always had an intense interest in their bodies. Historian Howard Eilberg-Schwartz writes: "If Jews were a people of the book, then the book was significantly a book about the body." Much of Jewish sacred text—the preponderance of the biblical book of Leviticus, for example—is devoted to regulating corporeal functions: bodily emissions, circumcision, skin diseases. Moreover, laws relating to the body were never purely scholarly; rather, they dictated the rhythms of purification rites, menstruation, ritual bathing, guidelines for eating, and when and with whom one may have sex.

This ancient Jewish attention to the body led the patristic fathers, Saint Augustine prominent among them, to condemn the Jews as a carnal people. A recurring theme in early Christian thought contrasted the lowly Jewish concerns of the flesh with the elevated Christian concerns of the spirit; Christianity's own demotion of the body came about as it absorbed Greek thought and retreated from its Jewish theological origins. The Greco-Roman attitude to the body was, however, itself equivocal. On the one hand, the Hellenists idolized the human physique—its sculptors evoked the splendor of the ideal torso, heroes emerged triumphant from the gymnasium, and the poets exalted the bravery of their military victors—while, on the other hand, their philosophers stressed the body's inferiority to the soul. Plato, the most influential philosopher for early Christianity, argued that the enduring, indivisible, and uplifting soul is clearly of a higher rank than the fleeting, divisible, demoralizing material body. These ideas also seeped into Jewish theology, most prominently in the work of the second-century Alexandrian Jewish philosopher Philo, who, uneasy with the blatant physicality of the Bible, strove to provide a more "spiritual" spin to the many bodily texts. Nevertheless, the antibody philosophy of the Greeks and

Stoics never attained the same importance in Judaism as it did in Christianity.

Fast-forward to the Enlightenment of the eighteenth century and the era of regnant rationality. Reason was now held to be supreme, and so Christianity was redefined as the preeminent religion of reason. Judaism, in contrast, was viewed as primitive and superstitious. The attacks on the Jewish corporeality continued, but now not because Judaism undermined the spirit, but because it undermined reason. We are talking theology here, but in their day-to-day lives, Jews were little concerned with metaphysical musings. In fact, most Jews were probably completely unaware of these Christian attacks on their carnality. Ritual attention to the body was even less a problem for the Jews living in Muslim countries, where the milieu shared little of Christianity's inclination toward bodily asceticism.

Our narrative turns especially ugly and ominous as we move into the nineteenth and twentieth centuries. Previously, the Jewish interest in the body was reviled, but now the Jewish body itself is vilified. Formerly, the problem was religious and therefore correctable by a change in religion. During the Middle Ages, for example, it was widely believed that the Jews emitted a persistent odor called the *foetor judaicus,* which they could lose by converting to Christianity. (The notion that Jews discharge an odious smell endured well into the modern era. The philosopher Arthur Schopenhauer wrote repeatedly of being overcome by the stench of the Jew and even refers to the noxious odor of Spinoza, a thinker he much respected.) From here on, the defects of the Jewish body were viewed as inherent, hereditary, racial, and incorrigible. Where before the conclusions about the Jew and his body were drawn from the articles of faith, now the framework was empirical science.

As the walls of the European ghettos fell and Jews were begrudgingly allowed into the larger non-Jewish world, they were met by teams of medical practitioners who took their measure, calibrated their foot size, analyzed their gait, gauged their gaze, explicated their noses, probed their neurological inclinations, and charted their diseases. The findings were incontrovertible: Jews were physically impaired. Jewish bodies were found flawed from head to toe. Already in 1804, an Austrian report recommended that Jews be released from the Austrian army because their feet were too weak. This was of no small consequence because without admission to the armed service Jews were effectively condemned to second-class citizenship. The French medical establishment proclaimed that Jews suffered from *claudication intermittente*, a diagnostic category described by Jean-Martin Charcot, the esteemed neuropathologist (and teacher of Freud) as chronic tension in the lower leg. This syndrome supposedly explained the peculiar Jewish gait and, by convoluted extension, the "typical hysteria of the Jewish male." These "scientific facts" were repeated with solemn certainty and given wide dissemination in leading journals and books. The only controversy in the scientific literature was whether these deformities were embedded in Jewish culture or, more portentously, in their genes. But either way, the sin of Judaism had become the embodied sin of the Jews. The discourse of Christian anti-Judaism had turned into the pseudoscience of anti-Semitism.

The Jewish nose wins the prize as the most clichéd of all Jewish physical features. In the last two centuries, it became the anti-Semite's favorite caricature and a central feature in the Jew's negative bodily self-image. The Jewish nose was the telltale sign, the physical characteristic that most distinguished the Jew and Jewess from the gentile. Most of the Jews of Eastern Europe couldn't care less about this nose business, since they couldn't enter the gentile world even if they wanted to. Traditional Jews everywhere didn't care either, since they didn't aspire to acceptance into the gentile mainstream. But for Jews who dreamed of assimilation, the Jewish nose posed as a severe impediment.

The "Jewish nose" was not just a slogan of the street. Sober scientists sought to weigh in with their research and explanations, and nineteenth- and twentieth-century medical literature brimmed with biological analyses of the Jewish nose. This was one popular theory: Smell is the highest-developed sense in animals and less important in humans, and because Jews are closer to animals on the evolutionary scale, they have longer noses and a better sense of smell than non-Jews. (This hypothesis was regularly conflated with the idea that Jews were a *mischling* people, a mongrel race interbred with blacks.) In the annals of peculiar science, a 1913 article entitled "The Nose of the Jew and the Quadratus Labii Superioris Muscle," in the prestigious journal *American Anthropologist*, surely deserves a place of honor. The article advances the novel idea that the long nose of the Jews resulted from their hereditary and habitual expression of indignation. In addition, the author informs us, Orthodox Jews, in particular, believe that this feature had a positive cultural value, and, therefore, through the process of selection, observant Jews have longer noses than less traditional Jews.

Other explanations tied the Jewish nose to sexuality. The

human male has two long fleshy protuberances on the center line of the front of his body—the nose and the penis—and the symbolic affinity between the two organs was already a popular notion in ancient times. The oversexed drive of the base Jew was insinuated by his protruding nose. It was left to Sigmund Freud and his (Jewish) psychoanalytic followers to propound the most detailed association between the nose and the penis, and, in particular, the psychological ramifications of the circumcised penis.

Is the whole Jewish nose business a myth? Are Jewish noses actually different from other people's? The question still peppers the American Jewish conversation. Back in 1914, an American social scientist, Maurice Fishberg, actually set out to find the answer. He examined four thousand Jewish noses in New York City and found that only 14 percent were aquiline or hooked, the shape that supposedly typified Jews. The other 86 percent had noses that were either flat or straight or something other than the classic Jewish nose.

In any case, many Jews who did have "typical Jewish noses" were eager to have them fixed. As soon as surgery made the procedure possible, these Jews lined up for the operation. The father of aesthetic rhinoplasty was a German Jew named Jacob Joseph, a man most earnest about not looking Jewish and who had dueling scars emblazoned on his cheeks to signal his acceptance into the upper crust of German society. Joseph proselytized across the country for his technique of "curing" the ungainly Jewish proboscis, and by the end of the nineteenth century the nose job was all the rage. (This is hardly the first time that Jews reshaped their bodies to pass into the gentile world. In ancient Rome, Jews who frequented the baths underwent painful operations to hide their circumcisions.) Joseph's surgical technique crossed the ocean and continued to be popular among American Jewish women throughout the twentieth century.

Jewish leaders of the time understood that cutting your nose to spite your race was a symptom of the problem, not a solution. There was an important question to face: Independent of their mean-spirited motivation, were these attacks on Jewish physical weakness true? Were Jewish bodies really malformed? Yes, answered many. Unlike their enemies, however, Jewish leaders attributed the defects not to heredity, but to cultural factors, including persecution. But, yes, Jewish interest in the body, they said, extended only to its functions, not to its competencies, and that had to be changed.

This new dedication to the body became a favorite slogan in Zionism's early stages, though some in the movement thought it an inessential distraction. Max Nordau, a physician trained by Charcot in Paris, and the vice-president of the first six Zionist congresses, led the mission to create the new ''muscle Jew.'' Nordau argued that the Jews had destroyed their bodies on the stinking streets of the ghettos and now must resuscitate themselves on the playing fields of Berlin and Vienna. The Jews had great promise, Nordau was sure: ''[The Jew's] greatest defect has been and is lack of discipline. . . . Nature has endowed us with the spiritual qualities required for athletic achievements of extraordinary quality. All we lack is muscle, and that can be developed with the aid of physical exercise.'' The new ethos of the reconstructed Jewish body became the driving ideology in the Zionist homage to the pioneer who puts away his books to work the soil.

Shalom Hedaya thinks this concern with the Jewish nose, and

by extension, the more general concern about "looking too Jew-ish," is peculiar to American Jews of European descent. Hedaya lives in the Syrian Jewish community in Deal, New Jersey, and insists that Sephardic Jews such as himself, unlike Ashkenazic Jews, were always secure about their looks. "Our noses were never—excuse the pun—outstanding." Hedaya traces the differ-ence not only to the physical features of the respective home countries, Arab versus European, but also to what he considers the "assimilationist attitudes" of Ashkenazic Jews. He does worry, however, that these assimilationist leanings are beginning to take root in his own community, and that Sephardic American Jews, too, are becoming insecure about their physical presence.

What About American Jews?

Just a half century ago, Jews paid the most horrific price in their history for their abject powerlessness. Eradicating weak-ness—and as important, eradicating the perception of weakness—became a cardinal Jewish imperative. To a significant degree, this imperative has been fulfilled. Israel thrives as a military might; Jews have not experienced such power in at least two millennia, perhaps ever. No matter what their political views are with regard to Israel's policies, nearly all American Jews cherish that military capability; even the children of the anti-Zionist Chassidim mas-querade in the uniform of the Israeli Defense Forces on Purim. Elsewhere, Jews are still vulnerable to periodic terrorist attack, but in general, this is a relatively safe period in Jewish history.

Here in the United States, American Jews enjoy unprece-dented confidence—in fact, never in their Diaspora history have Jews lived in a country where their security depended so little on their physical strength. And when retaliation is necessary, American Jews are ready. On the Chassidic streets of Williamsburg, one occasionally hears a cry of *"chaptz em"*—grab them—the Yiddish code words for emergency help when one is being attacked. The determination to fight back in this community is the sharpest indication of a new attitude among American Jews in general. In short, in the twentieth century Jews have experienced both the greatest weakness and the greatest power in their long history, a heady and confusing mix. When American Jews talk about their physical potency, you can hear the traces of both experiences in their covert anxiety and overcompensating braggadocio.

Self-protection, however, is not the same as physical confidence. Bob Margolis, a casting director in Los Angeles, recalls seeing pictures of Israeli pioneers in the earlier part of the century. "Here were our Israeli cousins working the soil with their Uzis slung over their sweating bare backs. Hey, we noted, Jews could look like this. But most of us saw ourselves as a continuation of the old Jews, the Jews of Eastern Europe whose shoulders were bent, too, but not from carrying rifles and rakes. We'd fight back if attacked, maybe, but we didn't have that ruggedness, that sweat of the Israeli pioneers. I remember reading in close succession the two big Jewish novels of the 1960s, *Portnoy's Complaint* and *Exodus*. What a stark contrast: Alexander Portnoy, the neurotic, masturbatory, whining American Jew, versus the debonair, dashing, and daring Israeli soldier, Ari Ben Canaan. Hardly a contest."

But American Jews *did* have their own physical role models, and they, too, were in uniform—on the country's playing fields.

American Jews and American Sports

At six feet eight inches, David Kufeld is the tallest Jew I've ever met. David, in fact, has a unique claim to fame: He is the only Orthodox Jew ever to have been drafted to the NBA (the Portland Trailblazers). David is now the director of the Jewish Sports Congress, a national organization devoted to encouraging Jewish participation in sports.

When I asked him how he thinks American Jews feel about sports, he answered: "Equivocally."

"Nine out of ten Jewish parents," Kufeld says, "wouldn't encourage their kids to pursue sports too enthusiastically. The prevailing attitude is, why pursue an activity that is not academically oriented? Why risk damaging your GPA? But the culprit isn't sports per se. They'd feel the same way about their child's involvement in a rock band. I always felt obliged to have interests outside of basketball. It was important to me that I was perceived as well rounded, not just as a ballplayer. In college I was editor of the newspaper and DJ on the college radio, and I'm sure that part of the reason I didn't become a phys-ed instructor was because I accepted the notion that sports were of secondary value for an intelligent Jewish young man."

What, then, is the equivocation, the other side of the coin? "It's the fact that American Jews are as sports crazy as other Americans," Kufeld answers. "Like everyone else, American Jewish youngsters turn to sports for their heroes, and that identification is especially strong if the athlete is Jewish."

Jewish jocks? An oxymoron, many said. Henry Ford's vile

anti-Semitism was eccentric, but not his view of the Jewish athlete: "Jews are not sportsmen. Whether this is due to their physical lethargy, their dislike of unnecessary physical action or their serious cast of mind, others may decide. . . . It may be a defect in their character, or it may not be; it is nevertheless a fact which discriminating Jews unhesitatingly acknowledge."

The numbers seem to support Ford's contention. Of the ten thousand people who played major league baseball since its inception, only about ninety were Jewish—less than 1 percent. The percentage of Jews in pro football since 1920 is .0025, twenty-five athletes out of ten thousand. Six Jews have skated in the National Hockey League in the past twenty-five years. (At one time, being Jewish was a plus in hockey. When the New York Rangers were just starting out in the 1920s, they needed to attract fans, so they changed the name of one of their players, Lorne Chabot, to the more Jewish-sounding Chabotsky.) Basketball was the exception when, for a time, Jews dominated the game in the big eastern cities, but now Jews have pretty much disappeared from professional basketball as well. Few Jewish athletes in any sport have been superstars. The B'nai Brith hall of fame honors dozens of Jewish baseball players, but their standards are relatively low—only two of their roster are in the baseball national hall of fame. A substantial number of Jews in the football and basketball halls of fame either played in college or were coaches, confirming the notion that Jews excel in brains, not brawn. The bottom line: The percentage of Jews in American sports has always been lower than their proportion in the population, and their presence continues to drop.

The Jews who did make the big time became all the more

important to the self-esteem of American Jews. Success at sports, after all, was (and perhaps is) *the* American seal of approval, and Jews desperately sought that recognition. Jewish triumphs in the ring, on the basketball court, baseball diamond, and football grid-iron exposed the lie of Jewish weakness and proved that Jewish boys could mix it up with the best. And as with all immigrant populations, sports also served as a critical bridge between fathers and their native-born sons. In his history of Jews in American sports, *Ellis Island to Ebbets Field,* writer Peter Levine describes this important generational link: ''. . . sports—watching it, play-ing it, or following it in the newspapers—permitted shared ex-periences identified as distinctly American that allowed opportunities for reconciliation and companionship between par-ents and children of different generations not always available in the day-to-day struggle to put food on the table.''

Perhaps because so few Jews are now celebrated sports fig-ures, it is difficult to appreciate the degree to which Jewish ath-letes became Jewish heroes. Their names were golden badges to aspiring young American Jews. Boxers such as Barney Ross and Benny Leonard, basketball greats such as Red Auerbach, Red Holzman, and Dolph Shayes, Olympic stars such as Marty Glick-man and, later, Mark Spitz, were national heroes, and Jews, too, mind you. And when these Jewish gladiators championed their religious affiliation, as they sometimes did, American Jewish pride flowed.

Robert Gurstein wants to talk about baseball. A history teacher in Milwaukee, he has a lifelong love affair with the sum-mer game. ''No sport entered the American Jewish psyche more than baseball,'' he exclaims. ''Hank Greenberg, Sandy Koufax—

these were super athletes and *ipso facto* super Jews. In fact, I became a Tiger fan because of Greenberg—what pride he instilled in all the Jewish kids on the block.''

If, as Gurstein suggests, baseball gave American Jews their bodies, so American Jewish writers gave the national pastime its soul. Malamud, Potok, Roger Kahn, and a coterie of Jewish novelists and sportswriters helped create the legends that would forever identify baseball with the supreme American values of individualism and fair play. These were also the values that would allow Jews to partake in the American dream. As Philip Roth writes in *Facts: A Novel,* playing baseball was a ''bestowal of membership in a great secular nationalistic church from which nobody had ever seemed to suggest that Jews should be excluded.''

Jewish writers Judaized baseball in the process. They approached sports as Jews. The holy relics of the old Jew were transformed into the holy relics of their new American bodies. Philip Roth again: ''The solace that my Orthodox grandfather could be expected to have taken in the familiar leathery odor of the flesh-worn straps of the old phylacteries in which he wrapped himself each morning, I derived from the smell of my mitt, which I ritualistically donned every day to work a little on my pocket.''

In this vein, writer Ted Soloratoff recounts how the Brooklyn Dodgers became part of his Jewishness:

The Dodgers were upstarts. Through most of the 1930s they were known for their ineptness and eccentricity. They were also smart, the first team to broadcast their games, the first to play night baseball. In sum, the Dodgers were the Jews of baseball; they even played in homey

Ebbets Field, whose cheap seats extended around the entire outfield, where the fans were all crowded together, just like in the Jewish neighborhoods of my relatives in the Bronx and Brooklyn. Seeing America more and more as a place where Jews struggled, scrapped, tried hard, looked for an edge, and got ahead, I took to the Dodgers as my team.

Crammed into one paragraph are all the traditional Jewish self-ascriptions now cast unto the Dodgers: inept, eccentric, and successful because smart. Jews weren't detached fans—they put their whole heritage into the endeavor. Yet for all this, one often hears that American Jews are a different breed of fan.

Abe Pluchenek is a successful stockbroker, an avid basketball player with an excellent jump shot, and someone with strong opinions about Jews and sports. I asked him whether he thinks Jews are any different than other sport fans. "Yes," he replied, "finally, for Jews it's still the brains, not the body that impresses. I was reading this book about Moe Berg, the baseball player who spoke twelve languages and became an American spy during World War II. Heroic stuff, magnificent character, who cares that he was only a mediocre player? You know how many times Jews remind me that Mark Levy, the longtime coach of the Buffalo Bills football team, attended Harvard Law School? You think that matters to anyone else? It matters to Jews. Still."

These conversations about sports reflect a larger, continuing uneasiness with the American Jewish self-image. As Pluchenek noted, the life of the mind is preeminent in the Jewish hierarchy of esteem—but bodies matter as well. They matter not just because we are all physical beings and the full life must include the refinements of the body, but also because of the peculiar history of the Jewish relationship to the physical. For centuries, Jews have been ridiculed for their supposed inferior physiques, emasculated by the charge that their men are less manly and deemed to be ridden with a host of genetic diseases. The Jewish response, as we've seen, has ranged from loud denial to disregard to acquiescence. Which perspective will dominate the conversations ahead? That all depends on whether American Jews are ready to shed the physical stereotypes that have become so much part of their collective psyches.

CHAPTER FOUR

The Jewish Battle of the Sexes

> *When there is no union of male and female, one is not worthy of beholding the* Shekhina *[Divine Presence].*
> Zohar

Part I. Gender Wars

> *Nobody ever wins the battle of the sexes. There's too much fraternizing with the enemy.*
> Henry Kissinger

Jewish men and Jewish women have a problem these days . . . with each other.

"Jewish women? Permit me to speak for my Jewish male brethren on this not-so-dear topic in our lives. Jewish women are: demanding, emasculating, carping, materialistic, strident, and sexually withholding. That's for starters."

"Jewish men? They're fine. That is, except for being nerdy, frightened by female success, and consumed by the lingering belief that they are forever entitled. I suppose it's not easy living your whole life as Mama's little prince."

These endearing quotes come, respectively, from a Jewish man in his early thirties and a Jewish woman of about the same age. Ironically enough, they present their harangue at a Jewish singles event which they are attending in order to meet a suitable Jewish spouse. In their pursuit to marry within the faith, these

two young Jews are now a minority, but in their aspersions about
the opposite sex, they echo widely voiced disapproval.

A recent UJA leadership weekend offered participants a smor-
gasbord of workshops on Jewish topics, but the largest crowd
thronged to a session devoted to the enmity between the sexes.
At a New York convention of like-minded leftist Jews sponsored
by *Tikkun* magazine, the most cantankerous meeting was entitled
"Jewish Women and Jewish Men: Love or War." On the other
coast, hundreds of Jewish students packed a UCLA Hillel conference to explain their disinclination to date each other. Jewish
male-female antagonism is the subject of similar encounters
across the country.

How serious is all this anger?

Extremely serious, say many Jewish leaders. For them, the
most frightening aspect of this gender conflict is its implications
for marriage: If young Jewish men and Jewish women don't like
one another, they aren't likely to marry one another, and if they
marry out of the faith, they aren't likely to raise their children
within the faith.

This is writer Anne Roiphe's concern:

The horrible statistics on intermarriage today reflect the
fact that our American Jewish culture has done a good
deal to make our Jewish children dislike and resent each
other. These complaints are openly expressed in books,
movies, jokes (Jewish mother, princess, prince). The joke
is on us because like the advertisements that are flashed
across the television screen, they sell us a bill of goods.
What they say is that Jewish women are somehow less

beautiful, less kind, more materialistic, prone to suffocating their offspring, ambitious but not helpful.

Along with blaming the popular media, Roiphe points an accusatory finger at fellow writers, such as Philip Roth, Saul Bellow, Bernard Malamud, and Alfred Kazin, for propagating the image of the Jewish mother as a "weary, unfulfilled, bitter soul" and for positing heroes "who learn about the world from the *shiksa* who is tall, blond and sexy in a way no Jewish girl could be." Jewish women, by contrast, are projected as aggressive and greedy. But these Jewish women, Roiphe emphasizes, are bitter as well. Having finally achieved the same education and privileges as their brothers, "they are now furious at the creature they snicker at called the Jewish Prince." The result, Roiphe concludes, is that "Jewish women too are ripe for plucking by the stranger who doesn't smell from smoke of this old battle."

Roiphe is certainly correct in pointing to gender hostility as a factor in the current high intermarriage rate between Jews and non-Jews, but that is certainly not its root cause—marriage across religious and ethnic lines is a national phenomenon that has more to do with the loosening of ethnic ties and external tolerance than internal strife. Many intermarried Jews are, in fact, deeply offended by the implication that a dislike of "their own" prompted them to marry non-Jews.

"I fume every time I hear this outrageous suggestion," says Steven Littman. "I met my wife at Tulane University ten years ago. Not only is she not Jewish, but her father is a born-again Baptist. I had some fleeting qualms about marrying out of the faith—very fleeting, I must say—but that had absolutely nothing to do with any prejudices I had about Jewish women. A person's religious background was never high up on my list of what counts. I dated my share of Jewish women too. And spare me the condescending psychobabble about one's attraction to the exotic 'other.' I wasn't reacting 'ethnically' when I married Christina. I married her because I loved her.''

Jews from deep within the Jewish camp also downplay the significance of these gender wars, but for other reasons. Robert Frankel is a librarian at a university that recently sponsored a symposium on gender relations among Jews. He considers himself a committed Jew and recently became engaged to a woman whom he also describes as ''intensely Jewish.'' ''There's a lot less here than meets the eye,'' he assures me, referring to the supposed difficulties between young Jewish men and women. ''I, too, was given to making disparaging remarks about Jewish women, and my fiancée says she'd do the same about Jewish men. When you hear these nasty accusations hurled across the aisles, you need to recognize that this is mostly posturing. It passes. When it counts, Jews like us who only seriously date other Jews judge the other gender as individuals. You need to remember, too, that men and women are always carping at each other, and this is another typical internal family spat. Only editors of Jewish magazines who have run out of story ideas herald this as a major Jewish problem. It isn't.''

Frankel's disregard for the seriousness of this conflict seems, to many, far too cavalier. Intermarriage aside, the very popularity of these ugly images of Jewish Princesses and wimpy Jewish men begs for explanation. Cross-gender anger might be a habit of the human species and it certainly existed throughout Jewish history, but never in that history has the stereotyping become prevalent or as biting among Jews as here in the United States. American Jewish humor is surely partly to blame—whole comedic careers have been built on these images—but comedians fish for attitudes that already thrive in the cultural stream; if the Jewish mother, the Jewish American Princess, and the Jewish nerd are comic figures, that's because so many Jews feel this way about them. The humor is just the surface—smoldering not too far below is a volcanic brew of anxieties about sexuality, materialism, and making it in contemporary America. That's why an examination of Jewish gender wars in the private conversations of American Jews quickly becomes an examination of the history of Jewish self-image in the past century. It's a volatile story.

Ladies First

> The Holy One, Blessed be He, said to Moses, "Go to the daughters of Israel and ask them whether they wish to receive the Torah." Why were the women asked first? Because the way of men is to follow the opinion of women.
>
> Pirkei D' Rebi Eliezer

> Hebrew: a male Jew, as distinguished from a Shebrew, an altogether superior creation.
>
> Ambrose Bierce,
> Devil's Dictionary

May 1981. Steve Steinberg takes a carving knife from his kitchen, walks into the white and silver bedroom, and stabs his wife, Elana, twenty-six times. Their two daughters are in the other room and hear their mother's screams. One calls the police. Steinberg concocts a story about two robbers attacking their house. His story quickly disintegrates and he is charged with murder.

In less than a month Steinberg walks free. He is acquitted on grounds of sleepwalking and temporary insanity brought on by his wife's behavior. Elana Steinberg, not Steve Steinberg, is the focus of the trial. The defense shows that she was a Jewish American Princess. A progression of witnesses testifies to Elana's incessant shopping, her habitual whining and complaining. In his summation, Steinberg's (Jewish) lawyer refers to her as a "bitch" and argues that her unending demands for clothing and furniture drove Steven to murder. The jury agrees.

The verdict in the Steinberg case was outrageous, of course, but it also demonstrated the degree to which the repulsive image of the Jewish American Princess had become part of the American idiom. As Janice Booker, author of *The Jewish American Princess and Other Myths,* correctly remarks, "The repetition and acceptance of these negative and damaging stereotypes, which pander to anti-Semites, become the accepted norm and are introduced into ordinary conversation as casually as the weather."

Through endless repetition, the JAP joke reinforces the two defining characteristics of the type: Jewish women live to shop and they don't like sex. Thus: You can tell a JAP has an orgasm when she drops her nail file. The JAP porn movie? *Debbie Does Dishes.* Jewish foreplay? Thirty minutes of begging. How to get a JAP to stop having sex? Marry her. Along with lightbulb, elephant, and Polish jokes, JAP humor hit its apex years ago, but it has managed a remarkable staying power in the culture ever since. One wonders why.

"Why? Because it's true." Sherry Etrog grew up in Great Neck, Long Island, a perennial contender for the title "JAP capital of America.'' She thinks the JAP tag is well deserved. ''Have you been doing some upscale shopping lately? If so, you'd know that JAP isn't some bigot's fantasy. Jewish suburban women, though of course not only Jews and not only suburbanites, *are* ravenous consumers. Young Jewish girls too . . . the Gap JAP.''

I asked Sherry, a school psychologist, if she considers herself a Jewish American Princess. Her quick answer suggests that she's discussed this before. ''Obviously, I don't think of myself as asexual or an addicted shopper. But would I rather spend an afternoon at Bloomingdale's than under the hood of a car? You bet. And would I mind a rich husband who let me use his hefty credit card to do my shopping with? Would I—where is he?'' Sherry also believes that it's hypocritical to condemn JAP behavior as some kind of vagrant Judaism or vacuous capitalism. ''First of all, when I say Jewish women are very devoted consumers, I'm not saying that's all they do. This past Rosh Hashanah I heard a fifteen-year-old walking out of shul say to her friend, 'My goal in life is to save the world and then shop.' The kid's priorities seem very contemporary Jewish to me. Look, well-off Jewish women are just doing what everyone everywhere does—all Americans want to live the good life. Why not enjoy the fruits of your labor, or, for that matter, your father's or your husband's labor?'' Sherry doesn't see this as undermining women. ''If Jewish women like to be taken care of, I say bully for them. Way to go. The assault on JAPs is based on pure envy.''

Michele is Sherry's sister. She, too, works as a school psychologist. Although they grew up in the same home and work at the same profession, the two sisters decidedly do not share the same attitudes about this subject. ''Don't fool yourself,'' Michele says. ''We certainly *are* dealing with bigotry here. Jewish women

111

aren't any more princessy than any other women in the culture. If anything, my bet is that they are far less. So why the rap on the Jews? I'll tell you why. It's called classic anti-Semitism. It's just a modern version of the old canard about the money-obsessed Jew who is also somehow sexually different, undersexed or oversexed. It galls me that Jews themselves, even Jewish women, even my otherwise intelligent sister, buy into this slander.''

Michele is especially upset with the entertainment media, which, she believes, is most responsible for projecting the JAP into the American vernacular. She mentions as an example the film *Private Benjamin*, which features Goldie Hawn running about in the army with her Louis Vuitton bag. ''Why is this woman Jewish? How many Jews, for goodness' sake, are likely to enlist in the army?'' Michele also names the movie *White Palace*, starring Susan Sarandon and James Spader, which depicts an utterly despicable Jewish family. ''The family's Jewishness had absolutely nothing to do with the plot. Ninety-eight percent of the country is gentile, the movie takes place in the Wasp Midwest, but they need to make this family Jewish.'' Michele runs through a string of Woody Allen films with negative portrayals of women, but the movie that most ticked her off was *The Heartbreak Kid*. ''The competition is stiff, but this movie deserves the prize for the most despicable piece of JAP-bashing anti-Semitic dreck. It's the story of a Jewish American Princess, played of course by a Jewish actress, who manages on her honeymoon to exhibit such nauseating mannerisms that after just a few minutes you're rooting for the hero to chuck his bride in favor of the *shiksa* enchantress, Cybill Shepherd. Naturally, the movie is directed by a Jew, a Jewish woman no less, Elaine May. What else did you expect?''

This much is certainly true: Whether or not they invented the JAP caricature, Jews certainly helped consecrate it. JAP-bashing is a regular feature of the Jewish conversation. As far as Claudia Setzer can tell, the JAP shows up *only* in Jewish conversation.

Claudia was raised as a Catholic in the Midwest and now teaches New Testament studies at Manhattan College. She is also an observant Jew, having converted to Judaism in 1979. I asked her how she responded to JAP jokes as a young woman back in Minnesota. Her answer is telling. "I couldn't say. I never heard these jokes. I can't speak for all America, or what it's like growing up in the Midwest today, but the term 'JAP' was meaningless to me back then. I think even today, if I repeated a JAP joke to my brother, he wouldn't get it—the assumption about Jewish women and their assumed materialism and disinterest in sex would go right past him. The only people I ever heard tell JAP jokes were Jews."

This isn't wholly surprising—groups often bandy derisive comments about each other that they'd consider offensive coming from outsiders. Scott Miller, a twenty-eight-year-old attorney living in Shaker Heights, Ohio (which, he advises, furnishes its own steady crop of Jewish Princesses), acknowledges a double standard when it comes to discussions about Jewish women. "You can bet that when Jewish guys get together, before long they'll be grousing about Jewish women. That's a regular subject of our private conversations. How self-indulgent Jewish women are. How unappreciative they are. How they belittle their men—in contrast to the more accepting, less demanding non-Jewish woman. But I'm definitely uneasy when I hear my non-Jewish friends denigrate Jewish women this way. It's different. Those are our sisters, girlfriends, and wives they're talking about."

113

Scott says he's somewhat uneasy when his non-Jewish friends joke about JAPs, but he's learned to tolerate the banter. "I realize that these jokes aren't meant to be hostile to Jews. JAP jokes are really behavior that's true of some women from all groups. The jokes aren't any more about Jews than Polish jokes are really about Polish people—the humor lies in the punch line, not the ethnic reference. Aren't we Jews unfairly thin-skinned when we object to this humor?"

The nonchalant tolerance behind these comments infuriates Dottie Swartz. She is, by her own description, a "Jewish feminist—or a feminist Jew." She expects that either label will make people think of a sixties radical, even though she was born in 1970. "But yes, I am disgusted by this kind of humor both as a woman and as a Jew.

"Every book about Jewish mothers or Jewish Princesses has the same two bullshit lines somewhere on the cover. One, 'You don't have to be Jewish to be a Jewish mother,' or Jewish Princess as the case may be. Two, a proclamation that the author of the book is Jewish. Well, what I want to know is, how come if you don't have to be Jewish to be these awful women, they always are? Why rag only on Jewish moms, not Jamaican moms or Greek moms or Hispanic moms? If all sorts of people are princesses, why pick on the Jewish ones? And it's obvious why they emphasize that the author of the book is Jewish. Because if a non-Jew wrote it, he or she would be accused, deservedly, of vile Jew-baiting. As if Jews can't be anti-Semitic. We all know what hogwash that is."

Dottie weighs in with her feminist side as well. It is no accident, she assures us, that JAP iconography developed at the same time as the feminist movement. Nor, she says, is it an accident that so many of the movement's pioneers were Jews: Betty Friedan, Gloria Steinem, Shulamith Firestone, Susan Brownmiller, Robin Morgan, Andrea Dworkin, among others. The attack on the JAP, she believes, is partly anti-Semitism and also an attack on women's equality. "The Jewish woman is in a no-win situation. Either she's a ball-buster for staying home, living an unproductive self-centered life, or she's a ball-buster for insisting on her own productive equality."

Author Niki Stiller also sees the JAP label as the creation of a more general male hostility to the new woman. She writes: "... I am afraid what has become clear in this age of transition is that many men, Jewish and gentile, would like to *shiksify* us all, Jewish as well as non-Jewish women, and that any woman who claims equality and respect will be hated and feared as much for her intellect as for her origins."

The intriguing question hidden behind all these exchanges is why conversations about the contemporary American Jewish woman so quickly turn to discussions about JAPs and the qualities that revolve around that profile. The reality, after all, is otherwise: Over the past decades, American Jewish women have managed an outstanding record of achievement. Spoiled? Sixty-one percent of Jewish women between the ages of twenty-five and forty-four are employed full-time. Nearly 63 percent of these women work as teachers, in the health professions, or in professional and managerial occupations. In a study conducted in the 1980s, only one of three Jewish women believed that women who stayed at home make better mothers. Interested only in shopping? Jewish women are the most highly educated women in the United States. Eighty-five percent of Jewish women under the age of forty-five have attended college, two-thirds have undergraduate degrees and 37 percent graduate degrees. The comparable figures for women in the general white population are 11 percent with bachelor's degrees and 6 percent with any postgraduate studies.

The discrepancy between image and reality is puzzling, and the answer lies in the dizzying transformations of the American Jewish woman these past three generations: from selfless immigrant *yiddishe* mama, to her daughter the suffocating Jewish mother, to her daughter, the reigning Jewish American Princess. Here, in capsule, is the saga.

The original *yiddishe* mama came from the old country with her Eastern European family, to whom she was the enduring icon of pristine maternal goodness. Al Jolson sang to her glory in his venerable "My Yiddishe Momme," recalling her unstinting love as she toiled in the sweatshops by day and in her kitchen by night, working hard so that her children wouldn't have to do the same, marching through hellfire to see her children to safety— and a law degree. She was the matriarch, the glue of the family, the one with "the business smarts in the house." She is now the *bubbie,* the grandmother or great-grandmother of most contemporary American Jews, a receding memory living on only in heirloom candlesticks, faded photographs, and Yiddish movies. This Jewish mother of the first generation spent her life in production, not consumption.

In her place, a new Jewish mother arose in the years following World War II. In sociologist lingo, this new Jewish mother belongs to the second generation of immigrants as depicted by the male third generation, a generation already ambivalent about its Judaism. She is another story entirely.

She is also not very likable. This Jewish mother is overbearing; the earlier generation's unflinching devotion is now suffocating manipulation. She meddles, ever determined to prevent her offspring from achieving the least bit of autonomy. She is castrating, controlling, and collusive. She is forever visiting the doctor. Preferably, her son is the doctor. If not, she'd like her daughter to marry a doctor; a lawyer wouldn't be so bad either. She hates her daughter-in-law. She has terrible taste and goes to the hairdresser too often. She also buys too much furniture. She makes too much food and she eats too much food. She is, overall, too much. Sure, she poses as self-sacrificing—"How many Jewish mothers does it take to screw in a lightbulb? None. It's all right, dear, I'll sit in the dark"—but you pay the price in guilt.

The Jewish mother reached her apogee in the 1960s, making steady appearances throughout the decade in best-selling humor books. She bitched her way into the serious novel too. Every study of postwar popular American Jewish culture devotes reams of paragraphs to Philip Roth's *Portnoy's Complaint,* a Jew-crazed novel which itself devotes copious paragraphs to the protagonist's Jewish mother. Mrs. Portnoy memorializes every banal slogan we associate with the archetype: the force-feeding, the cloying overprotectedness, the sagging, the bragging, and the nagging. (Father is a caricature too, though, tellingly, of much less importance than his wife. Roth gleefully contrasts the carefree gentile father drinking his whiskey with the constipated Jewish father drinking his milk of magnesia.) True to form, the Jewish mother of this lore lingers. She may have reached her heights decades ago, but like Woody Allen's Jewish mother-in-the-sky in *New York Stories,* she just won't go away.

For many social critics, what is pivotal here is the economic turn of this "middle generation" Jewish mother. Her husband is the sole breadwinner, so his self-worth is determined by how well he performs in his profession. For her part, the Jewish mother doesn't sweat at work, but she is still the consummate home-maker, fussing and fretting over her children and kitchen.

The Jewish mother's daughter, the Princess, doesn't sweat at all. Her story—in popular parlance—is that she works neither at a job nor at home; she produces nothing but consumes all. Sociologist Riv-Ellen Prell describes her contradictory image: "The Jewish woman is represented through her body that is at once exceptionally passive and highly adorned. She simultaneously lacks sexual desire and abundantly lavishes attention on her desire to beautify herself. . . . Her body is a surface to decorate, financed by the sweat of others." She cares for her body but is reluctant to share it with her husband. No wonder hubby feels cheated.

Even in this quick overview of the emergence of the Jewish American Princess, we cannot ignore the fact that the JAP is not only Jewish but also American. Scholars of American women's history point to the solid American pedigree of the princess. A century ago, you found her as Miss Southern Belle sitting on the porch of her plantation, stealing sips of mint julep, planning the next season's ball. Consumed by her conspicuous consumption, the American Princess was the subject of careful examination in Thorstein Veblen's seminal turn-of-the-century analysis, *The Theory of the Leisure Class*. Resurrected again, that's her dancing the night away, the flapper girl immortalized in *The Great Gatsby*. She's royal once more in the late-twentieth-century American television sagas of *Dynasty* and *Dallas*. And lo, she rides yet again, this time in her regal Lexus, adorned in shimmering holographic credit cards, reigning proud over her yuppie kingdom. The American Princess is as American as the apple pie she never baked—and she prowled the nation's shopping centers long before the Jews owned the stores.

On this account, the addition of the adjective "Jewish" to the time-honored concept of the American Princess is a classic immigrant strategy. The Jews arrive on these shores eager to imitate the dominant culture but uneasy about abandoning their own ways. The solution? Copy the governing gestures of success and call them your own. The marks of American triumph were always easy to identify. Buying. Having. Hence: the JAP.

Elaine Eckstein finds this analysis disturbing, not because it isn't convincing, but because it indicates how badly Jews have strayed. Elaine is a children's book writer, a mother of two children, and an active participant in her Jewish community in Denver. "I don't want to nitpick about whether Jews are more or less JAPy than other women. That's not what's important. What's important is that this unbridled commercialism is part of our capitalist lifestyle and maybe it's authentic American, but it isn't authentic Judaism. We Jews, and I include Jews from the Orthodox to the assimilated, have bought into mall mentality and, in the process, have distorted Jewish values. It bothers me a great deal."

Elaine Eckstein represents a third view on the status of the Jewish American woman. In one view, espoused by Sherry Etrog earlier in this chapter, Jewish women exhibit an extraordinary interest in accumulating material goods, but that's no cause for shame. This is a natural way to enjoy economic success. In a second view expressed by Michelle Etrog and others, Jews are no more consumer-oriented than anyone else, and the focus on Jews, the very term "JAP," is just a modern manifestation of antifeminism, anti-Semitism, and Jewish self-hatred. According to the third view, expressed here by Elaine Eckstein, Jews are indeed guilty of excessive materialism and that is a problem that must be redressed. Jews ought to reject the commercialism of contemporary American culture. But how does one go about making these changes? Elaine has her misgivings about a frontal appeal. "I don't like the behavior, but do I really want to join the chorus of JAP-thrashers? Jewish women aren't the only guilty ones and singling them out for criticism is unfair. My solution is to keep the criticism private, keep it within the Jewish conversation, not out there in the public."

Elaine's worries may be solved by time. The JAP phenomenon along with the jokes, the criticisms, and the defense may soon disappear. The Jewish American Princess has a daughter, and she's nothing like her mother.

Alexandra Leifer is a high school student in Chappaqua, New York. "JAP jokes are history," she says. "I haven't heard one in years." Although the term "JAP" is still very much part of her and her friend's vocabulary, Alexandra insists it no longer has any particular Jewish content. "JAP describes the way some girls act—and boys, too, for that matter—but it's not a Jewish thing. There's a Catholic girl in our class, Dawn? She's as spoiled as they come and sometimes we call her a CAP, you know, a Catholic American Princess, but usually we'd just call her a JAP. My parents think it's a loaded word because their generation is all caught up in worrying about how the Jews are doing, how they're being judged and all. It's not a problem for us."

Gilad Aronoff sees similarities between Alexandra's generation of American Jewish females and the Israeli women he grew up with. Gilad immigrated to the United States from Israel ten years ago and now works as a computer programmer in Raleigh, North Carolina. "This whole JAP business doesn't exist in Israel. Part of the reason, I'm sure, is that our girls spend two years in the army and that is hardly a shopping expedition. But it's also because these young women know who are they are and aren't anxious about assimilating into a larger culture—they *are* the larger culture. Here in America you also have a new generation of Jews not worried about assimilating. They, too, think they already belong to the larger culture, even though in this case it's not the Jewish culture, but the American culture. Whether that's good or bad is a different question. But I do think that because these kids are secure about their Jewishness, they can talk about Jewish Princesses without discomfort, unlike American Jewish women over the age of thirty, who seem to me a lot more self-conscious about their Jewishness."

And what about the attitude of the next generation of Jewish men toward Jewish women? Some observers expect them to ease up on their hostility toward Jewish women, but not always for enlightened reasons. As one fellow explained to me with an obvious trace of sarcasm, "Now that Jewish men so easily marry non-Jewish, they can stop being so angry with Jewish women." Be that unfair cynicism or psychological insight, the larger truth is that American Jews are successfully integrated into the wider American culture, and behavioral differences between Jewish women and the rest of the population are increasingly difficult to detect. It's a safe bet, therefore, that the bitter jokes and complaints about Jewish mothers and Jewish Princesses will eventually tire themselves into oblivion.

Schmoozing

... and Gentlemen

> *The definition of a computer: a Jewish accountant with a personality.*

> *So this Chassid dies, goes to heaven, and requests to see his rebbe, who had died several years before. They bring him to a room where he sees his rebbe sitting on a chair with a gorgeous blond shiksa on his lap.*
> *"This is heaven for the rebbe?" the Chassid asks.*
> *"No, stupid," he's told, "this is hell for the shiksa."*
> *Underground Chassidic joke*

American Jewish men haven't had it any easier than their female counterparts. They haven't had it easier *with* their female counterparts either.

"I don't get it," Howard Schonfeld says to me with an exasperated shrug that's incongruous with the bravado he usually exudes. Schonfeld is a bustling stockbroker given to upbeat talk and action. "I truly can't figure it out. I'm single, I have a decent profession, I make a decent living, I'm decent looking, a nice Jewish fellow, right? Every Jewish mother's dream for her daughter. So why do I get such grief from these women I date? The usual complaint is that I'm too removed from my feelings, too intellectual, that I have trouble expressing my emotions. Then I notice how these women swoon for gentile jocks with the emotional and intellectual depth of a piece of cardboard. But if I, by the way, even hint that I'm turned on by some hot Wasp actress, I'm guilty of treacherous self-hatred."

This doesn't seem to be a peculiar Jewish problem—stunted

male emotions are a grievance of women everywhere. A more typical and more distinctly Jewish criticism is actually the converse of Schonfeld's. Daniel Salzman, also in the dating phase of his life, claims to be a victim of this more common criticism. "Jewish women have no patience for Jewish guys who show any emotions. With other men it's a plus, but when Jewish men express their anxieties, they are immediately labeled as neurotic. Jewish women tell you how important family is for them, but if you call your mother with any regularity, you're a 'typical Jewish mama's boy.' Underneath all the talk about sensitivity, Jewish women think Jewish men are wimps."

I repeated Schonfeld's opposite experience to Salzman and asked him if this doesn't show how absurd it is to generalize about how Jewish women feel about Jewish men. "On the contrary," said Salzman, "it just shows that Jewish women have it in for Jewish men. Period."

It's easy to interpret these male grumblings as exercises in projection and insecurity, and perhaps that's what they are. Nonetheless, warranted or not, these accusations are widespread, and the irritation they evoke is palpable in the private conversations of American Jewish men. What makes the perceived scorn singe is that these attacks are but the most recent abuse Jewish men have received over the years—mostly from other men. Salzman's anxiety, in particular, resonates to a long tradition of degradation of the Jewish male's virility.

Marsha Stone is married to a non-Jew. She acknowledges that the image of the sexually neurotic Jewish male is an unfair caricature, and yet, "I must say that there's a sense of, how should I put it . . . 'physicality,' a comfort level with one's sexuality, that

I found lacking in so many of the Jewish men I grew up with. This is just me, but I was attracted to a certain 'unapologetic rawness' that I missed in Jewish guys. Jewish men intellectualize their sexiness, if you know what I mean. I'm not suggesting that I'd be happy with just the brawn; lucky for me my husband has a fine brain to go along with his fine body. Let me put it this way: I like that sexual ease that I think is more common in non-Jewish guys.''

Marsha's judgment is by no means exceptional; many Jewish women agree. If Jewish women grapple with a reputation of sexual unwillingness, Jewish men contend with a reputation of sexual underachievement.

Throughout the Middle Ages, Jewish men were demonized with all sorts of devilish physical traits including tails and horns. They were also deemed effeminate, women underneath their male exteriors—Jewish men were even thought to menstruate. In later centuries, European scientists shifted from demonology to the rhetoric of biology, but the attribute of female characteristics persisted. Jewish males were said to exhibit an unusually high incidence of "hysteria" which demonstrated their lack of masculinity (the word "hysteria" derives from the Greek *hysterikos,* meaning "womb," "uterus"). The eminent French scientist Frederick Galton prepared photographic plates of Jewish "gazes" which demonstrated, he submitted, the feminine/neurotic tendencies of Jewish males.

In this century, the association between the Jewish male's femininity and neurosis became even more emphasized in psychoanalytic theory. This, for example, is from Carl Jung: ''They [Jewish males] have this peculiarity in common with women; being physically weaker they have to aim at the chinks in the armor of their adversary, and thanks to this technique which has been forced on them through the centuries, the Jews themselves are best protected when others are vulnerable.''

One of the most vicious, peculiar, and surprisingly influential attacks on Jewish masculinity came from Otto Weininger. A Viennese Jew, Weininger converted to Christianity the day he became a doctor of philosophy, and he committed suicide at the age of twenty-three in the room where Beethoven died. His book *Geschlecht und Charakter* (Sex and Character), written in 1903, was widely read and discussed in intellectual salons all over Europe. In this book, Weininger (by all accounts a closet homosexual) argues that Jews are thoroughly ''womanized'' and that by allowing Jews to assimilate into their culture, European civilization was itself becoming womanized. The only way Europe could save its masculinity and save itself from this insidious emasculating Jewish disease was by ridding itself of its Jews (which explains why Hitler called Weininger the only decent Jew). Weininger's work influenced Ludwig Wittgenstein, Elias Canetti, D. H. Lawrence, and other important European writers. James Joyce, citing Weininger, claimed to have ''a pet theory that Jewish men were by nature women.''

This wasn't just idle European cultural chitchat. The image of the sexually deficient Jewish male not only sunk into the European mind-set, contributing to the horrors that followed, but crossed the ocean and took root in the United States as well. American Jews themselves helped plant those roots.

Back in Europe, the Jewish nerd/buffoon/*schlemiel* was a staple of Yiddish novels, song, and theater. In this setting, however, he was always a type, not typical, just one character in a cast with many sympathetic males. But in America, and in particular the world of contemporary film, this loser was transposed into the Jewish everyman. No one managed this public humiliation with more art (and venom, some would add) than Woody Allen. Allen fumbled his way across the planet's largest screens from Brooklyn to Paris with pit stops in such Jew-forsaken haunts as Butte, Montana, up there for all the world to see. Here was the Jewish male with all his stereotypical smarts intact, but all his sexual capacities pathetically stunted.

The reaction of American Jewish men to this image was complex. One approach was to play up their "female side," a tack many Jewish men still favor. Daniel Salzman's response speaks for many Jewish men: "Just what is the masculinity that Jews are supposed to lack? That we don't hunt, box, drink ourselves into a stupor, or beat our spouses? That we take seriously our responsibility to provide for our wives? That we have some psychological insight into our behavior? If there's a problem here, it's not with us, but with those who see this as some kind of lack of manhood. True, Jewish men fail to live up to the macho standards of others. Thank God."

But there's more to it. There's a little secret associated with this celebration of Jewish male "sensitivity," a wistful piece of faith that Jewish men sometimes share with one another in conversation. These Jewish men like to believe that non-Jewish women are especially attracted to them precisely because of these wholesome and gentle characteristics. As always, Philip Roth poignantly describes the reasoning of the Jewish male in heat.

Who knew that the secret to a Shikse's heart (and box) was not to pretend to be some hook-nosed variety of a goy, as boring and vacuous as her own brother, but to be what one's uncle was, to be what one's father was, to be whatever one was oneself, instead of doing some pathetic little Jewish imitation of one of those half-dead, ice-cold shaygets pricks, Jimmy or Johnny or Tod, who look, who think, who feel, who talk like fighter-bomber pilots.

Do American Jewish men still think this way? No, says Phillip Lowinger, a Chicago-based freelance writer with a concentration on science and technology. His work takes him across the country, and Lowinger concludes from his own observations that "Jewish guys are no longer obsessed with making it with non-Jewish chicks. It's no longer a special challenge, no longer a victory. Jews are just too much part of the world now. Anyway, everyone also realizes that the bit about sensitive Jewish men no longer flies. Jewish men drink with the best of them and some even beat their wives. Besides, who wants this sensitive image? Jewish men will tell you that all this gentility stuff is fine, but the fact is we can, damn it, jock it up with the best."

Stereotypes, however, don't evaporate quite so easily. As we close out the century, Jewish men are caught between an impossible series of demands: to become stars in their profession, but also to renounce the treadmill of ambition; to make money and lots of it, but to renounce the pursuit of wealth in favor of spiritual attainment; to get back to their bodies and shoot more hoops, but to devote themselves to intellectual pursuits; to get out there with the guys, but to stay home with the family. It isn't easy.

And so both American Jewish men and American Jewish women carry the luggage of demeaning labels, of themselves and each other. Roiphe thinks these attributions are at the root of the accelerating intermarriage rates—which turns an attitudinal problem into one of group survival. But just how serious is the intermarriage problem about which we hear so much?

Part II. Intermarriage: Breaking In and Breaking Up

What do you call the grandchildren of intermarried Jews? Christians.   *Milton Himmerlfarb*

The Jewish young man brings his Native American wife home to meet his mother. "Ma, this is my wife, Running Water." "Nice to meet you," says the mother. "I'm Sitting Shiva."

"You can bet on it. Every Jewish religious leader, every community professional, will tell you that the gravest problem facing American Judaism today is intermarriage. Every magazine article will call the situation an unmitigated tragedy." Zev Schwebel's tone conveys that he has a different view. "My unofficial advice," he says, "is to get past the rhetoric, past the presumptions, beyond the statistics. If you want to get into the really interesting territory, ask why it is a calamity. Watch the uniformity collapse. Suddenly everyone has different answers, if they have answers at all. Suddenly everyone's private agendas come to the surface."

While Jewish leaders bemoan the rising rates of intermarriage, the supposed threat, as Schwebel correctly suggests, does mean different things to different people. For traditionally religious Jews, the primary concern is spiritual. Every Jew has a Jewish *neshama,* a Jewish soul which is lost when the Jew marries out of the faith—when the wives of these marriages are non-Jews, so are the children. Organizational professionals focus less on the soul and more on the body politic. Intermarriage means, ultimately, fewer Jews, and fewer Jews means fewer votes and diminished political influence on Jewish interests here and abroad. (Another concern, less often admitted, is that fewer Jews also means fewer dollars for Jewish causes and their own organizations.)

Zev Schwebel isn't overwhelmed by any of these answers. He has been in the "intermarriage business" as an associate director of a major Jewish organization for fifteen years, knows all the players and all the studies. "I'm not denying that these worries are legitimate. They are, absolutely, and in combination they pose a serious situation. Nor do I buy the notion you hear these days that intermarriage is a welcome opportunity to expand the Jewish population. It doesn't work. We can argue about how much of our communal resources we should spend on combating the trend, but let's recognize that intermarriage diminishes our numbers and that's not a plus. What's not so clear to me, however, is all this talk about tragedy. Who says that, say, 3 million committed, Jewishly educated Jews is worse than 5 million Jews with only tangential connections to Judaism? In the Golden Age of Spain, one of the most prolific and productive periods in Jewish history, the total number of the country's Jewish population did not exceed 400,000 people. Numbers aren't everything."

Schwebel is especially perturbed by what he sees as the hyperbolic language that has become part of the campaign against mixed marriages. "When I see those direct-mail envelopes screaming 'Another Holocaust . . . here in America' and then find inside an appeal for money to fight the 'holocaust' of intermarriage, it makes my blood boil. This is an obscenity. Do these people think the evil of the Shoah was just about diminishing the number of Jews in the world? How dare they equate the horror of a Nazi with a couple that intermarries? This sort of talk is morally irresponsible, counterproductive, and just shows how self-serving some of these organizations really are.''

Discussions about intermarriage invariably touch hot buttons in the Jewish community. Most Jewish families in the country have confronted an intermarriage directly, and its prevalence has spawned a mini-industry of Jewish professionals, academic demographers, and policy makers. The consensus of these experts is that, Schwebel's reservations aside, the climbing intermarriage rate is very much a dire threat to the American Jewish community. ''I don't care what words you use,'' says one community professional, ''but I don't know what else to call the disappearance of most of the American Jews but a disaster in the making. Just look at the numbers.''

The numbers are certainly dramatic. Forty years ago, the Jewish intermarriage rate was below 5 percent, the lowest mixed-marriage rate of any religious group in the country. By 1970 it vaulted to 32 percent, and by 1990 it stood at an all-time high of 57 percent. More than half of the American Jews who married in the last decade have chosen someone who is not born Jewish. As of now, 69 percent of Jews are married to Jews, and that number continues to fall as these younger Jews intermarry at even higher rates. Mixed marriage is five times higher among Jews eighteen to thirty-four than among those over fifty-five years of age.

What happened?

Ruth Cohen's intermarriage experience hints at some answers. She describes her Jewish upbringing as "typical, not unpleasant but peripheral. You know the drill: a couple of years of boring Hebrew school, once-a-year visits to the synagogue, seders at Uncle Stan's, and discussions about Israel around the table at crisis times." Ruth married Francis Amato, an Italian Catholic, right after they were students together at Brown. "Some people warned me that our religious differences were bound to get in the way of our relationship. I assure you they haven't. Back at the beginning of our marriage we did talk about conversion. I had no intention of becoming Catholic and Frank might have more seriously considered becoming Jewish if religion meant more to me. For secular Jews like me, being Jewish is about culture and history, not religious persuasion, and you must recognize that it's a lot easier to convert to a set of beliefs or practices than to convert to a people. Quite understandably, Frank found it hard to understand why my being Jewish mattered to me, since I don't go to synagogue and I'm completely alienated from Jewish rituals. I mean, to what would he be converting?"

Ruth's father was "vaguely upset" when she married Frank, and her mother not at all. "But even my father couldn't really complain. I mean, how could Jews attribute anti-Semitism to gentiles for their reluctance to marry Jews and at the same time oppose Jews marrying gentiles? Jews are in a paradoxical vise. They want you to remain Jewish, refrain from dating Christians, but they also want an open society where Christians are not so Christian that they refuse to date Jews. Well, you can't have it both ways. Either you are like everybody else or you're not."

An assessment of the data on intermarriage in America leads to only one conclusion: If American Jews don't want to intermarry, they won't be like everyone else—because everyone else intermarries. The rapid growth in interfaith marriage is a countrywide phenomenon. Before World War II, Americans rarely married across religious lines, and that was even true of Protestants marrying Protestants of different denominations. As recently as 1957, 81 percent of Lutherans married other Lutherans, 83 percent of Baptists married Baptists, and 88 percent of Catholics married Catholics. When mixed marriages did occur, one of the partners usually converted, typically the wife; family harmony required that everyone in the household share the same creed. Then came the 1960s, and a seismic shift unsettled the ground underneath all religious denominations in the United States. Intermarriage rates soared, and spouses now insisted on retaining their own religious persuasions. The numbers tell the continuing story. Today 21.8 percent of married Americans, roughly 33 million couples, live in households where at least one adult has a different religious identification than the rest of the family. By the 1980s intermarriage between European ethnic groups became the norm, not the exception. Interreligious marriages were almost as common. Nearly half of young Catholics now intermarry, 70 percent of young Lutherans marry non-Lutherans, 70 percent of young Methodists marry non-Methodists, and 75 percent of Presbyterians marry non-Presbyterians.

The reasons for this change are many. For one thing, adults are marrying later—the average age of marriage in the United States moved up several years and is now twenty-six for men and twenty-four for women. The average age for Jewish marriages is actually higher than the national average and getting higher. In the 1950s three-fourths of American Jewish women were married before age twenty-five; today only 12 percent marry before age twenty-five. And Jews who marry non-Jews marry even later. Later marriage means less parental influence, less dependence on parents for financial and emotional support, and a lot more independent thinking. Add the current moral climate that highly values individual beliefs and it's not surprising that people marry whom they please and newlyweds no longer insist that their spouses switch religions for the sake of family unity. Moreover, when it comes to Jewish mixed marriages, America is the rule, not the exception. The Jewish intermarriage rate is much the same in France, Hungary, Italy, and the former Soviet Union. In Great Britain, for example, intermarriages are ten times more frequent than they were in 1960—in fact, there are a third to a quarter fewer Jews in England today than thirty years ago.

Why should American Jews really want to be different when it comes to intermarriage? The answer to most committed Jews is obvious. Catholic leaders can remain calm even though one in four Catholics in the United States is now married to someone who isn't. After all, American Catholics constitute 26 percent of the population, the largest Christian denomination in the country. But Jews are only 2 percent of the population to begin with, and the children of mixed marriages are not likely to be Jewish. Of the 770,000 children now raised in homes with parents of mixed religions, 25 percent are raised Jewish, 40 percent are raised Christians, and the rest with no religion at all. A total of 250,000 American households are Catholic-Jewish.

But most of the intermarried Jewish couples who make up the roughly million intermarried households (there are about 2.5 million Jewish households in the country) aren't dissuaded by these figures. In a study conducted for the Jewish Outreach Institute in 1995, 69 percent said that the differences in their religious background posed no difficulties in their relationships and 48 percent of intermarried couples said they had no interest whatsoever in becoming involved in a program that dealt with intermarriage. (Non-Jewish women married to Jewish men are twice as likely to be interested in learning about Jewish outreach programs than are non-Jewish men married to Jewish women.) The children of intermarried couples were even more disinterested in discussing intermarriage: 93 percent said it wasn't a matter of concern for them; 90 percent of children of intermarried couples marry non-Jews.

The incontrovertible fact is that interfaith marriages are commonplace in the United States. For many Jews, this is a welcome attestation to their complete Americanization. Intermarriage, after all, means not just that the *goyim* would play golf with you, not just that they would vote for you, not just that they would let you into their living rooms—but that now they would be willing to have Jewish children and grandchildren. It means Jews had made it from the boardroom to the bedroom.

Listening in on how American Jews talk about intermarriage makes it clear that there is no hard line between those who vehemently oppose it and those who gladly accept it. For many, the feelings are more ambivalent. Although they barely recognize it themselves, even Jews who are deeply opposed to intermarriage sometimes derive a tinge of pleasure when these marriages become high-profile demonstrations of Jews "making it."

Barry Smelzer, a twenty-six-year-old son of immigrants, recalls noticing this equivocal response in his parents' home. "We're all observant. Intermarriage, God forbid, is not even an issue. My parents would have immediate coronaries if any of their children even dated a non-Jew. But it was interesting to see how they read the news about Jackie Onassis spending her last years with Maurice Templesman, a Jew closely tied to the Jewish community. Templesman, by their own accounts, should have been seen as a good-for-nothing who lived with a *shiksa,* and yes there was that reproof too, but you could also detect the patent pride, 'See, here's President Kennedy's widow, the Queen of America, living with this identifiably Jewish man, in fact, his nephew davens in so-and-so's shul.' I guess particularly for my European parents, this was an astounding accomplishment.''

American Jews took notice: Jews were marrying into American nobility and power families. Within the Kennedy clan, Jackie O was not the first to consort with a Jew. Caroline, the president's only daughter, married a Jew, Edwin Shlossberg, in a Roman Catholic Church. Nevertheless, this would have hardly made the marriage palatable to the bride's grandfather, Joe Kennedy, a notorious anti-Semite. Governor Mario Cuomo's daughter married a Jew, and so did the granddaughter of Franklin Delano Roosevelt. Barry Smelzer is disturbed by this partial, albeit covert satisfaction with this marker of Jewish integration into American society. ''If we're going to survive as a people, we need to draw around the wagons,'' Barry explains. ''We can work with non-Jews, be friends, share our cultures, but we cannot merge our families. For American Jews, that's suicide.''

Barry is currently completing his doctorate in modern Jewish history and points to some unsettling parallels. ''Comparisons are always risky, but the recent historical record undermines the notion that high intermarriage rates suggest lasting acceptance. Let me give you some examples. In pre-Holocaust Poland, then the largest Jewish community in Europe, intermarriage rates were below 1 percent. The highly assimilated Jewish communities of

Germany, Italy, Holland, Australia, and Austria, on the other hand, had intermarriage rates that approach those of modern America. Germany, for instance, had an intermarriage rate of 26 percent . . . and not a good ending there, was it?''

American Jews can be usefully divided into three main groups with regard to their attitude toward intermarriage. One segment is unalterably opposed and believes we must do everything we can to stop this phenomenon; another believes that it is a fait accompli, a sign of social progress and no reason for distress; the third sector also recognizes the inevitability of intermarriage in a liberal, tolerant culture but is nevertheless uncomfortable with the phenomenon.

Lyddia Elster qualifies as a member of this large swath of ''accepting but uneasy'' group. Her son, divorced from his Jewish wife, married a non-Jewish woman a year ago. ''Happy? I'm not happy. But what are you going to do? This is how it goes these days. I think the media has a lot to do with it. You rarely see a program where a Jew is married to another Jew; I can't recall a single one. I remember back in the 1970s there was a show on TV, *Bridget Loves Bernie,* which featured an interfaith couple, and the Jews made a stink about this and the show was thrown off the air. Then intermarriage became routine. Do you remember the show *Chicken Soup,* an intermarriage sitcom starring Jackie Mason and Lynn Redgrave? It aired in 1989, I think. Anyway, the show didn't last long. It was canceled, not because it bothered people's religious beliefs, but because it bothered their taste, the show happened to be awful. Times had changed. Now you see intermarriage all over television: *L.A. Law, Rhoda, Cheers, thirtysomething,* and *Roseanne.* I mean, in all honesty, what could I expect different from my son? It's the world he lives in.''

The fact that Lyddia Elster's son is divorced deserves some notice in this context: Divorce, demographers tell us, is an important factor in the growth of Jewish intermarriage. The national divorce rate in the United States has exploded, tripling in the decades between 1960 and 1980. According to conservative estimates, nearly one of every two marriages that took place in the 1980s is likely to end in divorce. Half of all children under eighteen will have lived for some time with a divorced parent. The Jewish divorce rate has kept apace during this period, and that's a dramatic change from years past. In the old days of just a generation ago, Jews divorced at less than half the rate of Protestants and even often less than Catholics, who officially aren't permitted to divorce, but today 18 percent of American Jews have undergone at least one divorce, well within the national average of 15–20 percent, and younger Jews divorce even more frequently, at about the same rate as the national average of their peers. The tie-in to intermarriage is this: After divorce, Jews are more likely to marry non-Jews. Brandeis University researchers conducted a study of Jews married in the 1980s and found that 86 percent had married Jews in their first marriage, 70 percent in their second marriage, and only 54 percent in their third. Surely, part of the reason is that later marriages have less likelihood of bearing children, so those who have already raised Jewish children in their previous marriages feel freer about marrying out of their faith the next time around.

In addition to the increase in divorce rate, the reasons for the rise of intermarriage are, as we see, manifold: a greater willingness among non-Jews to marry Jews, lack of Jewish education, marriages later in life when parental influence is lessened, the influence of the media. Geography counts too, since as one leaves the more heavily populated Jewish urban centers, the pool of coreligionists is smaller: New York Jews intermarry significantly less than Jews elsewhere; in Denver, for example, the intermarriage rate is 75 percent. But whatever the causes, the effect is clear: Jews are intermarrying with abandon.

So what to do? Here is the current central policy debate.

On the one side are what we can call the "inreachers." In their view, the battle is basically over, and the bulk of American Jewry has lost. Steven Bayme, director of the Jewish Communal Affairs Department of the American Jewish Committee, is convinced that it is simply naive to think that large numbers of intermarried couples will become interested in Judaism. "Most mixed marriages have taken a walk and there's nothing we can do about it," he says. "To simply chase after people who have no desire to be chased is a misdirection of Jewish communal resources." When Jews live in an open society, free of blatant anti-Semitism, they intermarry with non-Jews. The level of Jewish education for most American Jews is pitiful, hardly sufficient to resist the temptation to lose oneself in the American culture at large. Intermarriage comes with the territory. According to the inreachers, the best response is to reach in. Put the effort in prevention and draw the circle around the inner core of committed Jews, give them your full communal and religious attention, amplify their Jewish education, nourish their ties to Israel, and protect their Jewish affiliations. The trade-off is that you lose heavy percentages of those uncommitted Jews who are outside your shielded circle—but these Jews on the outside are lost anyway, if not immediately, then in a generation or two. Any major effort to stem their further assimilation spreads Jewish resources too thin, threatens the inner core, and is doomed to fail anyway.

Strong support for this viewpoint comes from Zionist demographers, who see Israel as the only bastion of future Jewry, and the Orthodox, who oppose weakening Jewish legal strictures for the sake of welcoming intermarried Jews.

On the other side of this debate are the "outreachers." First, they insist, we have to stop seeing only the negative side of intermarriage rates. These marriages involve not only Jews marrying out but non-Jews marrying in, an infusion of new blood into the Jewish ranks. Though hardly enough, a substantial and increasing number of intermarried couples do raise their children Jewish. In any case, the American Jewish community cannot afford to kiss good-bye to the majority of Jews. True, intermarriage is less of a problem for Orthodox Jews, but they are only 7–10 percent of American Jewry, a proportion not likely to grow substantially in the near future. What of the other 90 percent of American Jews? The time has come to face reality, say the outreachers. There are more than half a million children of mixed marriages and that number will grow considerably. We need vigorous programs that encourage non-Jews married to Jews to join the tribe. American synagogues now sponsor "outreach programs" aimed at interfaith couples and that's the way to go. As Egon Mayer, one of the country's leading authorities on intermarriage, says, we need to move from "outrage to outreach."

Moreover, as other Jewish demographers point out, even if present trends continue, the consequences are not nearly as dire as the pessimists suggest. Steven M. Cohen, a leading sociologist of American Judaism, believes that the much publicized inter-

139

marriage rates are inflated, but that at any rate American Jews are becoming stronger, not weaker, in their Jewish affiliation. According to Cohen: "While thousands, if not hundreds of thousands, of mixed-ancestry Jews will be lost to Judaism, there will be millions of American Jews around, and a large—if not growing—fraction of this community will, relatively speaking, be highly involved in Jewish life. Thus, while the continuity of many Jewish families may be at risk, the continuity of an active American Jewish community is not."

This was Schwebel's view too, as we noted at the outset of this discussion of intermarriage. Numbers, he said, aren't everything. But as his critics remind him, while numbers may not be everything, they cannot be ignored. American Jews need a critical mass to remain a viable community, and they cannot take for granted that a substantial fraction of this community will be highly involved in Jewish life. This will take work. Rachel Cowan, a rabbi, communal activist, and herself a convert to Judaism, warns, "If one thinks of intermarriage as a kind of disease that requires an antidote, then we've already lost. The basic truth about intermarriage is that the Jewish community has been unable to make itself a place where its own young people want to spend much of their time." The stark truth is that if the American Jewish community doesn't make itself that kind of place, the intermarriage problem will be solved by itself—there will hardly be any Jews left to intermarry.

Part III. Sexy Jews

One who willfully does not engage in propagation of the species is like someone who has shed blood.

Talmud Yevamot

A Chassidic young man was extraordinarily nervous before his first sexual encounter with his new wife. "Relax," he's told, "you're not the first person to do this, you know. Your father had sex with your mother too."

"Yes," says the groom, "but that was with my mother. I don't even know this girl!"

In 1994 the National Opinion Research Center at the University of Chicago published the most authoritative contemporary picture of sexual habits of Americans. The major findings were summarized on the front page of the *New York Times,* and the study was widely discussed in books and articles. Less well publicized, but evident in the findings, was this bit of intriguing information: Jews have more sex than any other group in the United States.

Contrary to the mythology, Jews in America have more sex and more sexual partners than blacks. Contrary to the image of the nebbishy, asexual Jews portrayed in the movies and culture at large, and contrary to their own sexual self-image, Jews have significantly more sex than any other group in every category the study examined. Here are some representative numbers: 34 percent of Jews have had more than eleven partners since the age of eighteen, while the corresponding number for other Americans in this bracket is 20 percent; 42 percent of Americans have had

141

more than five partners since the age of eighteen—64 percent of Jews are in this category. Jewish sexual activity isn't only about promiscuity. Jews also have more sex in terms of frequency than any other ethnic group. And while advanced education generally correlates positively with increased sexual behavior, this alone doesn't explain these high Jewish scores—Asians, though highly educated, have less sex with fewer partners than the average American. The graffito in the Temple bathroom exhorts us to "put the id back in the yid," but these data suggest that if anything, we need to put the lid on the id.

Sex for Jews isn't the same as sex for Christians. It isn't that Jews have sex differently, but that they think differently about sex. Judaism and Christianity certainly influenced each other, and internal disputes about sexuality flourish within each religion; nonetheless, when you talk about sex, you can't talk about a shared Judeo-Christian tradition.

Benjamin Belzer, a sex therapist on Long Island, sees this divergence as beginning early in life. "If you are raised Jewish and try to imagine the best, most perfect human being in all of history, you don't think of someone who has been celibate. This holds true whether your upbringing is postmodern, assimilated, or Chassidic ultraorthodox. The holiest men and women of Jewish history were all married. Abraham was, Moses was, King David was, Maimonides was, as were all rabbis past or present. Ben Azzai is the lone exception, the sole celibate among the rabbis of the Talmud, yet it was he who declared that 'one who chooses not to procreate is the equivalent of a murderer.' These rabbis didn't merely opt to marry and have children—they had to: 'Be fruitful and multiply' is the first commandment in the Torah. In Judaism you cannot be a saint and a virgin." This brings to mind Lenny Bruce's routine that focused on this feature of Judaism, though with a lot less delicacy: "Unlike your people," he tells his non-Jewish audience, "our people were *shtuppers*."

The implications of this pro-sexual upbringing are difficult to overstate and are rarely stated at all. Even when Christians (especially Catholics) distance themselves from their religious upbringing, they tend to maintain a reservoir of respect for those who choose celibacy in the service of a higher cause. But in Judaism you get no points for lifelong chastity. In this instance, Jews are one with Muslims, Hindus, and just about every other religion in the world; of major faiths, only Christianity and some branches of Buddhism consider total sexual abstinence noble. It is also worth noting that the path of celibacy did not remain within the strictly Christian sphere, but crossed over to the domain of scholarship. For more than two thousand years until the twentieth century, no major, first-tier philosopher in the Western world (with the exception of John Stuart Mill) was married. (A few apparently did have sexual encounters.) This list includes Saint Augustine, Aquinas, and, of course, all the church fathers, and also Descartes, Leibniz, Locke, Berkeley, Hume, Kant, Hegel, Schopenhauer, Kierkegaard, and Nietzsche. Spinoza, the only Jew who qualifies for a place in this pantheon of great philosophers, was also a celibate, but Spinoza renounced his ties to his mother religion. Jewish scholars were invariably married.

This is not to suggest that Judaism promotes an unmitigated hedonistic approach to sex. It doesn't. Jews, in fact, have an equivocal attitude toward sexual license, and as historian David Biale has shown in his masterful overview *Eros and the Jews,* this oscillating viewpoint stretches all the way from the present back to biblical times. Both tendencies come to the fore in conversations about sex among contemporary Jewish Americans.

Ultraorthodox Jews are unusual in this regard. They are not in the habit of discussing their sexual lives with outsiders, nor, for that matter, among themselves either. Talking about sex in a personal context violates codes of modesty, and sexual references are regularly clothed in euphemisms and allusions. Beresh Manis, a thirty-five-year-old Chassid living in Williamsburg and a father of seven (six girls and a boy), is much more forthcoming in his conversation with me than are most of his friends. We speak in Yiddish with a sprinkling of classical Hebrew, but Beresh surprises me by occasionally dropping a current, state-of-the-art American idiom. Beresh is more ''out there'' than his cohorts, and wants to be certain that his remarks are not misconstrued, and his views not be taken as representative of other Chassidim. I assure him that I can spot the anomalies. There aren't many.

Yes, he's heard the rumor that Chassidim have sex only between the sheets. ''Whoever invented that nonsense?'' he wonders. We recall the Talmudic debate on whether sex is permitted in the daytime and the view held by the rabbis in the Palestinian Talmud that a couple should be naked during lovemaking. One can justifiably conclude that in rabbinic Judaism, when sex is permitted, just about any kind of sex is permitted. ''It's true that traditional Judaism frowns on sex without marriage, but it also frowns on marriage without sex,'' Beresh adds, making his case for the sexual openness of Chassidism. ''Mystical texts, especially the Kabalah, are full of sexual imagery, and that tradition has much importance in the Chassidic outlook.''

The Jewish Battle of the Sexes

Tracing Jewish sexual practice to Kabalistic speculation is always complicated and self-selective, in contrast to the influence of the Halacha, Jewish law. Here the rules are explicit, detailed, and, for observant Jews, definitive. While rabbinic Judaism, as do all traditional religions, posits reproduction as the central purpose of sexual congress, the Halacha also underscores the importance of sexual pleasure for its own sake. Moreover, a case can also be made—and many contemporary rabbis make the case repeatedly—that the Halacha is overtly sympathetic to female sexuality (particularly when one considers the times in which these rules were codified). In Jewish law, sex is a woman's right and a man's duty. The male sexual obligation, the law of *onah,* derives from the biblical description of the male's duties in marriage: "he must not withhold from the woman her food, her clothing or her conjugal rights" (Exodus 21:10). The Talmud, accordingly, stipulates that a wife has a right to divorce if her husband withholds sex from her; but a woman need not have sex with her husband if she finds him repulsive. Many texts also overtly recognize the woman's pleasure in sex—the Mishna in Talmud Sotah, for example, remarks, "A woman prefers little food and sexual indulgence to much food and continence."

Nachmonides, a leading thirteenth-century sage, specifically calls for gentleness in lovemaking and recommends that men help their wives reach orgasm first. At least one Talmudic rabbi held that unlike the Christian notion that even lust in the heart is a form of adultery ("I say to you that every one who looks at a woman lustfully has already committed adultery with her in his heart": Matthew 5:28), one may conjure up another woman's image if that helps in making love to one's wife, provided the other woman is not his other wife. The text is silent, however, about the permissibility of the woman thinking about another man.

The Talmud also stipulates how much sex is appropriate—it depends on one's profession. According to Rabbi Eliezer, men of independent means should go at it daily, twice a week for laborers, and once a month for camel drivers. Scholars should have sex more often than others and especially on Friday night, the holy Sabbath. Rabbi Moshe Feinstein, the preeminent Orthodox rabbinical authority in the United States after World War II, ruled that because women in our generation live in a culture that promotes sexual arousal more so than in previous generations, scholars should be especially conscientious to have sex at least twice a week.

Soshana Twersky has little patience with this litany of texts. "Spare me," she pleads. "What, you're going to trot out Talmudic dicta that show the rabbis as sexual progressives? I'm sure you can, as I'm sure I can match you one for one with some text or ruling which is antisexual. There is, after all, a central notion that the sexual urge is the result of the *yetzer harah,* the evil inclination. And when it comes to women, I'm sure I probably can come up with three antiwomen texts for any one you find favorable. Let's get back to the basics. In Halachic Judaism masturbation is prohibited. Homosexuality is a capital offense. Premarital sex, even holding hands, is verboten. The mingling of the sexes is forbidden, as is any encounter which may lead to illicit sexual arousal such as pornography, uncovered female knees, mixed bathing, or even the sound of a woman singing." (These prohibitions are directed primarily at men because they, not women, might succumb to "spilling seed." Similarly the biblical

146

injunction against homosexuality applies to males, not females.)
"A strict Orthodox man will not be alone in a room with a
woman other than his wife, nor will he shake a woman's hand.
So let's not pretend this tradition is at the cutting edge of sexual
revolution, okay?"

Soshana Twersky grew up Orthodox but is no longer. She is
part of a growing chorus of Jewish women activists who believe
that Judaism must go further in eliminating its sexist traces. The
issue, Soshana says, isn't so much about Jewish law as it is about
the entrenched customs that surround those laws. What especially
bothers her is the hypocrisy she sees permeating these discussions. "I'm tired of hearing this self-serving defense of the Jewish attitude toward sexuality. At least the ultra-Orthodox tell it to
you straight: Any public display of sexuality is an abomination;
women should have less participation in Jewish ritual than men;
women cannot be witnesses in a Jewish court; women are tempt-
resses that must be kept away from the perpetually horny men;
and, in general, wives should serve their husbands. With them
we know where we stand. Contemporary Iran is their model state.
It's the more modern traditionalists that irk me. Laws that make
menstruating women untouchables are now advertised as a wonderful way to reinstill love for one's wife. Rules requiring women
to cover up their bodies are excused as showing respect for
women. And on and on with the apologetics. Give me a break.
The fact is that rabbinic Judaism is plenty uptight about sex and
a backwater for the liberation of women."

Texts do prove little—there are more than enough to confirm
any agenda about Jewish sexuality. Twersky is certainly correct,
too, in noting that custom has as important an influence as the

law in determining the sexual lives of traditional Jews. The intense debate among observant Jewish women is how much of this custom can be altered without jeopardizing the law. Soshana Twersky answers with this joke:

A yeshiva boy asks his rabbi if it is permissible to dance with his wife. The rabbi shakes his head and rules that he ought not. It is unseemly.

"But we can have sex anytime we please on the days she is permitted to me?"

"Absolutely," says the rabbi.

"In the missionary position?"

"Sure."

"With my wife on top? From behind?"

"Any position is okay," says the rabbi.

"Oral sex? Cunnilingus?"

"That too is allowed."

"How about sex standing up?" asks the student.

Here the rabbi balks. "Actually that should be avoided. It might lead to dancing."

For most American Jews, these debates about Jewish law and Jewish custom are utterly irrelevant. Most American Jews are not observant and they couldn't care less about the strictures of Jewish law. When they talk about sex, they rarely talk *as Jews*. Nevertheless, the perspective of Jewish tradition forms the context, if only subliminally, of their attitudes toward sex, for Jews, unlike Christians, lack even the residue of the notion that sex is a sin. At the same time, American Jews are citizens of America and participate in a culture where the push and pull of sex is constant, the contradictory celebration and castigation of sex unrelenting. Added to this confusion are the aspersions Jewish men and women cast on each other's sexuality, attributions that are all the more ironic and disturbing when one considers the comparative health of the sex lives of contemporary American Jewish men and women.

CHAPTER FIVE

From Self-Criticism to Self-Loathing

I'm not a Jew. Only Jew-ish (you know, I don't go whole hog).
Beyond the Fringe

The Jewish ability to internalize any criticism and condemnatory remark and castigate themselves is one of the marvels of human nature. Aaron Appelfeld

Two Jews lined up against the wall to be shot by a firing squad are offered blindfolds. One shouts, "Absolutely not. I will face you scoundrels straight on."
"Shush. What's the matter with you?" whispers the other Jew. "Don't ask for trouble."

Part I. Self-Criticism

Jewish Guilt

"It's ridiculous. I'm walking home and this homeless guy asks me for some money to buy a coffee, pizza, bus fare to Hoboken, the usual recitation. Most normal people walk by. Me, I can't just shake my head, say no, sorry. I'm compelled to mutter something about not having spare change on me. Tell me, why do I have to make excuses, apologize to this bum on the street? And it's not just the panhandler. I'm uncomfortable when a doorman opens the door for me, I can't handle getting a shoeshine in public, I'm afraid to ask the waiter to take back a spoiled bottle of wine. I behave as though I'm partially to blame for all the world's inequities. It's my Jewish guilt."

A similar lament from another Jew: "Looking back, I think

we should have insisted that Jessica continue with her piano lessons. She started, stopped, started, stopped, and finally we caved in and let her get away with giving it up altogether. We made a mistake. Maybe it's my Jewish guilt, but I believe it was our responsibility to have kept her at it."

On and on, Jews complain about their shortcomings. They should call their parents more often, they should clean the house more frequently, they should get more serious about working out, they should have read that best-seller, written thank-you letters, paid bills, called their friends. The confession always ends with the same refrain: "I guess it's my Jewish guilt acting up." Which is interesting, you see, because my gentile friends give me the exact same speech about *their* sins of omission, without, of course, the annotation blaming their lapses on their Jewish heritage.

Perhaps this whole bit about Jewish guilt is just silly, I tentatively propose to a group of Jews enjoying Sunday brunch in an apartment on the Upper West Side of New York. Perhaps Jews don't feel guiltier than any other people and it's time they stopped acting as if they do. Actually, guilt is only a bridge to the larger topic I want to discuss—the general Jewish tendency toward self-criticism—but we never get there. Jewish guilt remains the morning's focus.

"You think maybe Jews aren't more ravaged by guilt than other people?" asks Raffi Spira incredulously. Raffi owns a restaurant in Queens and seems to be without even a trace of personal anxiety. He is convinced, however, that anxiety is a Jewish characteristic. "I don't doubt that non-Jews on occasion experience remorse. Catholics mostly, I suppose. But Jews clearly have a major market share in the guilt business. Just listen to the way Jews forever inflict guilt on each other—parents on their kids, kids on their parents, spouse on spouse, God on the entire Jewish people, the Jewish people on God, everyone complaining about the shortcomings of everyone else. Feeling contrite is part of the Jewish birthright. It's all part of the Jewish neurosis.''

On the other hand, Rebecca Adler, our host that morning, thinks my proposal has merit. ''I must say that I, too, am tired of this Jewish-guilt bit,'' she says. ''The whole notion is nonsense *narishkeit,* a crock. I happen to do psychological research for a living, with an emphasis in related areas, like narcissism, shame, self-esteem. I'm still waiting to see a single piece of solid empirical research showing that Jews feel more guilty than others. I haven't come across any such data, and it's not for want of trying. Why Jews insist on promoting this self-image is beyond me.''

But with just a smidgen of pressure, Rachel acknowledges that she does have some thoughts on why Jews do this guilt number on themselves. ''Guilt,'' she theorizes, ''is just one trait in a mass of neuroses that Jews regularly attribute to themselves. The laundry list is long: Jews are hypochondriacs, Jews whine, Jews are worrywarts, Jews are anal-compulsive, Jews are orally fixated. I guess at one time being Jewish really did define people's lives, so every *meshugana* blamed his hang-ups on his Jewishness. This sort of labeling obviously continues. I still hear Jews refer to their Jewishness as an explanation for their hemorrhoids, insomnia, cellulite, why they love gambling, why they hate gambling, why they excel at sex or why they fail at sex, eat too much, diet too much. It's the same with guilt, which automatically gets labeled *Jewish* guilt. The only thing really Jewish about the guilt is this penchant for criticizing yourself and then calling it Jewish.''

Indeed, guilt is just one example of this tendency of American Jews to see themselves as neurotically driven or ''psychologically overwrought.'' This self-image emerges regularly in books, on the screen, and in private conversations but is not wholly self-induced. From the end of the nineteenth century and through much of the twentieth, scientists asserted with supreme confidence that Jews were more neurotic than others, that they suffered from a chronic nervousness that manifested itself in all sorts of behavioral deficiencies—the only debate was whether this condition was congenital or the result of stressful environment. (There were stranger suggestions too: A Jewish psychiatrist, Abraham Meyerson, proposed that Jewish mental anxiety was the result of thinking too hard and too often.) Recent data indicate that, in fact, Jews suffer from lower rates of psychosis than most other ethnic groups, but the perception of the neurotic Jew doggedly persists. Feeling guilty and constant self-criticism are seen as part of this neurotic pattern.

''Whoa, hang on a minute.'' Dr. Michael Marx, a Boston heart surgeon, has little patience with this interpretation of guilt as neurosis. ''Self-criticism is not unhealthy and is one of our great strengths. The lack of it is other people's weakness.'' According to Marx, to their credit, Jews have always been relentlessly self-critical, forever picking at their emotional scars. ''Already in the Bible, the trait appears with the rebukes of the prophets. The call for repentance is an ongoing demand throughout the Jewish calendar. It's no accident that the holiest day of the year, Yom Kippur, is devoted to communal confession. On every major holiday, Jews recite the prayer *umipnay chatuaynu,* which blames their exile on their sins. Every Saturday, rabbis admonish their congregation for its spiritual failures and exhort the members to improve. Come to think of it, I suppose that criticizing Jews for being too self-critical is itself very Jewish. The truth is, it wouldn't hurt if more Jews returned to some serious self-criticism.''

One hears this often: Jewish guilt is built into the very structure of Judaism. Rabbi Harlan Wechsler, in his book *What's So Bad About Guilt?,* explains that connection: ''Deep in the Jewish tradition, deep in the psyche of the Bible, is a human being who can experience guilt. And it is true, whether one seeks to praise the fact or bury it very deep, that the culture of the Jews is a culture rooted in that conception of a human being. More than guilt's a problem, it is second nature to Jews.''

Freud, who wrote a great deal about Jews, guilt, and Jewish guilt, thought much the same. In *Moses and Monotheism* he presents the ''Freudian'' argument that the Jews experienced a deep anger with God, the analogue of a murderous hostility to the father, and that hostility gave rise to guilt, which, in turn, gave rise to extremely stringent ethical ideals. Freud interprets these rigid rules as characteristic of ''obsessive neurotic reaction formations.'' Psychoanalytical literature is replete with explanations of Jewish guilt as a reaction to the rigors of Jewish laws.

The psychological explanation for the phenomenon of Jewish guilt doesn't ring true in America, however, for here most Jews aren't religious. They don't beat their breasts in the synagogue and they are not chagrined about their irreligious ways. And yet, the cliché about Jewish guilt is commonplace among assimilated, not traditional, American Jews. Try an "it's my Jewish guilt" routine among a group of fundamentalist observant Jews and you'll get blank stares—they won't know what in heaven's name you're talking about.

According to Rabbi Zvi Blanshard, the absence of the Jewish-guilt syndrome among traditional Jews points to a fundamental feature of Jewish modernism. Rabbi Blanshard has plenty of occasions to think professionally about this topic. He is a senior lecturer at the Center for Learning and Leadership (CLAL), and in addition to his rabbinical degree, he holds a Ph.D. in philosophy and is a practicing therapist. Although in his clinical practice he finds no higher incidence of guilt feelings among his Jewish patients than his non-Jew ones, he does agree that Jews have dealt with guilt for a long time, certainly in their texts and literature. "Assimilated, nontraditional American Jews joke about guilt because they have inherited this Jewish culture, this religion, which transmits a sense of responsibility, but they have not inherited the institutional apparatus for expiating that guilt. Not just the Jews, by the way—a medieval Catholic could go to church, confess, and be done with it, but it's more complicated for a modern Catholic." But why confess at all? I ask. Why bother? "Because guilt that festers becomes psychologically unhealthy," says Blanshard. "If you are a nonpracticing Jew, what do you do? You could deny your guilt, but that's never easy . . . or you make a joke of it. Freud was right in judging humor, even self-deprecating humor, as a sophisticated and in many ways a healthy way of dealing with this sort of anxiety."

The Jewish spiel on guilt has been traced to religious strictures, emotional background, Jewish history, and creative mixtures of these various explanations. For example, combining history and psychology, Mortimor Ostow, a contemporary psychoanalyst who has written widely on Judaism and psychology, suggests: "Misfortune creates a feeling of guilt. This is a common clinical observation. The feeling of guilt seems to arise from a sense of helplessness and recedes when the helplessness recedes. It is this mechanism that accounts for the guilt frequently countered in Jewish thought and writing. Where tragedy is absent in Jewish history guilt does not appear." Nearly every conversation among Jews about Jewish guilt is sure to produce some other innovative explanation.

Rhonda Beth Auerbach likes the psychological spin on Jewish guilt but thinks it doesn't go far enough: "Forget the religious stuff. Rules against eating pork aren't what cause Jewish guilt. Jewish self-criticism is not about ritual, it's about the way Jews feel and think about their inner lives." Rhonda owns a boutique in Greenwich, Connecticut and is a self-proclaimed "people observer." "Sure, in some broader sense Jewish traits are based on Judaism," she acknowledges, "although it may be the other way around. But if you ask me, the reason why you get so much of this Jewish self-criticism, Jews yakking about their inner anxieties all the time, is because Jews are an introspective lot. Jews are talkers and they constantly talk about their feelings. They don't feel more than others, they just notice it better. You think it's an accident that so many of the high-profile therapists who write books about guilt and neuroses are Jewish?"

These conversations rarely end here. Talk of Jewish self-criticism inevitably spills into a conversation about the price Jews pay for this habit. The cost, or so it is commonly suggested, is happiness.

Can Jews Be Happy?

Why don't Jews drink?
It dulls the pain.

The renowned children's author Maurice Sendak, author of the popular *Where the Wilds Things Are,* says that as a child he spent a lot of time with the Italian neighbors across the hall. Only later did he discover that they were not Jews. Growing up, he thought that Italians, in contrast to his own family, were just happy Jews. According to common folklore, non-Jews can manage unalloyed, mindless, purposeless, uncomplicated fun—but not Jews. Jews feel bad about feeling good. Woody Allen reflects that turn when in his most Jewish persona he remarks that we've progressed from sex without guilt to guilt without sex. Oh, Jews laugh, all right, and are even better at making others laugh, but underneath, in the texture of their daily lives, they are a serious, even solemn lot. You hear this charge repeated often, most insistently from younger Jews.

Jason Solomon, a seventeen-year-old student in Pasadena, is unusually reflective about the importance of pleasure in his life. "I'm an affluent teenager in Southern California, so of course I'm supposed to be a spoiled kid only interested in a good time. That's not it, though. It's the heaviness around me that gets to me. The message I get at home, from my teachers in Hebrew school, is always the same. Work. Achievement. Learning. Make a contribution to society. Those are good things, sure, but what about the importance of *my* happiness, what about *my* joy? I never hear about that. On Yom Kippur my rabbi gave this sermon about

157

how the pursuit of happiness as a basic human goal was an American invention taken over by the advertising industry, but never a Jewish ideal. Jews are about obligation, you know, service to God and one's fellowmen and all that, and how we can't just pursue happiness when others have none, that sort of thing. Well, I think having a good time is a legitimate goal. Maybe all that history of Jewish suffering makes it impossible for Jews to chill, but why should I perpetuate that suffering?"

Solomon's complaint had been foreshadowed decades earlier with even more bitterness by Alexander Portnoy, Philip Roth's seminal protagonist and the twentieth century's proof text of American Jewish neurosis. Portnoy fantasizes about his father enjoying an affair with a gentile woman and the emotional repercussions that are sure to ensue:

Yes a regular Jewish desperado, my father. I recognize the syndrome perfectly. Come, someone, anyone, find me out and condemn me—I did the most terrible thing you can think of: I took what I am not supposed to have! Chose pleasure for myself over duty to my loved ones! Please, catch me, incarcerate me, before God forbid I get away with it completely—and go out and do again something I actually like.

You hear often that traditional Judaism teaches a wariness about indulging one's pleasures, but as usual, the truth is more nuanced, more complex; classical Judaism provides a medley of voices about the pursuit of joy. Passages abound in the Talmud remonstrating against licentiousness and physical indulgence—at one point the rabbis even proscribe singing in the wake of the destruction of the Temple. On the other hand, Jews are exhorted to "serve God with joy." Rav (in the Talmud Yerushalmi) says that in the world to come we will be required to give an accounting for every opportunity we had to enjoy a legitimate pleasure but refused without sufficient cause. This range of attitudes is reflected in the Hebrew language itself, which is flush with synonyms for "joy" (*deetza, reena, simcha, chedva, sasson,* etc.). It has, of course, at least as many words for "suffering."

This equivocal attitude toward pleasure manifested itself throughout Jewish history. Every now and then new movements sought to introduce pleasure as a Jewish virtue. Chassidism, developed in the eighteenth century, was the most successful, but also most controversial. A central doctrine of Chassidism was ecstatic, fraternal celebration in the service of God, but its promotion of drinking, singing, and dancing deeply offended the established Jewish powers of the time. In more recent years, Zionism, too, has been challenged for its anti-ascetic strains. Hermann Cohen, the illustrious Jewish philosopher of the early twentieth century, commented to Franz Rosenzweig, the other illustrious Jewish philosopher of his day, that the problem with Zionism was that "those fellows want to be happy." Gershom Scholem, who reports this conversation in his autobiography, adds that "this is the most profound critique of Zionism ever."

Elky Rabinowitz is sure that Jason Solomon's carping about his parents' antihedonism is, after all, no more than standard teenage chafing. Elky spends her days with this age group as a teacher in a Boca Raton local high school and contrasts her students with her own Jewish peers and the many senior citizens in her neighborhood. "I can't see any difference in attitude between the Jewish kids and Christian kids when it comes to wanting to have a good time. Everyone complains that their parents get in the way. The Jewish adults I know are another story. These ancient texts you quote don't matter—whatever joy Jewish religion allows, Jewish history has expunged.

"Let's face it," Elky continues, "you think of Jews, you don't think of a happy-go-lucky people, and given the tragedies of Jewish history, that's hardly surprising. Jews can be joyous, sure, but never totally joyous, never joyous with abandon. At the end of the Jewish wedding ceremony the groom steps on a glass and shatters it to recall the destruction of the Temple two thousand years ago so that even the most festive celebration commemorates suffering. Maybe the next generation will be different, but as far as I can tell, contemporary American Jews can't totally relax. Not yet. Despite our success, Jews are still too unsettled, too unsure to get cozy in the easy chair. That's especially true for the older Jews around here, even though they've come here to Florida to retire and take it easy. This century has been just too ghastly for Jews. Too many memories."

Persecution, however, may not be what separates Jews from their comforts. Some suggest the inhibition against pleasure is rooted in Jewish ethical teaching: You're taught not to feel too good in a world with so much pain. Sigmund Freud tells the joke about the rich Jewish baron who, deeply moved by a beggar's tale of woe, rings for his servants: "Throw him out. He's breaking my heart." Freud concludes, "There really is no advantage in being a rich man if one is a Jew. Other people's misery makes it impossible to enjoy one's happiness."

"I think that is the heart of it," says Joann Berofsky, who took this perspective to heart and became a social worker in Detroit. "You remember how your mother made you eat? She'd ask, 'How could you throw away your vegetables when millions of people are starving in China?' Your wise-guy answer telling her to send your portion to Shanghai missed the point. Other people suffer, it's your business. So you end up feeling lousy, feeling guilty when you feel satisfied. It's a no-win situation."

Such is the American Jewish conversation about guilt, suffering, and perpetual self-criticism. First, they argue about whether Jews do, in fact, indulge in an inordinate amount of self-judgment. Then, assuming that they do, they argue about why they do, spinning theories that weave through history, Talmud, ethics, and psychotherapy. Next, they wonder if the next generation of American Jews will be as self-critical. Finally, someone proposes that only a neurotic people could spend so much time discussing whether they are neurotic. And the discussion begins anew.

These discussions proceed, for the most part, amiably, often humorously, tongue in cheek. But when the line between self-criticism and genuine self-degradation becomes blurry, the conversation grows serious. Jews have a long-standing awareness of self-hatred. It has a painful familiarity.

Part II: Jewish Self-Hatred

Why was Moses not permitted to enter the Promised Land but Joseph had his bones brought there for burial? Moses was punished because he concealed his Jewishness from the man whose daughter he wished to marry. He posed as an Egyptian, not as a member of the enslaved tribe. Joseph, on the other

*hand, throughout his stay in Egypt never denied his Hebrew
background.*   *A midrash*

*Why hate yourself when there are so many willing to do it for
you?*   *A good question*

"Jewish self-hatred? Doesn't exist, a misnomer."

The man leans in to me, halving the distance of the small
table between us. "Hey, don't get me wrong, I know lots of Jews
who hate Jews, hate the fact that they are Jewish. They'd never
admit it, though, not in a trillion years. But just listen to them
talk, observe their attitudes. Jewish bar mitzvahs are loud and
obnoxious, but Italian street festivals are picturesque. Paintings
dealing with Jewish motifs are kitsch, but drawings of other ethnic groups are delightful folk art. Every Jewish crook on Wall
Street is proof of the venality of Jews in general."

"Well, yes," I say. "Members of minority groups tend . . ."

He cuts me off and leans still closer. "Spare me the sociology
crap. The self-deception of so many Jews has got to be unique.
I was recently on a train in Pennsylvania listening in as this cosmopolitan Jewish woman talked to a man she took for an Amish.
She was going on and on, telling him how she commended his
determination to continue his heritage—that's the way she
talked—admired his dedication to dressing in the manner of his
forebears and carrying on the Amish language and customs. The
whole spiel. The man politely informed her that he wasn't Amish
but a Jewish Chassid. I won't ever forget the look of disgust on
that woman's face. Typical. Sophisticated Jews dutifully respect
nuns for wearing their ancestral habits but are embarrassed by
the attire of Chassidim, even though, and maybe precisely because, that's how their own great-grandfathers dressed."

This sure sounds like self-hatred, I say. "Oh no," he answers.

"I assure you, none of these people hate themselves. So-called self-hating Jews love themselves. They love themselves so damn much that they see themselves as better than their own people."

Psychotherapists beg to differ with my friend's coffee shop exposition. In their view, ethnic self-hatred is a genuine problem for the individual himself, flowing from a lack of self-esteem, too little self-love, arrested self-regard, or some other favorite psychophrase. The self-hate phenomenon, they point out, is common to members of all minority groups, black, Irish, Asian, Jews. In explaining its occurrence, the literature invariably invokes the work of the early-twentieth-century German Jewish social psychologist Kurt Lewin, who advanced an influential analysis of self-hatred as "identification with the aggressor." Lewin's thesis is that low-status minority groups desire a share of the respect and rewards enjoyed by the higher-status group. But the low-status group is frustrated when denied access to the upper echelon and this leads to aggression. Ah, but what to do with this aggression? It can't be directed toward the dominant group, which enjoys power and is the ideal. So it turns inward and against itself, resulting in self-hatred and pathology. Lewin focused much of his theory on Jewish self-hatred. According to this analysis, the Jew is bitter because society won't allow him to look like and live like a gentile. The Jew, unwilling to be antagonistic toward the master culture he so admires, becomes hostile to his own people, the Jews.

Sounds plausible, especially as an explication of Jewish self-hatred of the past, but how does it explain the endurance of contemporary American Jewish self-hatred? American Jews don't think of themselves as a low-status group, and its members can look and live like non-Jews. Jewish self-hatred seems to have its own peculiar, pernicious, and seemingly persistent properties.

If one doubts that Jews traffic in degrading self-images, consider this list:

Jewish guilt
Jewish lawyer
Jewish mother
Jewish businessman
Jewish wedding
Jewish landlord

In the pubic lexicon this is not a complimentary crew of characters and characteristics. They, and many more that spring to mind, are caricatures of course, which is precisely the point. True, we could as easily produce a companion list of widely embraced complimentary qualities of American Jews—charitable, smart, funny, talented—but the ready acceptance of negative clichés does insinuate the fragility of Jewish self-esteem. Jews use these terms as much as anyone.

"What bothers me most," says Janet Peterman "is the self-deception. There's a Jewish guy I work with, Henry, who typifies what I mean." Janet does computer graphics at a small firm where the casual corporate culture promotes a lot of talking. "I'm pretty out there with my Judaism, so the conversation sometimes comes around to Jews. Henry invariably gives me this crap about how Jews are unethical businesspeople, conniving, aggressive, chauvinistic. What pisses me off is that he always claims that he means only to be constructive. He always begins his rant with 'it hurts me to say this . . . but.' That's the standard mask of self-haters—they're pained, of course, but high calling forces them to say these unpleasant things about their own people. Henry never has anything good to say about Jews; it's always constructive criticism.''

This sort of self-hating Jew is a relatively new phenomenon. Jews had always interacted with the host non-Jewish population in which they lived, and managed to incorporate and Judaize aspects of gentile culture without diminishing their own identity or dignity. The Hebrews adopted the Canaanite calendar, Palestinian Jewry absorbed Roman methods of legal codification, the Jewish liturgy adapted Arabic music, Spanish Jewish philosophy assimilated Greek thought, and more recently, Eastern European cuisine is now identified by Jews as Jewish food. Being part of the non-Jewish world rarely caused feelings of inferiority, and among the great stars of Jewish history were leaders and scholars prominent in both communities: Abravanel, minister of exchequer in Spain; Maimonides, physician to the emir of Cairo; nasi Don Joseph, adviser in the court of the Turkish sultan, are just a few of many such examples. Jews were persecuted, but they rarely entertained doubts about the advantage of being Jewish. They believed, after all, that they were the chosen people, morally and religiously superior to the heathens around them, and that their oppression was part of a Divine scheme, a plan, moreover, that has them triumphant in the final chapter.

The term ''Jewish self-hatred'' attained official ''status'' with the 1930 publication of *Das Judisiche Selbthass (Jewish Self-Hatred)*, by the acclaimed writer Theodore Lessing. (Lessing himself was apparently something of a self-hating Jew, but that wasn't enough to save him. The Nazi leader Hermann Göring personally arranged to have Lessing shot to death.) The term may belong to the twentieth century, but the attitude already became a serious concern earlier, with the advent of the modern era of Western Europe and its invitation to Jews to join the larger non-Jewish culture. For the first time in the Jewish Diaspora in Christendom, the Jews were invited in not just as marginal visitors, but as full-fledged participants in society's music, art, philosophy, political conversation, and culture.

For many Jews, this was an offer they could not refuse. But the offer came with a price—the Jews would have to purge themselves of their old habits, and the tariff was often tantamount to a rejection of all things overtly Jewish. For many, this was also an invitation to Jewish self-hatred. Jews soon began to mimic the prevalent anti-Semitic mood of the period and sometimes led the way. Throughout the nineteenth and early twentieth centuries, Jews were prominent in the production of patently anti-Jewish literature and science. For example, an Italian Jew, Cesare Lombroso, known as the father of modern criminology, developed a schema of the criminal type which utilized the stereotypical descriptions of Jews in the anti-Semitic literature of the period. Self-hatred began to take its toll. Consider: Throughout all the thousands of years of persecution, except for those self-inflicted deaths committed as *kiddush hashem,* religious martyrdom, the suicide rate among Jews was almost nonexistent. In modern, assimilationist Germany, the Jewish suicide rate exceeded that of German non-Jews by a ratio of nearly three to one.

What about the rise of Jewish self-hatred in the United States? Jay Freitag thinks it wasn't a major problem before and it isn't now. In his view, Jewish self-hatred is best understood as a lack of self-confidence caused by the immigrant experience. "My grandparents came from the 'other side,' my mom's folks from Russia and my dad's from Austria-Hungary. They were uneasy about their old-world Jewishness when they settled here in Baltimore and were determined to become 'real Americans.' Some old-world inheritances were beyond their control, like their Yiddish accents, which of course their children made fun of, and became the bread and butter for a generation of Jewish comics. But I wouldn't call that self-hatred. That happens to all immigrants and their children.''

Freitag also recalls how the determination to assimilate sometimes brought about its own unintended ironies. ''Take the business about names. These Jewish immigrants weren't happy giving their kids names like Moshe or Mendel or Mordecai. They wanted to give their Jewish kids these classy Anglo-Saxon names—the names, no less, of the landed gentry of England. So their sons became Milton, Seymour, Sidney (my father's name), Harold, Bernard, Irving. And within one generation these names, of course, became unmistakably Jewish. Would you call this self-hatred? Hardly. No, I'd call it the desire to feel part of one's new country—a universal desire. And, by the way, Moshe, Mendel, and Mordecai were once non-Jewish names too.''

But not all are as sanguine about Jewish self-hatred in America. Sasha Levinson, a senior editor at a national fashion magazine, has a number of Jewish colleagues who, as she puts it, ''wish they could just escape their Jewishness.'' Sasha finds this attitude perplexing. ''I'm not talking about immigrants—I'm talking about third-, fourth-generation Jews. These are young people, my generation of thirty-year-olds. They celebrate Christmas with gusto and not Chanukah at all, will have nothing to do with their traditional relatives, have no interest in sending their kids to Hebrew school. They just want to be Americans, they say, as if being Jewish and being American were contradictory. This isn't a reaction to anti-Semitism; it's a profound uncomfortableness with their Jewish identity. And it sure isn't unusual.''

That many Jews are uneasy about their Jewishness is surely nothing new, nothing remarkable. But committed Jews are less forgiving when this self-hatred is manifested publicly by celebrities and Jewish intellectuals.

Shale Blanco is not an academic, nor does he work for a Jewish organization. But he keeps his own tabs on Jews who, in his unambiguous opinion, have worked against the Jewish interest in America and are recognized as self-hating Jews. ''Unfortunately,'' says Blanco, a forty-nine-year-old marketing executive in Boston, ''the list is long. And it goes back many years. Remember Walter Lippmann? In his day, he was considered the dean of newspaper columnists and he had enormous influence on politicians as well as other journalists. Here's a guy who writes about everything that takes place in the world, but not once about the destruction of European Jewry, which was not exactly a non-event. Already back in 1922, he wrote to Lawrence A. Lowell, the president of Harvard University, applauding Lowell's efforts to impose a quota on the number of Jews allowed into the university. He writes about the 'many distressing and personal social habits' of Jews and how his sympathies are with the culturally superior non-Jew. Lippmann was truly harmful to American Jews.

''Or consider a self-hating Jew like Lillian Hellman, who, in her play, changed Anne Frank's diary to make Anne's suffering result not from her being Jewish, but from fascism in general. She was sued for this concoction and lost. Or William Kunstler, who devoted much of his career to defending, out of court as well as in court, terrorists and murderers of Jews. Or Hannah

Arendt. Here's an intellectual powerhouse who spent much of her youth as a Zionist and wrote insightfully about anti-Semitism. But after the war she turns away from her fellow Jews and, notoriously, back to her Nazi lover, the philosopher Heidegger. The capstone of her Jewish self-hatred was her much heralded but thoroughly inaccurate book of 1963, *Eichmann in Jerusalem: The Banality of Evil*. Arendt refers to Eichmann's captors as Zionists, to the prosecutor as a Galician Jew with a ghetto mentality, and has the gall throughout the book to make it seem as if the Jews were as responsible for their deaths as were the Nazis. The book, so bereft of compassion, was published less than twenty years after the Shoah, when the wounds were still so fresh. Arendt's longtime friend the great scholar Gershom Scholem wrote that Arendt suffered from a fundamental lack of *ahavas yisroel*—a love for her fellow Jews. He was right.''

When you discuss famous self-hating Jews in America, one name that invariably comes up is Woody Allen. Allen is a complex figure. No doubt he would consider himself a proud Jew, but many Jews would find that ascription ironic. Blanco does. ''Just look at his movies and stories. He continually portrays Jewish men as weak, abject objects of pity and Jewish women as unsympathetic, cloying shrews. Traditional rabbis are always made to look like buffoons.'' Allen infuriated many Jews when he wrote an op-ed piece for the *New York Times* in 1988 condemning Israel's response to the Palestinian *intifada*. Allen wrote that he was ''appalled beyond measure'' by the ''violent and cruel'' behavior of Israeli soldiers.

''I remember how I felt reading that [Allen's op-ed piece],'' a woman named Aliza said to me in a conversation about Jewish self-hatred. "Here was a major Jewish director who in his work steadfastly avoids any reference to anything positive about Jews, or makes any reference to Israel or the Holocaust. He had nothing to say about the slaughter of children in Maalot, the terrorism, the massacre of Jewish athletes. Nothing. Did he—or those like him—ever show up at a rally for Soviet Jewry? Fat chance. But now this apolitical artist decides to weigh in with his moral condemnation of the terrible Israelis. Thanks for your advice, Woody. Where were you when we needed you? I mean, who the hell invited Woody Allen to become the conscience of American Jewry?"

In a subsequent article written as a response to the furor engendered by his op-ed piece, Allen wrote: "Now I have frequently been accused of being a self-hating Jew, and while it is true that I am Jewish and don't like myself very much, it's not because of my persuasion. The reasons lie in totally other areas—like the way I look when I wake up in the morning, or that I never could read a road map." The flippant response just made Jews even angrier.

"Woody Allen as an individual isn't the issue," says Blanco. "He's representative of the type. He admits he's Jewish, even revels in it in some way. He probably thinks his politics reflects his idea of Jewish values. But at the same time, he never pays his communal dues. And his comedy, especially his early work, lives off Jewish stereotypes that have nothing to do with the real world of Jewish men and women. His is the perfect example of self-hating Jewish humor."

Jewish self-hatred and Jewish humor—the one topic inextricably leads to the next. It is inconceivable to think of twentieth-century American humor without thinking of Jews; Jews as stand-up comedians, gag writers, the writers of television sitcoms, humor books, and comic films. According to a *Time* magazine survey in the 1970s, more than 80 percent of all professional comedians in the United States were Jewish. Not all American Jews are funny, but it sometimes seemed as if all the funny people in America were Jewish. In the past couple of decades alone, more than a hundred volumes of Jewish humor have been published. (The definition of a Jewish joke? ''A joke that no gentile understands and that every Jew has already heard.'') The comedy is wide and various, spanning the insult humor of Don Rickles and Jackie Mason, to the sweet humor of Danny Kaye and S. J. Perelman. And part of that treasure of Jewish humor is a heavy dosage of self-hatred.

The Jewish quip is often self-reflexive; Jews are its own target. One Jewish comedian is asked, ''Isn't Jewish humor masochistic?,'' to which he answers, ''No, and if I hear that question one more time, I am going to kill myself.'' Sigmund Freud, who had an abiding interest in Jewish humor, wrote: ''I don't know whether there are many other instances of people making fun to such a degree of its own character.'' Freud noticed—and you don't have to be a Freud to notice—that the punch line of a Jewish joke often socked it right to the Jewish jaw. But why? What drives Jews to unleash this self-abuse? Why those countless jokes about Jewish weddings, Jewish business practices, Jewish lawyers and accountants? The answers flow down the academic chute in a torrent of doctoral theses and learned exposition, but every Jew around a dinner table has his or her own theory as well.

Sheila Sternberg writes funny copy at an advertising firm in Washington, D.C., and thinks of humor as a coping strategy. ''I think the explanation for Jewish humor is pretty straightforward. Jews in the old world lived amidst degradation, hunger, and the constant threat of annihilation, so they turned to humor to help them cope with their terrible conditions. They used parody to transcend their dingy surroundings. That's a fancy way of saying life stinks and making jokes helps.''

Yes, but this doesn't seem to explain the self-flagellation, the unpleasant stereotypes, making yourself the butt of your own jokes. The answer must lie elsewhere. ''It assuredly does,'' says Sam Hasenfeld, a New York City expatriate now teaching English in Memphis. ''Jews take the hostility directed to them and turn it inward. It doesn't take much insight to realize that humor functions as a defense mechanism. Jewish comics deflect that hatred into laughter. The Jew says, 'You don't have to make fun of us . . . we can do that ourselves—even better.' I'm not saying this is a sign of psychological health, but whoever thought humor was the result of mental serenity? How many great Wasp comedians do you see marching out of Iowa?''

If this analysis is accurate, then Jewish humor should begin to disappear as Jews become more and more entrenched in American culture. And that apparently is just what is happening, though the reason may be less the result of Jewish acceptance than Jewish ignorance. As American Jews know less about their heritage, Jewish humor becomes increasingly contentless. These days the only Jewish jokes are ''Jewish style'' jokes of the kind you see on *Seinfeld*. Moshe Waldoks, rabbi, professional Jewish humorist, and editor of the best-selling *Big Book of Jewish Humor,* regrets the loss: ''I've been doing Jewish humor gigs around the country for years. And more and more it becomes less and less possible to make references to Jewish terms and Jewish heritage. The audience just doesn't get it. I talk about Jewish *nochis,* Jewish pride, and they think I mean Jewish nachos, some kind of Jewish Tex-Mex food. For most of this century, Jews shared ethnic markers, such as foods, holidays, language, folk Judaism. Now Judaism requires expertise and most Jews can't make the connections.''

Self-disparaging humor is a pointed manifestation of the more general self-hatred that arises from an internal clash of identities and a corresponding clash of values. Michael Lerner believes this is precisely the situation facing younger American Jews. Lerner, the editor of the magazine *Tikkun,* has himself often been called a self-hating Jew who, say his critics, espouses ''viciously anti-Israel views'' and is a ''favorite display Jew of the news media . . . the ultimate authority on the misdeeds of Israel.'' But Lerner has little regard for these critics and says, ''Most of the younger people I know see *me* as the crazy Zionist. I am trying to drag these young Jews back into Judaism, into caring about Jewish issues, and these critics attack me for being disloyal?'' But Lerner explains to me why he thinks Jewish self-hatred is a serious problem in the country. ''The internalization of negative and anti-Semitic images of Jews is very, very deep. Genuine value differences are at work here. Jews are a heavily moral and intellectual culture and America is a heavily pleasure-oriented and anti-intellectual culture. So over and over again, as Jews try to assimilate into America, they come across these non-Jewish values and hate important qualities of their own. Part of the assimilation process is to reassure yourself that you are a good American, and that includes no longer focusing on your Jewishness. On a superficial level that could be all right—there are aspects of the immigrant culture which should be jettisoned—but in general this attitude is very dangerous.''

American Jewish self-hatred will certainly take different forms in the next century, but it isn't likely to disappear. Noted Jewish scholar Jacob Neusner explains why a solution is not at hand. ''What, then, is to be done? In my view, nothing at all. Once one has explained a problem and persuaded people of its importance, he is supposed to announce the solution, found an organization, and ask people to write out checks. Everyone feels better. People have *done something*. But organizations administer no cure for self-hatred. It is part of the Jewish condition; it is the Jewish part of the human condition of self-devaluation.''

Self-hatred is ugly, and for American Jews it is a problem they must acknowledge and deal with, but it is a problem that exists within the Jewish family. Some Jews, however, take self-hatred a step further. They step out of the family altogether and become enemies of the community. These are Jewish traitors and the subject of the next chapter.

CHAPTER SIX

Enemies Within: Jewish Traitors

The best in man can only flourish when he loses himself in a community. Hence the mortal danger of the Jew who has lost touch with his own people and is regarded as a foreigner by the people of his adoption.   Albert Einstein

A friend of mine just named his newborn son Gideon. Pretty name, Gideon. "We were all set to name him Noam," he tells me. Pretty name too—means "pleasant" in Hebrew. "Do you know why we didn't?" he asks me. "Because of Chomsky. People will hear his name and think of Noam Chomsky. We'd rather not have our child associated with a Jewish traitor."

"Traitor" is a harsh word. Like murder, treachery is a capital offense. Every community has a consensus about its core values, the sacrosanct convictions upheld by all within the fold. A traitor is unfaithful to these perceived vital interests. But it isn't easy to be a traitor. You must betray someone or some group that reasonably expected your loyalty; you must anticipate the harm of your actions or, at minimum, be grossly negligent by not anticipating those harms; you must go well beyond mere criticism and align yourself with the enemy. Whether Noam Chomsky meets these conditions is surely a matter of dispute, but American Jews do share a sense of who is and who is not on their side.

If you can determine whom the community considers its traitors, you can determine its core values. Who are American Jewry's traitors? What are the community's core values? Listen to American Jews and you immediately understand why one needs to be extremely cautious in answering these questions. First, the American Jewish community is extraordinarily fluid and diverse, and few convictions are held by all. Any answer must provide a lot of room for difference. Second, and perhaps more important, these core beliefs are in flux. The bedrock issues of older Jewish adults are no longer the firm concerns of younger Jews. What will the next generation of American Jews deem as their basic, inviolable beliefs? What will they consider their most vital interests?

Transitions in Jewish core beliefs are not new. For example, religious belief, or the lack of it, is no longer a criterion of belonging. Ages ago, you could be excommunicated for heresy, for denying central tenets of the Jewish faith, but it's been centuries since all or even most Jews adhered to the same theological beliefs. Today's Americans Jews dress in all sorts of religious stripes and their beliefs run the theological gamut; you find Jews swaying in prayer in old-time fundamentalist synagogues and you find them holding forth in intellectual forums at humanist-atheist congregations. Eating pork makes you a sinner but not a traitor. Orthodox believers bitterly excoriate the godlessness of a Bialik, Ben-Gurion, or Golda Meir, but they don't doubt the fealty of these individuals to the Jewish people. The upshot: You can advance pretty much any religious belief and still remain within the compass of the American Jewish community.

The same is true of politics. Here, too, Jews espouse ideologies that map the political expanse, and the divisions are fierce. The recent Jewish history of political beliefs is a cross fire of communists, Bundists, Yiddishists, right-wing Zionists, left-wing Zionists, and everything in between. In the United States, particularly in recent decades, American Jews have been heavy hitters in both liberal and conservative ballparks; invariably, each side claims to represent authentic Judaism. When it comes to Israeli affairs, the internal political quarrel among American Jews is especially acrimonious—no debate in the American Jewish community has been as nasty as the ongoing dispute over the moral duty (according to some) or destructiveness (according to others) of American Jews voicing their displeasure with the foreign policies of the Israeli government.

Not all differences, however, are permitted within the American Jewish community. Maverick ideas are acceptable, but there are limits—for without limits, a community loses its self-definition. Some viewpoints are so extreme that they are perceived as coming from outside the family, as attacks on the community's core.

Here are three viewpoints that currently qualify as treachery by the bulk of American Jews.

Jews for Jesus

> Feivel sees his old friend Mendel on the street and asks him how it goes. Mendel shrugs and says nothing much has been happening and in turn inquires about events in Feivel's life. "Actually, something major has occurred," says Feivel. "I've converted to Christianity. In fact, I'd like you to do me a favor and become a Christian as well."
>
> "What? Me convert?" exclaims an incredulous Mendel. "Why would I do something like that?"
>
> "It's like this," Feivel explains. "If you convert, I'd have at least one Christian friend."

Jewish custom mandates that you sit *shiva*, enter a period of mourning, when a child dies or converts. If your child deserts Judaism to join another religion, he or she no longer exists for you. This is a solemn business. The primary devotion of the traditional Jew is to the Jewish people even beyond allegiance to one's biological family. One can't take apostasy more seriously than this.

Ethan Lewinter didn't sit *shiva* when his twenty-seven-year-old sister converted to Christianity five years ago, but he still finds it difficult to come to terms with her decision.

"It's incredible to me. I understand that religion in America is not a matter of fate, but of faith—no one *has* to belong to any particular religion anymore. Okay, so you don't want to be Jewish, but why be something else? Why *shmad* [convert]? It might sound smug, but I can't fathom deserting Judaism in favor of a derivative religion like Christianity or Islam. My sister's case is probably typical, though. Like so many other Jews here in St. Louis, she knows very little about Judaism and converted because she wanted to marry her husband, who takes his Christianity seriously. I think it's inexcusable. I admit to being ashamed of her because what she did is shameful."

Ethan Lewinter's other sister, Samantha, doesn't share her brother's embarrassment. "This was a free choice. My sister didn't have to convert—no one forced her and she could have done just as well in her career as a Jew. I may not agree with her decision, but then she doesn't like my politics either. We're both adults, we should respect each other's point of view."

The actual number of Jews who convert to Christianity— 280,000 of contemporary American Jews have chosen to do so— is about the same as the number of Christians who convert to Judaism. But Jews are a numerical drop in a sea of other religions, and the threat of absorption is ever-present. Deserting Christianity means leaving the religion to a billion and a half other Christians, but every Jewish defection counts and hurts. No wonder converts out of Judaism attract so much ire from their former coreligionists.

It's not a new story. Throughout their history, Jews forsook Judaism, sometimes en masse, for Baal, Hellenism, Christianity, Islam, or whatever religion dominated their time and place. One difference prevailed, however. Earlier, the appeal of other creeds was rarely the central allure for the conversion—more frequently, the motivation came at the point of a blade. Even noncoerced conversions were only quasi-voluntary, begrudging, calculated attempts to secure an easier life. When the noted poet Heinrich Heine became a Lutheran in 1825, he made it clear that he did so not because of some new theological insight, but because he wished to advance his career. "The baptismal certificate is the ticket of admission to Western culture," he said. Similarly, the esteemed philologist-historian David Chwolson famously explained that he joined the Russian Orthodox Church out of conviction, the conviction "that it was better to be a professor in St. Petersburg than a *melamed* [grade school teacher] in Eysshishok," the Lithuanian village from which he hailed. These converts did not consider themselves turncoats, nor were they so considered by other Jews, who if not sympathetic at least appreciated their plight.

Because American Jews have no such incentives, their conversions evoke deep disappointment and resentment among members of the Jewish community. Nonetheless, even while the depth of anger varies, few American Jews consider apostates traitors, actual enemies. That characterization is usually reserved for Jews who not only reject Judaism for another religion but engage in mischief against Jewish interests by actively seeking to have other Jews follow in their path. Members of Jews for Jesus fall into this category.

When Jews bump into *Jews for Jesus* missionaries in airports and train lobbies, some just walk by, some stop to glare, a few to argue—but nearly all are discomforted. Raphael Jacobowitz, now in his eighties, explains his abhorrence: "I know I should ignore them, but they make me livid. I'm not personally religious, so it's not about theology. I'm not surprised by the subterfuge either—that's how missionaries work. They come on so friendly. 'Let's get ready for Passover,' their literature says. 'Shalom,' they call out, 'we are fellow Jews, Hebrew Christians who expand our Judaism to welcome Christ the Savior into our lives.' Well, if they are so determined to live as first-century Hebrew Christians, how come they run around with kiddush cups, prayer shawls, and skullcaps and all the other trappings of modern Judaism? I'll tell you why. Because the basic aim of this organization is to entrap Jews and turn them into Christians. I was around at the time of the Holocaust and it infuriates me when I see Jews working to diminish our numbers." Jacobowitz says he usually makes some passing comment to them. "Just last week I told this fellow, 'You probably are a complete ignoramus about Judaism. But okay, you don't want to be Jewish anymore. Fine, go, good riddance. But don't come back after my grandchildren.' "

This attitude is evoked even among Jews who consider themselves thoroughly assimilated. Twenty-three-year-old Alicia Stern has no active ties to the Jewish community. "I can't read a word of Hebrew and have been to synagogue just a few times in my life—for bar mitzvahs." She says that she would have no hesitation in marrying a non-Jew if he was the right man. Nevertheless, she is offended by Jews for Jesus. "Considering how distant I am from Judaism and the Jewish world, you would think these people wouldn't get me. But they do. I can't say just why, but even though I don't personally do anything Jewish in my life, I still consider myself part of the Jewish people, and I'm very uncomfortable with these people who are trying to get Jews to stop being Jewish."

This deep-seated antipathy of so many Jews to such organizations recalls the history of trouble Jews have suffered at the hands of their own apostates.

From the theological perspective, the participation of Jews in other religions, albeit strained, isn't automatically contradictory. Jews practicing Buddhism are the clearest example of this ideological tolerance. The numbers aren't certain—definitions of religious identity are always imprecise—but according to the best estimates, the majority of Buddhists in the United States, and most of their leaders, are Jewish. BuJews, as they are sometimes called (another, much smaller group of Jews practice Sufism, the mystical branch of Islam, and are called Jewfis), often insist on retaining their Jewish identification, and not without credibility— the theology, or more accurately, the nontheology, of Buddhism does not blatantly contradict Jewish belief.

Eric Abner is happy being described either as a Buddhist Jew or a Jewish Buddhist. "Traditional Judaism just didn't do it for me. I never liked the tribalism, the separateness, and I didn't like the God of Judaism either. Buddhism offers a way of belonging to the universe that is liberating and connected. But over the past years, through my studies of the Kabalah, I've begun to see how Judaism also teaches this 'oneness,' and my sense of the Jewish

God has also changed. I can't belong to a standard synagogue, but I do now celebrate some of the Jewish holidays in my own way and with like-minded individuals. I love being able to combine both traditions and I invite other Jews to do the same."
While many Jews consider his religious lifestyle "wacky" or offensive, and believe that people like him never get beyond just surface Judaism and surface Buddhism, they do recognize the possible compatibility of these particular beliefs. They also realize that this sort of religious persuasion is likely to remain on the fringe for a long time to come.

Conversion to Christianity, on the other hand, always posed special religious and social problems for Jews. Early on, Jews had to decide whether these early Hebrew Christians really counted as converts. Christianity, after all, began as a branch of Judaism: Jesus was an observant Jew, all of the apostles were Jewish. With the exception of Luke, all the books of the New Testament were written by Jews—they married as Jews, observed the commandments and holidays as Jews, and died as Jews. All that distinguished them from their coreligionists was their belief that Jesus was the Messiah.

After the destruction of the Second Temple, the Tana'im, the first rabbis of the Talmud, branded the Christians heretics and denied the sanctity of their scriptures; nonetheless, Christians were still regarded as Jews, albeit renegade Jews. That changed with the evangelical program of Paul. Proselytizing to the gentiles, Paul allowed conversion to Christianity without requiring circumcision, without requiring adherence to the dietary laws or most other biblical commandments. You could, that is, become a Christian without becoming a Jew—and that's when the Tana'im drew the thick line in the sand and proclaimed the

Notzrim (Nazarenes, as these Christians were called) non-Jews and expressly prohibited marriage with them. The doctrine became emphatic: You could not be both a committed Christian and a committed Jew. By the end of the first century, the Romans, too, recognized the separation of the two sects and did not require Christians to pay the *fiscus judaicus,* the Jewish poll tax. From the Christian perspective, the division grew apace so that by the time of the later Gospel of John, all Jews were viewed as Pharisees and enemies of Christ.

Few Christians converted to Judaism. The usual, but by no means uniform, Jewish reluctance to encourage non-Jews to convert to Judaism was rarely a unilateral decision. After Christianity became the official religion of the Roman Empire under Constantine, the Code of Justinian decreed the death penalty for any Jew who tried to convert a Christian to Judaism and for the Christian who converted. The Code of Omar under the Muslims proscribed the same law and the same penalty with the same prohibitive effect. Conversion from Christianity to Judaism became a genuine possibility only with the advent of a tolerant modern Western world. According to respected estimates, the number of Christians who have converted to Judaism in the United States in this century is more than the total number of Christians who converted to Judaism in all of previous history.

Non-Jews who convert to Judaism are generally held to be Jews in every way—thus, most rabbinical authorities rule that converts to Judaism should say the prayer ''Our forefathers, Abraham, Isaac, and Jacob.'' Conversions in the other direction, from Judaism to Christianity, are more problematic legally. Rashi, the eleventh-century commentator, reflects the dominant view that a Jew who converts is still Jewish: Once a Jew, always a

Jew. Other rabbis ruled that the sin of conversion is sufficient to exile one from his or her Jewishness. The Israeli government amended its Law of Return, which extends automatic citizenship to all Jews, to exclude Jews who convert to other faiths.

Jewish history is replete with instances of converts from Judaism who urged their new Christian benefactors to destroy Jewish texts and institute harsh penalties on the Jewish community. This history has little impact on the way Thomas Pollack, a medical supplies salesman, reacts to the Jews for Jesus missionaries he meets on his business trips. "I have a vague recollection of hearing about Jews converting and then making trouble for Jews, but that's the long-ago past. It was different then. Those guys worked for the church when the church had real power and was out to get the Jews. The Jews for Jesus characters I run into now and then in the subways and airports aren't getting anyone into trouble. I've heard them on the radio and they sound pleasant enough. To me they're just another bunch of religious crazies who hawk their goods in the great American religious shopping mall. They're a mild irritation, not a major threat. I just ignore them. I've got bigger worries."

So do most Jews. Every several months Jewish magazines feature an article on missionaries to the Jews, but few Jewish organizations see them as a major threat to the integrity of the American Jewish community. Jews for Jesus is part of a larger umbrella group of messianic groups who call themselves Jewish Christians. Their ritual service is an amalgam of traditional Jewish liturgy and fundamentalist-evangelical Christianity, and their theology is a studied mixture of Jewish and Christian beliefs. Outside of their churches, they are a busy bunch—proselytizing to the Jews is an expensive proposition. Philip Abramowitz, director of New York's Jewish Community Council's task force on cults and missionaries, estimates that messianic Jewish groups spend $100 million annually trying to convert American Jews, and Jews for Jesus (composed of nine constituent American organizations and five overseas) devotes an estimated yearly budget of $10 million to $12 million to this task. How successful are their efforts? The Messianic Jewish Alliance of America claims a membership of over 100,000 "Jewish believers," but Rabbi Tovia Singer, director of the New York Office of Jews for Judaism, an organization set up to counter missionary organizations, puts their number at closer to 8,000.

Whatever the real numbers, the Jews for Jesus movement is a blatant violation to most American Jews. To Jews, these missionary movements are a reminder that Judaism is still a small, vulnerable minority in a sea of Christianity. Jews who join these groups are seen as traitors by American Jews from across the spectrum of belief and practice.

Jews Who Seek the Destruction of Israel

> The creation of the state of Israel has rendered the greatest service that any human institution can perform for individuals—it has restored to Jews not merely their personal dignity and status as human beings, but, what is vastly more important, their right to choose as individuals how they shall live.
> Isaiah Berlin

Cognitive psychologists are making enormous strides in getting a fix on how the psyche manipulates data and forms beliefs. No one, though, has yet satisfactorily solved the problem of self-deception, our dogged ability to hold, simultaneously and steadfastly, two contradictory beliefs. Examples abound, and they include the mantra "I'm not anti-Semitic, I'm just anti-Israel." Does the person who makes this proclamation genuinely believe this? Perhaps, but when Jews hear someone spout this line, they immediately translate: "Here before me goes another anti-Semitic bastard." It doesn't matter if the speaker is a non-Jew or a Jew.

In the ephemeral world of theory, one could, supposedly, be anti-Zionist and not anti-Jewish, but in the real world of blood and politics the distinction is empty. Everyone knows this—especially Jews and their enemies. When terrorist organizations want to retaliate against Israel, they shoot up a crowded synagogue in Turkey, rake a van filled with Jewish teenagers on a bridge in New York City, or blow up the local headquarters of Jewish organizations in Buenos Aires. The terrorists could not care less whether their victims are religious or atheists, favor or oppose the ordination of women rabbis, advocate or reject negotiations with Syria, give money or not to the United Jewish Appeal, label themselves socialist or neoconservative. All that matters is that they are Jewish. No one is surprised by their choice of targets because everyone accepts the intimate connection between Jews and the Jewish state.

Over the past decades, American Jewish organizations have conducted ongoing studies to monitor the level of American Jewish commitment to Israel. The difficulty of quantifying "commitment" is readily apparent, but a shared, visceral, reflexive devotion to Israel endures and transcends all the differences in the many ideologies of American Jews. Absolutely secular Jews feel this way, as do Jews who affiliate with the ultraorthodox Neturei Karta, a group who will settle for nothing less than a theocracy in Israel. Nearly all American Jews have some emotional identification with Israel. The emotional aspect of this identification emerges most forcefully in times of crisis.

On March 4, 1995, the Islamic fundamentalist group Hamas detonated a tremendous bomb on a crowded street in Tel Aviv, killing dozens of men, women, and children. A day before, a terrorist had murdered dozens by exploding a bus in Jerusalem, and a week before that another bomb killed dozens on the same bus route. Rivy Isaacson recalled how she felt the day she heard about the Tel Aviv bombing and a conversation she had with her coworkers at a department store in Chicago where she works as a buyer.

"I was emotionally exhausted. It was now day after day that you saw these pictures of dead bodies, you heard the wailing sirens, the cries of mothers. As a Jew, this hit home. It hit home in a way that I recognize it can't for some non-Jew in Wyoming. I remember sharing my horror with my coworkers who weren't Jewish. They were duly sympathetic, yes it was terrible they said, but they weren't moved in the same way I was. Why should they be? They reacted the same way I do when I hear about a bomb in Belfast or Kashmir. It isn't a matter of which is objectively worse—when someone in your family passes away, it isn't just another person among thousands who died that day. When Jews hear about a terrorist blast in Tel Aviv, they understand that it could have occurred in front of their home in Malibu, Paris, Casablanca, anywhere. For Jews, these terrorist acts are never experienced as isolated events, but always as yet one more assault in a long history of violence against innocent Jewish men, women, and children. Any Jew who can stand apart emotionally from these events isn't one of us."

Crises such as terrorist bombs may evoke tribal attachments, but that intensity does not generally carry over into normal life. In one national study, for example, 47 percent of American Jews under the age of forty scored "high" on attachment level right after the Iraqi Scud attacks on Israel during the Gulf War, but only 34 percent in the age bracket soared as high two years earlier during quieter times. More generally, studies indicate that attachment to Israel is steadily becoming less of a factor in how most American Jews define their Jewish identity. In the comprehensive 1990 National Jewish Population Study, 10 percent of Jews polled reported being "extremely" attached to Israel, 20 percent "very" attached, 46 percent "somewhat" attached, and 24 percent said they felt no attachment at all. Most noteworthy is that levels of commitment to Israel have steadily receded most among younger Jews.

Jenna Helfine, a twenty-eight-year-old physical therapist in Westchester, New York, typifies this new and growing estrangement. Jenna does not consider herself a Zionist, although she says she would be greatly upset if Israel were destroyed; she has no immediate plans to visit the country, though she'd like to, but a trip to Italy comes first.

"Israel is a reality. Not a hope, not a dream. It's been around now, for what, a half a century? My mother was only seven when it became a country, for goodness' sake. Those old struggles, the rah-rah Zionist songs and speeches, you know, the Exodus days, were important back then but that's history. Israel doesn't need my help. I know many Jews my age are still emotionally tied to Israel. They'll root for Israelis at the Olympics, and feel proud when an Israeli makes an important scientific discovery. Yes, and they are embarrassed too when Israel screws up and kills innocent

Arabs. I feel attached too, but it's not a major thing with me. I wish Israel well, but the truth is that we can survive without each other just fine.''

No doubt Jenna can survive without Israel, but not all are as sanguine when it comes to the survival of American Jewry without Israel. David Schoen, a professor of modern history at a college in Virginia who previously taught at Haifa University, sees a complex relationship between the two Jewish communities. "Let's talk numbers for a minute. At the moment, more Jews live in the United States than anywhere else, including Israel. Indeed, never before in Jewish history have as many Jews lived in a single sovereign polity as the number of Jews who live in the United States. This will not be true much longer: Given current population trends, in a decade or two, more Jews will live in Israel than in the United States—already, more Jewish children are born there than here. The important shift, however, will not be demographic, but cultural and spiritual. Now you've got two centers of Judaism. Each community pursues its own twists and turns, sometimes marching in lockstep with one another, sometimes finding themselves at a distance, moving in opposite directions, but Jews in both Israel and the United States are ever mindful not to stray too far away from one another and always keep close tabs on how the other fares. My own guess is that before too long, even those who don't see it this way now will acknowledge that Israel has become the dominant center of Judaism, the true Jewish home, if not geographically then spiritually.''

Beth Moskowitz doesn't agree at all. "Please, I've heard all this before.'' Beth is mildly involved with her Reform Temple in Phoenix and expects to be even more involved when her child enrolls in the Hebrew school there, but says that she has more than enough opportunities for a rich Jewish life if she wanted one. "American Jews are thriving, and thriving Jewishly in our own American way. America isn't Israel—we have are own convictions, tastes, and goals. The well-being of Israel is certainly part of my Jewish consciousness, but we are two distinct Jewish communities. For too long we treated Israelis as if they were our own invention, our tough younger sibling with the rake on his shoulder, the funny hat on his head, lots of brains and courage— weren't we proud—but who needed our monetary support and cosmopolitan advice. That sort of condescension should have been put to rest years ago. But now these Israelis talk about American Jews as if we are the assimilated, Jewishly inept, lost younger brother, and only they can show us the way back. Thanks a lot. I think it's time, instead, for mutual respect."

The relationship between Israel and Americans has gone through some difficult passages these past years: the *intifada,* the assassination of Yitzhak Rabin, the peace process, the post–peace process bombings, the change of government in Israel. The war in Lebanon in the 1980s in particular "embarrassed" many American Jews, and a few saw this as an occasion to abandon Israel completely. One individual, an official at the American Civil Liberties Union, in a letter to the Jewish magazine *Shma*, expressed his long-standing reservations about Israeli chauvinism and "repressive nationalism" and then writes, "I have experienced the war on Lebanon of the past few weeks as a turning point in Jewish history and exceeded in importance perhaps only by the end of the second commonwealth and the Holocaust. I have resisted the inference for over thirty years, but the war on

Lebanon has now made clear to me that the resumption of political power by the Jewish people after two thousand years of Diaspora has been a tragedy of historical dimension.'' This sort of hyperbole is not totally absent, but it is rare—only a tiny percentage of American Jews are overtly opposed to Israel's existence.

Indifference to the survival of Israel marks one immediately as an outsider, a Jew who no longer belongs to the Jewish community. An even fewer number of detached American Jews not only have no special affection for Israel but think all American Jews should renounce their ties to Israel, and they vocally express their denial of Israel's legitimate standing as a nation. They believe Israel should be cut adrift from the concerns of America and American Jewry. To the vast majority of American Jews, these Jews are traitors.

Holocaust Denial

> There is one thing worse than too much talk about the Holocaust and that is hearing people say there is too much talk.
> *Rabbi Arnold Wolf*

> If there is one thing worse than talking too much about the Holocaust, it is talking too little and the one thing worse than talking too little is talking incorrectly.
> *Michael Berenbaum*

> Holocaust denial is no more about the Holocaust than the medieval claim that Jews poisoned the wells was about water quality.
> *Kenneth S. Stern*

If anything marks one as an enemy of the Jews, it is the denial of the Holocaust. It is the ultimate blasphemy. No other issue so offends contemporary Jewish sensibilities. Other political pronouncements from the left or the right can be overlooked, finessed, but not one that minimizes the Shoah. After Jesse Jackson said he was tired of hearing about the Holocaust (in addition to some other insulting remarks), it took him decades to wash away the anger of the Jewish community toward him. When Patrick Buchanan defended Nazi war criminals, he disgusted all Jews permanently. To Jews, this wasn't just another point of view, but a display of insensitivity bordering on cruelty. Rarely does any Jew engage in such rhetoric, although a few Jews have come perilously close to lending these deniers succor and support.

Within these brick boundaries of decency, however, new attitudes are emerging about the permissibility of rethinking, not the extent of the Shoah itself, but our communal response to it. This is new, and it took a generation's distance from the catastrophe to dare raise the needed questions. But, it must be emphasized, these are the hushed conversations of the recovery room, tinctures on open wounds. The parameters of acceptable talk are under consideration, and any Jew or non-Jew who enters the fray without the requisite apprehension is immediately recognized as the dangerous outsider who does not belong. Because the Shoah is the central backdrop to all current Jewish conversation—dozens of books on the calamity continue to be published each year—we need to examine in some detail the limits and constraints on these exchanges.

American Jewish discussions about the Holocaust can be usefully divided into three categories: the role of the Shoah in teaching about Judaism; the impact of the Shoah on the religious spirit of Judaism; and a reexamination of why events went so terribly wrong and the lessons we can learn from that experience.

A view once submerged but now increasingly vocal sees American Jewish organizational life as too invested in the Holocaust, especially as a pedagogical tool to younger Jews. Benjamin Klein works for a major Jewish educational organization, and though he rarely states his view in public, it is, in fact, shared by many: "Let's get real. Eighty-five percent of American Jews are born in the United States. A majority are third-generation Americans. The Shoah is an event that happened 'over there' many years ago and is increasingly remote from American Jews. No one, God forbid, is trying to diminish the memory of the tragedy. Of course it still weighs heavily on American Jews. Broadcasters, for their part, know they can still squeeze out an occasional television movie of the week on the subject. But substantively, the Shoah resonates for fewer and fewer American Jews, and the more we harp on it, the more distance we put between young American Jews and Judaism."

Klein is also down on Holocaust museums, and the parade of books and films on the Shoah that pour forth annually. "I think that as an introduction to Judaism and Jewish life they are counterproductive. Entitlement to suffering is a lousy reason to belong to a heritage," he says. "The net effect is that young Jews are turned off from Judaism. Who wants to be Jewish if all it means is that other people want to murder you?"

The critics of what some call America's "Holocaust Judaism" believe that Jews need to focus on the positive elements of Judaism and not the lachrymose approach to Jewish history—Jewish history as a chronology of pogroms and persecution. The more cynical among these critics add that a self-serving industry has been built to put the Holocaust at the forefront of Judaism.

As the saying goes, "There is no business like Shoah business." "It's time," they urge, "to stop putting the Holocaust as the centerpiece of our sales effort."

A number of recent studies support Klein's intuition, but many young Jews have very different experiences. Lisa Levine, for example, a twenty-one-year-old junior at a large midwestern university who had just completed a course on the Shoah, found her studies of that period extremely important to her reawakening Jewish identity.

"The Holocaust course is by far the most popular 'Jewish' class in the university. For many of us, it's the only course we take with Jewish content. I'm sure the professors in the Jewish Studies Department would like to have the same enrollment for their Bible and medieval Jewish philosophy classes, but they don't. For many Jews my age, the Holocaust is our introduction to Judaism. All my friends saw Spielberg's *Schindler's List*. It was as if we felt a religious requirement to see this movie. And maybe we did. I don't think we should stop here with our Judaism, but the Holocaust is something that grabs you immediately. It forces you to think as a Jew, for many of us, for the first time."

Mark Ringler is also offended by the idea that too much attention is paid to the Holocaust by Jewish educators. "Teaching the Shoah is not a market ploy, not a sales effort," he says, "but a response to a harsh reality." He tells me this story. "I'm a businessman now, but back in my early days I took courses at the Jewish Theological Seminary in New York and was a student of the great Jewish theologian Abraham Joshua Heschel. This was back in the early days of protest against the treatment of Soviet Jews, before their persecution became a popular cause. We were extremely frustrated. We were out there every day, screaming, complaining, sending letters, expressing our anger, but no one reported our demonstrations. We were totally ignored. We asked Rabbi Heschel what we should do. He answered, 'You don't understand. You don't cry because you want results. You cry because it hurts.' Well, I think we Jews are still hurting terribly from the Shoah. Education, selling Judaism, warning others . . . all this is secondary. We talk about the Holocaust because we're still in great pain."

Along with the creation of Israel, the Shoah is the major event in the last two thousand years of Jewish history and it happened just a generation ago. On many measures, the Shoah is arguably the worst single event that occurred in human history, and it happened to the grandparents, uncles, aunts, and cousins of American Jews. You don't lose more than a third of your people, a million and a half of your children, and not stagger through the next phase of your history. The lives of American Jews, as do the lives of all Jews everywhere, proceed under this over-whelming shadow. That's why American Jews are so deeply of-fended when Jews and non-Jews suggest that we forget about the Holocaust and its perpetrators and move on.

The problem—profound, wrenching, and immediate—is how best to keep that memory alive. For some, the answer is clear: We must talk to people where they live, and that means through the channels of popular culture and popular media. Others find this route demeaning of the Shoah, or worse. The esteemed play-wright David Mamet has this to say about *Schindler's List:*

Schindler's List, ostensibly an indictment of the German murder of the Jews, is, finally, just another instance of

their abuse. The Jews in this case are not being slaugh-
tered, they are merely being trotted out to entertain. How
terrible. For, finally, this movie does not "teach," it does
not "reach a great number who might otherwise be ignorant of this great wrong." It is not instruction, but melodrama. Members of the audience learn nothing save the
emotional lesson of all melodrama, that they are better
than the villain. The very assertion that the film is instructive is harmful. . . . *Schindler's List* is an exploitation film.

It is notoriously difficult to present the Shoah through art. It
is notoriously difficult to present it any other way. What makes
the argument over how best to present the Shoah so agonizing is
that this is one of those unusual instances where opposing sides
of the debate genuinely mean well and the passion is distributed
equally.

Less controversial but as disturbing is the growing awareness
among American Jews that the uniqueness of the Holocaust is
disappearing in the whirlpool of language. *The* Holocaust is becoming *a* Holocaust. Shifra Halpern, a writer for Jewish newspapers and magazines, is adamant about using the term "Shoah,"
rather than "Holocaust," when referring to the destruction of
European Jewry in World War II. "First of all, the word '*Holocaust*' is a Greek translation of the Hebrew word *olah*, meaning
a sacrificial offering to the Lord. The theological implication is
readily apparent—the 6 million Jews who perished were *kur-
bonot,* sacrificial lambs. I find this notion repellent. I'm also re-
pelled by how every tragedy, no matter what the scope or intent,
is now a 'holocaust.' Every harsh prison is a concentration camp,
every brutal policeman a commandant, anyone to the right of Bill

Clinton is a fascist, every atrocity a genocide, and anyone who survives a bout with a disease or an adversity is a survivor—a compatriot of those who made it through Auschwitz. Language has gone rancid. The Holocaust has become one big metaphor. I think the least Jews deserve is to have their own name for their own unique catastrophe.''

What galls other Jews is the notion that the Shoah is somehow over, part of a dead past. The Holocaust is certainly not history for them or the people in their lives. Not one of my uncles and aunts and cousins who survived the concentration camps and are still alive goes to sleep without a sedative: They are terrified of the dreams that will come in the night. Chaim Glickstein is forty-eight years old and a child of survivors. He talks about the enduring effects of the Shoah in his own life. ''My father's nightmares still haunt me. It's not over for me either. I'm obsessed with Nazis and have been all my life. The imagined torture scenes, the revenge fantasies, are my constant companions. I try to banish all that. I don't read books about the Holocaust, I don't see movies on the subject, it all makes me crazy. I think about my parents being tormented, their siblings murdered before their own eyes, and then I think of their faceless murderer eating sausage in his cozy home in Bavaria and I go into a rage. I think it's my responsibility to kill the bastard, but, of course, I will never do more than imagine myself doing so. I have an excruciating toothache and I immediately flash to the cousins I never met choking to death in the gas chamber. I once told myself in a fit of rationality that all this fantasizing was unfair. I was spending hours of mental duress, but their actual murder didn't take that long. The ruse didn't work, though. I did a calculation—that's how crazy this is: Disregarding the fact that most of these individuals spent months of torture and anguish, even if you allot just ten minutes of agony for each Jew who died in the Shoah, that comes to 60 million minutes. It would take me 596 years, about 600 years, of full-time twenty-four-hours-a-day-with-no-sleep pain to match their suffering. This is nutso thinking, I know . . . but it's the sort of weird stuff that I bet all survivors' children engage in.''

It has been a bit more than a half century since the electrified wires of Auschwitz were cut down and the remaining Jews liberated. In a people's history, especially a people as ancient as the Jews, half a century ago is yesterday. Most American Jews are not plagued by images of the Shoah the way Chaim Glickstein is, and so fail to recognize that, as a community, the Jews are still reeling from the terror even if they seem to be standing erect and confident. The effect of trauma often works that way.

The consequences of the calamity permeate contemporary Jewish theology too. The Holocaust has dramatically changed the religious terms of Judaism. A rabbinic sage of the twentieth century, Rabbi Yisroel Meir HaCohen, the Chofetz Chaim, said: ''For the believer there are no questions, and for the nonbeliever there are no answers.'' But the Shoah posed unavoidable questions even for the most pious and demanded answers even from the most skeptical. All recent Jewish philosophy revolves around the issues raised in ''Holocaust theology.'' These questions are not just metaphysical playthings for recondite scholars and academic journals; every Jew who thinks about his or her Judaism has to work his or her way through this labyrinth. When American Jews talk about God and God's relationship to Jews, they immediately turn to the Holocaust. Or to put this another way: The Holocaust made all Jews into theologians. How could it not?

The Shoah begs for interpretation, and the interpretations span the spectrum of beliefs: from a call for renewed fundamentalism to a justification for outright atheism. But because the trauma is shared by all Jews, and every response has a modicum of plausibility, there is an unusual level of tolerance in discussions about the religious meaning of the Shoah. Provided one enters the conversation with the appropriate deference to the enormity of the tragedy, almost any opinion is given a hearing.

I vividly recall experiencing that tolerance in my early years. At the table in the shul I attended each Sabbath sat two Jews, Reb Shmuel and Reb Lyzer. Reb Shmuel had been a *dayan,* a judge in the Jewish courts in Hungary before the war, and apparently was renowned even as a young man for his erudition and religious devotion. He survived Auschwitz, but his wife and three children were murdered there. Reb Shmuel was now an atheist, and in all the years I knew him, I never once saw him actually pray. The prewar Chassidic world was the world he knew, and he attended its communal functions, came to shul regularly with his two sons from his new family, and would spend hours there discussing scholarly texts. But he ceased to believe. Across the table, Reb Lyzer had the opposite reaction. He grew up as a "modern" educated young man in Cracow, not particularly pious. He, too, was a concentration camp survivor. Now, extremely devout, he wore a *shtreimel* (a Chassidic fur hat) and a long beard and prayed fervently. Reb Shmuel once said to me, "After all I went through, how could I continue to have faith?" In a startling refrain, Reb Lyzer said to me, "After all I went through, how could I not have faith?" They were good friends and immensely respectful of one another.

Holocaust theology produced a richly articulated series of approaches to how Jews could continue—or discontinue—their faith. The central issue in Holocaust theology is theodicy, the problem of evil: How can a loving, all-good God allow evil in the world? The question had been asked in every generation, but never with the immediacy and poignancy of the generation of the Shoah. For Jewish thinkers, the challenge is profound and visceral—could they still teach a Judaism that posits a special relationship between God and Jews, a God, moreover, who loves His people? The ground rules of this debate were well expressed by Rabbi Yitzchok Greenberg: "No statement, theological or otherwise, should be made that could not be credible in the presence of burning children." The traditional Orthodox reaffirmed the view that the Shoah was yet another sign of God's displeasure with His wayward Jews—because of our sins we suffer. This desolation was, perhaps, the most terrible of punishments in a string of previous calamities, but not theologically distinct. Other theologians, such as Richard Rubenstein, went all the way in the other direction. Auschwitz, he argued, was simply too much. To speak of a loving God after the burning and gassing to death of a million and a half Jewish children was simply obscene—the God of Jewish tradition had died in the camps. The poet Yaakov Gladstein wrote, "The Torah was given at Sinai and returned at Lublin."

Emil Fackenheim drew a critical lesson from Auschwitz, a 614th commandment: no posthumous victories for Hitler. Jewish survival is now a new binding imperative. Elie Wiesel insisted on the uniqueness of the Holocaust and argued that the impossibility of understanding this "Kingdom of the night" was intractable: "One cannot conceive Auschwitz with God, nor can you conceive of Auschwitz without God." The discussion continues among American Jews, ever feverish, ever intense, ever respectful.

Historians of the Shoah also give each other much room to maneuver, but again only within appropriate appreciation of the magnitude of the horror. Some scholars accentuate the uniqueness of intent, the German obsession to exterminate the Jews, while others concentrate less on the conception of the Shoah than on its process, the functional depravity that results from the corrupt state with advanced technology at its disposal. Whatever the analysis, looking back at these times automatically gives rise to painful questions about how Jews might have acted differently. There has been a quiet, internal controversy about who is to blame for the apparent failure of leadership, about who could have done more, who was selfish, who was culpably negligent, and what lessons we can now learn. Understandably, a generation ago, this reflection would have been deemed callous, but now a considered, scholarly reexamination is underfoot. But even beyond the academy, American Jews sense that these are questions they will have to deal with as a community. One proceeds gingerly here, for this is where the anti-Semite revisionists congregate and the self-hating Jew finds the door ajar.

Marcel Vishnitzer smokes too many cigarettes, and his office is cluttered with pieces of cloth and leather strewn everywhere. One wonders how he gets any work done, but his ladies' handbag business has been a going concern for twenty-five years. Vishnitzer grew up in Budapest and his parents managed to get him to Switzerland during the war. He is the only survivor in his family. We talk about what went wrong, how the Jewish leadership could have made different decisions. He cuts me short. "Every analysis of the Shoah must begin and end with one realization: The worst possibility was the actuality. So any direction you or anyone suggests that Jews should have pursued—they should have been more active, less active, more careful, less careful, louder, quieter, engaged in more armed response, engaged in less armed response—anything is plausible, because nothing could have been worse.''

Vishnitzer stares ahead, trying to come to terms yet again with the reality. ''Yes, it couldn't have been worse for us, and they, the Germans, couldn't have been more successful. Such devotion to a cause! For twelve years the extermination of the Jew was a German priority. At the cost of their own soldiers' lives, trains and trucks that were needed for their war effort were diverted to bring Jews to the gas chambers—the murder of Jewish babies was worth the price. They didn't get to achieve their ultimate goal of exterminating every Jew in the world, but they came close enough.''

The totality of the Shoah is a crucial feature in understanding its impact on the American Jewish consciousness and why any Jew who discounts its effect on the Jewish psyche is deemed an enemy of the people.

Are there any such Jews? ''Certainly,'' says my friend, the one who named his child Gideon, rather than Noam. ''My problem with Chomsky—and he represents other Jews with similar attitudes—is his utter insensitivity about the impact of the Holocaust on his fellow Jews. For decades now, this brilliant man, the most influential linguist of our time, and a scholar of Hebrew as well, unrelentingly lends his prestige and rhetorical skills to the cause of making Israel look bad. Bad enough. But he really went over the top when he wrote an essay which appeared in 1980 as the forward for a book by the neo-Nazi Robert

Faurisson. Faurisson, who was suspended from teaching and brought into court for defaming witnesses and scholars, was, by all accounts, a small-time crackpot, sometime academic, Holocaust-denier active in France's far-right political scene, for whom the Shoah is a Zionist hoax. Chomsky wrote an essay defending Faurisson's right to freedom of speech and condemning efforts to stifle his free expression. Chomsky's name is at the head of a petition supporting Faurisson's 'just right of academic freedom' and identifying him as someone who has been 'conducting extensive historical research in the Holocaust question.' Chomsky compounded his problems by claiming that he saw 'no proof' that Faurisson was an anti-Semite. 'After all,' Chomsky wrote, 'is it antisemitic to speak of Zionist lies? Is Zionism the first nationalist movement in history not to have concocted lies in its own interest?' Chomsky, of course, insists that Faurisson's claims are horrific lies. He defends his defense as addressing solely the civil liberty issues. But why in this wide world of beleaguered writers should Holocaust-deniers, of all people, deserve the benefit of a leading intellectual figure? Why is a Jew providing this benefit?''

Jews all over the world cluster their fear and identification around the Holocaust, and to tamper with the distinctiveness of this horror is to alienate Jews everywhere. As Elie Wiesel reiterates but never too often, "While not all victims were Jewish, all Jews were victims." All Jews were persecuted—the assimilated and the ultra-Orthodox, communists and nationalists, German Jewish poets and Greek Jewish cobblers, the aged and the infants. American Jewish children who are raised with even a minimal knowledge of their Jewishness absorb the sweep of this inclusive extermination. The vicarious projection is potent and shapes their nightmares—they, too, would have died in the crematoria. It wouldn't matter what they looked like, what they believed, or how they acted. *The Diary of Anne Frank* could easily have been their story. They learn that fifty years ago, one of the most powerful nations in the world, with the assistance of some countries and the silence of all others, gassed children to death by the millions. And American Jewish children then make the next brutal leap. It could happen again, this time to them.

The Shoah has become the "shared sacredness" of all Jews. "Sacred" is an odd term to describe this inferno. But it is sacred in the sense that one enters this world with one's head bowed and with terrible fear. Any Jew who does not respect that sense of awe is treacherous to Jewish pain and Jewish survival.

Holocaust survivors are dying out, and soon none will be alive. In a few decades, even their children will become old. The Shoah will recede from the center of Jewish consciousness; this is the natural path and solace of time. Israel, in all likelihood, will continue to flourish and experience a new set of glories and difficulties. American Jews will assuredly continue to assimilate, and those who remain committed will diverge into secular and religious camps. Few, however, are likely to exchange their Judaism for Christianity.

So what will bind the next generation of American Jews? Will it be a newfound Jewish spirituality? A rebirth of anti-Semitism? The temptation to guess is strong but, finally, useless. What is clear, however, is that without fundamental shared interests, the communal viability of American Jews will disappear. Traitors, we noted, are those who threaten a community's core interests; heroes are those who defend those same core convictions. Without common purpose, American Jews will have no one to betray them, but also no one to inspire them. Indeed, a critical role of future American Jewish leaders will be to define and crystallize those core values that define the American Jewish community in the century ahead.

CHAPTER SEVEN

Jews Talk About Non-Jews

> *When they asked the Jewish philosopher Franz Rosenzweig what Jews thought about Jesus he replied, "They don't."*
>
> *Worry about your own soul and the next person's body—not the reverse.*　　　　　　　　　　　　*The Kotzker Rebbe*

Part I. Jews Talk About Non-Jews

> *Gentile: of or pertaining to any people not Jewish.*
> The Random House
> Dictionary of the En-
> glish Language

Talk about chutzpah! More than 99 percent of the human race is defined negatively as other than that 1 percent, the Jews. But this division, however numerically skewed, was an essential feature of the self-identity of both groups—the Jew defined himself as not the other, not the gentile, while the Christian identified himself as not the other, not the Jew. Each assured themselves that they had different traits, different destinies. The term "gentile" is, of course, meaningful only to Christians and Muslims who belong to the biblical tradition, not to Hindus, say, or the Hopi, but, then again, it is in Christian and Muslim countries that Jews have lived these past thousands of years.

Throughout those millennia, Jews expended a lot of energy thinking about how gentiles think about Jews. Their survival depended on getting it right. They often got it wrong. But how

206

did—and do—Jews think of non-Jews? This is, of course, too broad a question to answer comprehensively in a single chapter or in several volumes—attitudes constantly shift in time and place. Our focus here is the attitudes of contemporary American Jews, and we should emphasize at the outset that most of this group are descendants of Eastern European Jews from whom they inherited so many cultural values and customs. These include beliefs about the *goyim* which were marinated in the unpleasantness of the East European experience, and refer, in particular, to the peasantry among whom the Jews lived. You find this outlook expressed explicitly as a running theme in Jewish literature, Jewish humor, Jewish song, Jewish idiom, and in many private Jewish conversations.

Here a few of the attributions that pepper Jewish lore:

Non-Jews drink (*"Shicker iz ah goy"*—"Drunk is the gentile"—according to the old Yiddish lyric).
Non-Jews don't have warm family relationships.
Non-Jews hunt.
Non-Jews are lacking in compassion.
Non-Jews are prone to violence.
Non-Jews lack intellectual acumen.
Non-Jews may be honest in business but they are unimaginative.

Edith Margolis says that while this list might be a "bit too provocative and maybe too much of a generalization," it does reflect the sentiment of her Jewish friends in her retirement community in Vero Beach, Florida. "Yes, of course Jews act differently. Why make believe otherwise? What, you think Jews run around with what do you call those machine guns, assault weapons? No, Jews argue with their minds, not their hands. One of my friends likes to point out that Fisher is a Jewish last name, Hunter a gentile one. I also hear people complain that Jewish parents pester their children all the time, but, believe me, a little pestering doesn't hurt and it's a whole lot better than the lack of interest you see in non-Jewish families. Next door to me is this Christian family. The kids went off to college or wherever and that's it—the parents hardly ever hear from them and they consider this normal. Call me old-fashioned, but I don't call this normal. To me, family still counts, education still counts, talking, not fighting, still counts. To me, Jewish values still count.''

Do most American Jews retain these beliefs about non-Jews? No. Familiarity sometimes breeds contempt, but when it comes to prejudice, familiarity more often breeds understanding. A recent survey by sociologist Steve Cohen suggests that antigentile prejudice is rapidly diminishing among most segments of American Jews. Although a majority in the survey thought that Jews are different than non-Jews, an even larger majority said that Jews weren't any better than non-Jews. Why the change in attitude? Part of the explanation is that nearly half the American Jews surveyed claimed to have a close friend who wasn't Jewish, and the percentage is even higher among younger Jews. The modern media, moreover, provides Jews with a more intimate look at how non-Jews live than they had access to before. American Jews see on the screen and personally know too many brilliant, gentle non-Jews who love their children, respect their wives, drink in moderation, and tolerate other faiths to make the old clichés sound anything but hollow.

Seventeen-year-old Karen Summers is delighted to be leaving Monmouth County, New Jersey, to start college at Baylor in the wilds of Texas, and is glad that the last big piece of schoolwork she did in high school, her senior thesis, was on the topic of ethnic stereotyping. "As a Jew, I think I'll need that information in the Midwest. My subject was the image of Jews among non-Jews and vice versa. In particular, I looked at the way these ethnic images were portrayed in comedy. It was a real eye-opener. Someone gave me a tape of a Lenny Bruce routine where he divides the world into Jewish and goyish. Jewish turns out to be sort of equivalent to urban and ethnic so that Italians qualify as Jewish, so do families in general, and for some reason, big bosoms are Jewish too. Then I heard a tape of Jackie Mason's Broadway show where Jews are portrayed as people who know nothing about operating boats but everything about running businesses, nothing about how to fix cars but everything about how to eat in a restaurant."

Karen found these classic Jewish comedy routines only intermittently amusing. "The truth is, I couldn't relate. This sort of stereotyping belongs to my parents' generation, my grandparents' even, definitely not mine. At least half my friends are Christian. Some celebrate different holidays, but other than that, I can't tell any difference between them and my Jewish friends. They don't know more about cars, that's for sure."

Chipping away, too, at the distinctions between Jew and non-Jew is an increased honesty among American Jews about their own foibles. The Jewish alcoholic is no longer an oxymoron but a recognized problem in some Jewish communities. Cities with large Jewish populations have organizations that deal with violence in the Jewish family. And, though still comparably rare, Jews have managed to master the arts of the hoodlum, the crook, and even the murderer and assassin.

This development is hardly surprising. For centuries, Jews have repeated to one another in whispers of tired experience the old Yiddish maxim *"Vie ist Christelzich azoi Yiddlezicht"*—"As the Christians do, so do the Jews." Sometimes this is said with resignation and a hint of anger, other times with a judicious acceptance of inevitability. In America that inevitability is undeniable; even the most traditional segments of the Jewish population have adorned the trappings of modernity—from sneakers and fast-food establishments to cellular phones and modems.

But what about religiosity? How do American Jews feel about the religious commitment of Christians? Are the Jews better off when non-Jews are more religious or less? This is a topic of intense private discussion among American Jews, and the differences are sharp and angry.

Background is important here. On most measures, the United States is an exceedingly religious country. More than 40 percent of Americans attend church regularly—only Ireland and Poland have a higher rate of churchgoers. In Sweden, by way of contrast, only 4 percent are regular churchgoers, and in England the rate is only modestly higher. Some 96 percent of Americans say they believe in God, 76 percent believe in the divinity of Jesus, and no other Christian country has a higher percentage of its population professing a belief in the devil. The contrast with the religious behavior of American Jews is startling. American Jews, unlike American non-Jews, are overwhelmingly irreligious— fewer than 15 percent of Jews consider themselves observant.

Most Jews do not attend synagogue regularly, and of those who do, a high proportion show up for reasons of ethnic identity and community, not religious persuasion. Only a tiny fraction of Jews believe in an afterlife and Jews are more likely to become atheists or agnostics than those raised in any other religion. Not surprisingly, many of the most prominent Jewish leaders of the century have been thoroughly nonreligious. American Jews have clearly gone their own way on the religious front.

Shawn Ehrenreich thinks the determination with which American Jews have distanced themselves from religion has "helped undermine the Christianity of their Christian neighbors," and that, he believes, is "senseless and self-destructive." Ehrenreich lives in a Detroit suburb, and though brought up in an assimilated, irreligious home, he is now an observant Conservative Jew, or "conservadox," as this sliver of religious persuasion is sometimes called. He is adamant about the need—from the Jewish perspective—to promote a greater religious climate in the United States. "American Jews don't live in a vacuum; like everyone else, they are molded by their environment. When the non-Jews are religious, the Jews stay Jewish, and when the majority culture believes in nothing, the majority of Jews believe in nothing. That's what happened. Most American Jews have become not Jews for Judaism, not even Jews for Jesus, but Jews for nothing."

Ehrenreich is aware of the discrepancy between the continuing religious affiliation of American Christians and the non-religious orientation of American Jews. "Yes, this is precisely the great irony. American Jews made a mad dash to assimilate into American culture, but the one aspect of their lives that they did not want to emulate was this national religiosity; instead, they bought into the vast spiritual emptiness, the other beckoning side of American culture. For the life of me, I can't understand why Jews get so worked up about prayers in the school or a religious symbol on a public lawn, but don't get upset about the gigantic billboards that drape our cities and highways celebrating the latest violent movie. I'm not talking about constitutional issues here. I'm talking about gut response. This isn't an appeal to right-wing extremism; it's an appeal to reality. There *is* a cultural war going on in America, and the question for us Jews is, whose side are we on?''

Naomi Rabinowitz, a graduate student in Jewish history at UCLA, disagrees vehemently. "That view just doesn't bear up under scrutiny. The fact is, Jews do better when Christians, and Muslims too, are less involved with their churches and mosques. From my reading of history, there seems to be a pretty straight correlation between Christian religiosity and Jewish suffering. That's been true throughout the centuries of crusades and po-groms.'' Rabinowitz points to the recent history of the Holocaust as confirmation of her claim. "Here, stark and bold, is the un-settling equation: Wherever Christians were devout, Jews died. In the most faithful Christian countries like Poland, Slovakia, and the Baltic States, the percent of Jews murdered was highest, usu-ally with a major assist from the local God-fearing population. In the least religious countries like Denmark, 90 percent of the Jews were saved, largely because of the help of the local un-God-fearing population. Yes, I know, unlike those horrible immoral Scandinavians, the religious Ukrainians and Austrians were ex-ceptionally moral—after all, they didn't screw around and have abortions. They just helped murder Jewish babies.''

The extrapolation from World War II surely needs tempering. The United States is not Europe and, let's not forget, Stalin was an avowed atheist and murdered Jews too. Rabinowitz acknowledges that there were important exceptions in Europe and that the analogy between there and the United States is complicated, "but the larger point holds true," she insists. "Jews just don't do well in very religious countries. America has a remarkable heritage of religious freedom, but that's all the more reason for Jews to fight vigorously to preserve that freedom. Don't Jews see that?" Rabinowitz has recently signed on with a Jewish organization devoted to maintaining the wall of separation between church and state, and is upset by the efforts of Orthodox Jews to help lower that wall. "What on earth do the Lubavitchers think they're doing when they send amicus briefs to the court in support of allowing religious symbols in municipal squares on Christmas? Sure, they care about menorahs, not crèches, but how foolish, how shortsighted, to imagine that an increased Christian presence in the public arena will help their own cause. Do they forget that Jews are just a drop in the bucket here?"

American Jews do sometimes overlook just how small a percentage of the country they really are, and that blind spot helps explain why they are so chagrined when people point to the Christian character of the country. Naomi Rabinowitz recalls how everyone was at the throat of the governor of Mississippi, Kirk Fordice, who in the course of a speech at a GOP governors' convention referred to the United States as a "Christian nation." "Judeo-Christian" was the proper term, he was told. "Who are we kidding here?" Naomi asks. "He was just refusing to be politically correct. May I remind you that it was a Supreme Court justice who declared a century ago in *Holy Trinity Church v. U.S.* that this is a Christian country. A minority view, sure, but not a dead one. Pat Robertson's fundamentalist television show, the *700 Club,* reaches tens of millions of viewers who share his dream of a Christian America. His America has little room for a liberal, secular Jew such as myself, and despite what they'd like to believe, there would be little room for Lubavitch either.''

Ask an American Jew whether he believes that Jews benefit when Christians are more religious, and he's likely to answer along the fault line of his own religious inclination; religious Jews, not surprisingly, are more likely than irreligious Jews to favor a more prominent religious presence in the American town square. But one issue that cuts across religious persuasion among American Jews is the fear of anti-Semitism.

When Jews talk about non-Jews, they invariably talk about how non-Jews talk about Jews. Every week, Jewish magazines highlight some act of bigotry, and every year sees a crop of new books on the subject of anti-Jewish discrimination in America and the world. Despite the apprehension, however, anti-Semitism in the United States is comparably mild; American Jews are more comfortable and safer in this country now than they have been anytime, anywhere, in the whole history of their Diaspora. Nonetheless, while the anxiety might be low-grade, not more than a whisper, it is never absent entirely. Given the barbarous brutality of the century and the eruptions of hate that mar the contemporary American landscape, even the most secure American Jew must assent to the poet Karl Shapiro's dictum that ''Any Jew that isn't paranoid is crazy.''

Gitty Einhorn is a thirty-three-year-old Orthodox Jew living in Monsey, New York, a mother of seven, who hopes, ''Godwilling, to have a few more.'' Her views about how Jews ought to relate to non-Jews are as typical of her ultraorthodox community as is her large family. ''Let the Christians be Christians, *gezunteheit* [with the best of health],'' she says. ''And our job is to be as Jewish as possible. We go our separate ways.'' But with just a little prodding, Gitty reveals her profoundly suspicious sentiments about gentiles and their attitudes toward Jews.

"Eysov Soyneh L'yaakov," she says, quoting a phrase well known to Jews brought up in traditional Jewish homes. The literal translation of the phrase is "Esau hates Jacob," but the names are always understood as referring to the gentile hatred of Jews, an enmity that is presumed to be perpetual. "I'm sorry if this sounds too old-fashioned, but this is the way it is. The *goyim* despise Jews." She quotes a comment by the sixteenth-century Rabbi Loew, known as the Maharal of Prague: "There are two types of non-Jews: those who simply scorn us and those who actively try to destroy us." For Gitty, when it comes to anti-Semitism, the non-Jew is guilty until proved innocent. "Some non-Jews *are* innocent of anti-Semitism," she assures me. "We must not forget the righteous gentiles who even risked their lives to save Jews, but we should also not forget that they are the exceptions." Gitty is also convinced that interfaith exchanges between Jews and non-Jews cannot bridge that prejudice. "Only assimilationists and fools believe they can. Anti-Semitism will cease only in the end of days when both Jews and Christians and everyone else return to their own true religious paths."

Gitty's views share a striking affinity with classical Christian theology—both interpret the Christian persecution of the Jews as the result of Divine will: For these traditional Christians, Jewish suffering is a punishment for their failure to abandon Judaism, while for these traditional Jews, Jewish suffering is a punishment for abandoning true Judaism.

While most American Jews are repulsed by this notion of an inherent, perpetual hatred of Jews, they also recognize that anti-

Semitism is a reality that distinguishes themselves from their Christian neighbors. Michael Willig, a dentist in Scranton, Pennsylvania, is only marginally Jewish by most criteria. Jewish by birth, he is an atheist by conviction, and his wife, Andrea, was raised Presbyterian. He and his family attend no religious services and do not contribute to any religious institutions. Willig emphatically rejects the notion that gentiles are intrinsically anti-Semitic, "nor extrinsically, for that matter," he adds. "I don't think most American non-Jews are anti-Semitic at all. Believe me, I hear the word *goy* a lot more than I hear the word *kyke*." Nevertheless, Willig does believe that the persistence of anti-Semitism anywhere in the world generates a different life experience for Jews. "Non-Jews don't appreciate how Jews everywhere live in constant trepidation, if only subliminally. The fear is buried below the conscious level and it's difficult to translate without sounding alarmist, but when I look at my daughters, I'm aware that somewhere on this planet, at this very moment, there are people who want to murder them, as they want to murder all Jewish children. Unfortunately, some of these people have the money, means, and ideological connections that can transform them from barroom haters to real-life killers. They've done it on a mass scale half a century go, and if allowed, they'd do it again." Does this perception alter the way he deals with non-Jews? "Not at all," says Willing. "As I said, I don't believe anti-Semitism is a significant problem in the United States, and my decent non-Jewish neighbor here in Scranton is certainly not responsible for the nutcase at a fascist rally in Munich or Montana. But this fear, this existential insecurity, is authentic and it sets Jews apart."

Recent studies confirm the optimistic side of Willig's remarks about contemporary America. Anti-Semitism is in decline and has been for the past forty years. "Overt anti-Semitism is simply no longer a factor in American life," concludes Jerome Chanes, editor of *Antisemitism in America Today*. Other studies suggest that American Jews are not ready to accept that conclusion. In one classic example, in 1985 about a third of the affiliated Jews in San Francisco said, in response to a questionnaire, that Jewish candidates could not be elected to Congress from their area. Yet, at the time, three out of four congressional representatives from that region, two state senators, and the mayor of San Francisco were in fact publicly identified Jews. In a repeated refrain, American Jews say they feel comfortable in America yet also express their continuing concern about anti-Semitism: Tell an American Jew that another Holocaust is imminent or even possible and you will be accused of paranoia, but tell the same Jew that anti-Semitism does not lurk in the country and you will be accused of naiveté.

Jewish antennae remain set to the on position, fine-tuned and sensitive, ever ready to pick up even the slightest murmur of Jew-hatred. Some of these murmurs of anti-Semitism sound like rumbles, however, when they assault basic issues of Jewish survival and identity. These sensitive core issues, as we might expect, parallel those that mark the traitors within American Judaism. But, coming as they do from outside the Jewish community, these attacks from non-Jews have a different complexion, a distinctive sting.

Judaism Is an Anachronism

> *The Constitution of the United States is a marvelous document*
> *for self-government by Christian people. But the minute you*
> *turn the document into the hands of non-Christian people and*
> *atheist people, they can use it to destroy the very foundation*
> *of our society.*   *Pat Robertson*

> *Whatever unease Jews felt in an American culture dominated*
> *by Christianity ain't nothin' compared with the anxiety in store*
> *for Jews and everybody else in a culture dominated by rav-*
> *ening atheists (sometimes mistakenly called "humanists") in-*
> *cluding, it should be noted, for the atheists themselves.*
> *Midge Decter*

Evangelical Christians pose a monumental dilemma for American
Jews. Only a minority of American Jews are comfortable with
the social agenda of this Christian group, but nearly all Jews
approve of its support of Israel; the Christian right's promotion
of Israel has been strong and steady, stronger and steadier than
any other segment of the Christian population. They have en-
dorsed Israel with their rhetoric, their money, and their politics.
The problem is, they love Israel for the wrong reasons. In their
eschatological vision, a Jewish Israel is the necessary precursor
to the conversion of the Jews and the Second Coming of Christ.
Israel, indeed the Jews themselves, are but a means to a Christian
end.

Should Jews forge alliances with groups that offer needed
support of Israel but also profess a theology that downgrades
Judaism? One side of the aisle argues that Jews ought to take
their friends where they find them, that Israel can't afford to be
choosy about its supporters, that what counts is not theology, but

behavior, and on that account the Christian right scores among the Jews' best friends. The other side contends just as vigorously that behavior can only be judged along with the motive that informs it, and on that measure, fundamentalist Christianity is Judaism's enemy. You can catch this debate in every Jewish organizational meeting in every Jewish community in the country.

A less publicized but equally vehement debate centers on the even more delicate issue of religious tolerance. Should Jews expect or demand that Christians respect the integrity and theological viability of Judaism? Can Jews legitimately insist that Christians recognize the eternal authenticity of Judaism?

Not everyone thinks so. Leah Orlowick is an ordained Conservative rabbi in Birmingham, Alabama. She is, by her own admission, at odds with most of her colleagues when it comes to dealing with Christians who think of Judaism as a superseded religion. ''You've noticed how Jewish organizations respond in horror anytime some Christian minister says something about God not hearing the prayers of a Jew or the eventual conversion of Jews to Christianity. I don't understand this hypertouchiness— maybe it has something to do with living here in the Christian South. It seems to me that it isn't our business to dictate to Christians how to be Christians, to tell them what they should or shouldn't believe.'' Orlowick points out that to have the courage of your convictions means not only maintaining that you are right but maintaining that those who disagree with you are wrong. ''Well, guess what? Some Christians are convinced that the Jews are wrong. As a result, they would like to see all Jews eventually converted to Christianity. Where do we get off telling Christians that they can't have that goal? And we Jews, too, have the equal right to believe that pagans, say, are wrong . . . that's part of what it means to belong to a particular faith. The important question is what you do with those beliefs. You can't impose your faith on anyone, you can't deny the right of others to believe as they wish, but you don't need to alter your own faith to make all faiths equal.''

In 1996 Southern Baptists proclaimed a special effort to con-vert the Jews. I asked Orlowick if she is also accepting of this missionary effort. ''Well, there are issues of mutual respect that are a factor here,'' she acknowledges, ''and the line between missionary activity and imposition is not always so clear. But I will say this: Jews can do with more confidence. Religious ar-guments belong in the marketplace with all other ideas, political and economic. I'd like to believe that in this open arena Judaism can at least hold its own. To repeat, I just don't think we should dictate to other religions what they may or may not believe.''

Alicia Pomerantz hosts Christian-Jewish exchanges in her home in Washington, D.C., and believes that Orlowick is not only wrong but dangerously so. ''What world does she live in? This isn't about theological niceties, it's about Jewish survival.''

Pomerantz is angry with what she calls ''misplaced toler-ance.'' ''Let me remind you of the recent research which shows that significant numbers of Christians with traditional religious upbringing continue to think of Jews as the people of the Bible, that is, in religious, cosmic terms. I'm constantly amazed at how even well-educated Christians see 'the Jew' as a mythic character. They see Christianity as fulfilled Judaism, the older religion re-placed by the new. In effect, then, Jewish history ends with the arrival of Jesus. As a Jew, I find this outrageous. Do you realize the implications of this view? Jews aren't a real people. We have no authenticity, no evolving history, let alone a viable religion. Sorry, but to me this is rank anti-Semitism. Jews don't insist that they are the only legitimate religion in the world and they should demand that others respect their legitimacy as well.

"And one other thing," Pomerantz continues. "After years of hosting these events in my home I've learned that if Jews don't demand their self-respect, they won't get it from non-Jews. And in that case, they don't deserve it."

Leah Orlowick again: "Spare me the rhetoric of self-respect, please. And rank anti-Semitism? Time for a quick reality check. Ninety-six percent or so of the country is Christian. We Jews can't pretend that it is otherwise. Some of these Christians are triumphalist, hoping for and expecting the eventual domination of their faith. Well, guess what? Jews would be pretty embarrassed if some of our own triumphalist literature were better known. I can show you many texts where Jews declare themselves inherently on a higher spiritual level than all non-Jews. And if you're willing to wade through all the apologetics, the hemming and hawing, I can bring you to Jews who still today believe in this natural superiority. So let's not be hypocrites. Anyway, if you really do believe in religious tolerance, it seems to me you have to extend that tolerance to fundamentalist religious beliefs as well."

The theological interpretation of Christianity as superseding Judaism has a long history, even in the United States. John Adams, the second president of the United States, was gentler than most in concluding a pro-Jewish, proto-Zionist letter as follows:

"Once restored to an independent government and no longer persecuted, the Jews could possibly, in time, become liberal Unitarian Christians." (Adams wasn't far off—a substantial proportion of contemporary Unitarians are Jews.) The evangelical wing within Christianity that continues to believe that Judaism must disappear in the scheme of human history is relatively small. American Christians are, after all, an extremely diverse group; more than 150 million people are affiliated with a church, of which there are dozens of denominations. How American Jews respond to Christians who deny the authenticity of Judaism depends to a large degree on how they interpret their own Judaism and where they draw the limits of tolerance.

This division among American Jews nearly disappears entirely, however, when it comes to the survival of Israel. They differ, of course, often bitterly, on the proper course of Israeli policy, but as we saw in the previous chapter, that exchange obscures the solid consensus that lies underneath those differences. As a result, non-Jews sometimes underestimate the enduring American Jewish sensitivity about Israel. Sometimes non-Jews underestimate their own negative biases against Israel and Jews.

The Anti-Israel Anti-Semite

> The hasty invention of Israel has poisoned the political and intellectual life of the USA, Israel's unlikely patron. Unlikely, because no other minority in American history has hijacked so much money from the American taxpayers in order to invest in a "homeland." ... a religious minority of less than two percent [the Jews] has bought and intimidated seventy senators (the necessary two thirds to overcome an unlikely presidential veto) while enjoying the support of the media.
>
> Gore Vidal

Yemen has three times as many people as Israel. Zaire has eight times as many. Indonesia, forty. So why is Israel in the news every day and not these other countries? Committed Jews care about Israel; that's understandable. Palestinians are invested in Israel's activities. That's understandable too. But why the harangue from a non-Jew in Omaha on why Israel should be more forthcoming in making peace with Syria? Why is a gentile woman in Dallas who doesn't know Laos from Venezuela so indignant about the Israeli response to West Bank violence? For that matter, why does her neighbor insist that Israel give back no land at all and remain the only power in the region? Why does everyone seem to have an opinion about Israel?

Some of the answers are obvious: Israel is in the middle of a politically charged part of the world and its policies have a direct effect on the foreign policy aims of the United States. Religious factors also play a role. After all, Israel is the Holy Land and has religious significance to all Christians. Publicity also has its economic and social benefits, and Israel itself sometimes helps promote this focus. But many American Jews find this attention to Israel suspect, especially the negative attention. The issue does not concern the right to criticize. Everyone has that right. Nor does the issue concern the content of the criticism, which may be correct in the particulars. What American Jews find troublesome is the question of standing, whether one is in a position to criticize.

Barry Sturm, a thirty-year-old financial planner in Los Angeles, had just returned from a year in Israel and was disturbed by all the comments he heard about Israel in the American press. The year's absence, he believes, helped give him a new perspective. "Let me put it this way," he said intently. "I'm mildly interested in the strife between the Tamils and the Hindus in Sri Lanka, and if pressed, I can give you my poorly informed take on the good guys and bad guys in that quarrel. The truth is, though, that this conflict is not a genuine concern in my life; I have never lost two minutes of sleep worrying about which party will win over there. That's why a Sri Lankan would be justifiably annoyed if I started making speeches about the situation in his country. Well, I feel the same way about non-Jews and non-Arabs pontificating about Israel. I'm not talking about some expert foreign policy wonk, but your average clueless American. These folk are entitled to their opinion, but my response is, who the hell asked you for it? What's it to you? You want to spout? Go spout about the Kurds. And that goes triple for those Americans who devote their careers working for anti-Israel organizations with names like Middle East Justice Watch or something like that. I ask myself, what makes these people choose this particular spot on the globe to focus their venom? But you see, we all know the answer. They attack Israel, but they mean the Jews. Let's face it: Anti-Israel is the modern wrapping on old-time Jew-bashing."

Non-Jews who are anti-Israel are furious with this equation, insisting that their anti-Israel views have nothing to do with a hatred of Jews. In principle, Jews will allow that possibility. Given Israel's enduring military security and the bitter internecine battles within the Jewish community over Israel's direction, American Jews are now prepared to give wider berth to anti-Israel sentiments than was true in previous years. But American Jews are not ready to brook anti-Israel criticism from non-Jews who have not first established their general support for the country.

"I was out there in the barricades with my sisters, all right," Susan Pfeiffer recalls, thinking back to her protest days of the late sixties. "Pro-feminism, antiwar, pro–civil rights, and anti-Israel. But even those of us who weren't uncomfortable with the anti-Israel rhetoric were jarred soon enough when the sentiment became overtly anti-Jewish. In fact, I believe that the adoption of anti-Semitism contributed to the new left's demise, but that's another story. The point is that my friends and I were slow in recognizing the anti-Zionism talk as just the cloak for the anti-Semitism lurking underneath. I don't make that mistake anymore."

Susan's husband, Harlan, warns against generalizing too quickly. "It's just unfair not to allow non-Jews to make the same comments or hold the same beliefs as Jews without being accused of bigotry. Jews need to lighten up about criticism of Israel. And they will as American Jews recognize that the Jewish state is secure and stop seeing every altercation there as heralding the collapse of the country. When that happens, they'll give non-Jews a little more breathing room."

Perhaps. But there is one issue that is likely to remain sacrosanct and about which Jews are of one mind—there is no tampering with the Shoah.

Demeaning the Shoah

Even when it is not the overt focus, the Shoah permeates every discussion by Jews about the fate of the Jews. It hovers in

the background, usually unarticulated, a black backdrop, the unspoken subtext that contours how secure Jews can be in a genṭile
world as they enter the twenty-first century.

Let's not shy away from the hard truth. For many Jews, the
unspoken lesson of the Shoah is that they cannot trust Christians
with the lives of their children. Tens of thousands of Christians
with crosses around their necks sent millions of innocent Jews
and millions of other innocent men, women, and children to their
horrid deaths while many of their fellow Christians cheered. Too
many priests and ministers encouraged the hatred as even more
looked on and did nothing. Certainly, these murderers and their
enthusiasts were not acting as true Christians. And millions of
other Christians, with crosses on their necks too, fought valiantly
to defeat the barbarism of Nazi Germany. But that is the precise
point: What went wrong with Christianity when so many could
stoop to such brutality and do so in the name of Christ? As
theologian Eliezer Berkovitz writes, "In order to pacify the
Christian conscience it is said that the Nazis were not Christians.
But they were all the children of Christians."

Why hasn't this shaken Christianity to its roots? Why is the
Shoah just a problem for Judaism?

Marilka Zweig asks me this question rhetorically, adding a
weary shrug. She spent the war as a teenager alternating between
labor camps and hiding in the woods near her hometown of Lodz,
Poland. She begins by talking to me in English but soon switches
to Yiddish. Back in her mother tongue, she dispenses with politeness: "When I hear people talk of Christianity as a religion
of love, I don't know whether to laugh or cry. Understand, I am
not blaming the Nazi savageness on Christianity. I myself was
saved by a Christian who did what she did because of her com-

mitment to her religious ideals. But I also know what her neighbors believed, how Christianity was taught in the old country, and what it taught about Jews. No Jew in hiding would have dreamt of walking into church to seek refuge from the Nazis; in many cases, that would be just a sure ticket to SS headquarters.''

The church Marilka refers to is the Catholic Church, and no survey of the American Jewish conversation should neglect the bitterness that Jews the world over retain toward the church in Rome. Because the resentment is rarely expressed in the polite forums of interfaith meetings where the agenda is contemporary concerns and mutual respect, and because that anger is primarily directed to Catholicism in Europe, not America, most American Catholics are not aware of the depth of the rage. Younger American Jews, removed as they increasingly are from the events of the world war, have less of that rage, but among older Jews, and especially East European immigrants and their children, the anger is sharp and enduring.

Ron Mirsky was born in the United States in the late 1940s. His mother immigrated from Poland in the 1930s. His father, also from Poland, is a concentration camp survivor. Mirsky works for a real estate management firm in Hartford, Connecticut, and is the father of three daughters. Although he doubts they personally will feel the rancor he inherited, he thinks ''Jewish history'' will certainly remember this betrayal. ''We Jews, like everyone else, have our cast of villains, but our enemy list is especially long and ancient. The scoundrels shift positions as the years go by, but some, like Hitler and his henchmen, have earned a secure place at the top of the chart. One niche or two below sits Eugenio Pacelli, otherwise known as Pope Pius XII. When my parents would mention his name, they would add, *Y'mach shmo'*—'May his name be erased'—the gravest curse in the Jewish lexicon. I heard this sentiment expressed regularly about that pope. Only later did I fully appreciate the significance of this: To hundreds of millions of Catholics, this man was His Holiness, the Prince of the Church—to us he was a Nazi collaborator.''

The record of Pope Pius and the Catholic Church in general during the Holocaust is a mixed bag at best. Catholic priests and nuns were among the few genuine heroes during the war, and many courageous clergymen risked their lives to hide Jews in their schools and monasteries. It is also true, however, that even more European Catholic clergymen ignored and sometimes encouraged the hatred of Jews at the time of their greatest peril. Ron Mirsky says that his reading of that period's history leaves him with ''a fury in the very gut of my being. Here's a church that excommunicates sinners for relatively minor sins but couldn't see fit to excommunicate two of its most famous sons, Hitler and Goebbels. It never got around to even condemn the Nazi SS, whose membership was mostly Catholic. Perhaps worse still is the way the Catholic Church protected Nazis after the war. Disgusting. And that they never apologized for their behavior is the most galling of all. Given that history, how am I as a Jew supposed to react when I read that the contemporary pope, John Paul II, confers a church knighthood on that lying Nazi bastard Kurt Waldheim?''

Mirsky's twenty-three-year-old cousin, Robin, thinks all this indignation is useless. ''That's Europe, that's history,'' she says. ''As far as America is concerned, our soldiers, Catholics and everyone else, gave their lives fighting the Germans. To me as a Jew, the Holocaust is a big deal, but I can't expect my Christian friends to care as I do—I mean, really now, their lives weren't in the balance, they didn't lose uncles and aunts to the gas chambers, they weren't the next victims in the event of an Axis victory.''

But American Jews do expect to be allowed to nurse their wounds, to grieve for their dead, and to care for the maimed that still walk among them. They don't want to be told that the Holocaust is old news and that we all have to move on. Most Americans exhibit that decency.

Some do not. Public officials with obvious anti-Jewish positions are rare these days, but when they show up, they come from both sides of the ideological wings: Ramsey Clark, a former attorney general, is a leftist who publicly supports known anti-Semites, as does Patrick Buchanan on the right. Because Buchanan is an acclaimed journalist and presidential aspirant, he serves as an especially useful example of why American Jews read national political news through the prism of their own nation's history and why they believe they cannot yet relax their guard even in the United States. During the presidential election of 1996, many commentators alluded to Buchanan's anti-Semitic rhetoric, but these columns failed to capture the depth of impact Buchanan's candidacy had on the American Jewish psyche.

''Buchanan is over the line. He messes with the Holocaust.'' Alexander Rifkin, a political science professor at a college in upstate New York, has been tracking the Buchanan record for years because, as he says, ''Buchanan's national acceptance despite his overt anti-Semitism belies the notion that Jews are fully respected as a group in the United States.'' Everyone is familiar with Buchanan's anti-Israel remarks, which include calling Congress ''occupied Israeli territory'' and blaming the Persian Gulf War on Israel's ''amen corner'' in the United States. ''But okay,'' says Rifkin, ''suppose you explain away all that as a foreign policy difference. The problem is that this anti-Israel rhetoric is just the icing to Buchanan's mean-spirited anti-Semitism.''

Rifkin continues his litany. ''When Patrick Buchanan 'raises questions' about Zyklon-B gas and the capacity of the Nazis to have murdered as many Jews as they did, American Jews are mortified. Why is this man doing this? Why such cruelty to his fellow American citizens, the Jews who survived the camps and now live in the United States? Buchanan lends his name and imprimatur to Holocaust-deniers by repeating charges of a 'Holocaust survivor syndrome,' which includes, as Buchanan puts it, 'group fantasies of martyrdom and heroics.' A right-wing ideologue who excoriates liberals for their softness on crime, he comes to the defense of mass murderers like Karl Linnas, Arthur Rudolph, and John Demjanjuk. Buchanan asks, 'You've got a great atrocity that occurred thirty-five, forty-five years ago . . . why pour millions of dollars into investigating that?' He urged Jewish leaders to stop protesting Reagan's visit to Bittberg, 'and be good Americans.' He is credited with penning Reagan's characterization at the Bittberg cemetery of German soldiers and SS troops as 'victims of the Nazis as surely as the victims of the concentration camps.' And despite all these horrendous comments, he is accepted as a credible, respectable, potential presidential candidate of one of the nation's two major parties. This is appalling stuff. What I don't understand is why only American Jews are appalled and not the rest of the country.''

Part of the answer is the distance between the Shoah and contemporary concerns, a distance not relegated to non-Jews. Although American Jews are uniformly vigilant about any tampering with the historicity of the Shoah, repeated studies indicate that, by and large, younger American Jews don't share the same visceral response as their parents.

Jessica Landau, a junior at Brown University, expresses a view representative of many in her generation. "I understand that the Holocaust has deeply scarred Jews everywhere, and it will take a long time for the trauma to heal. And I have no tolerance for anyone who belittles the suffering—how could you? But I think my parents' generation sees everything through that Holocaust lens and that distorts reality. I don't mean to sound callous, but I sometimes feel like saying 'enough already.' I know what happened, yes it was horrible beyond belief, I get the point, can we please move on? Now if I, a Jew, feel that way, what can you expect from a non-Jew? It's unfair, ridiculous to call them anti-Semitic just because they respond this way."

The desire to move Jewish attention away from a focus on the Shoah to other matters is more an argument about emphasis than substance: For all Jews, the Holocaust is a defining moment in Jewish history. It is, of course, also a defining event in *human* history. The Holocaust confirmed once and for all—and this is surely one of the most significant lessons of the twentieth century—that culture itself cannot prevent cruelty and sadism. The Nazi commandant who sat in his well-appointed office, sipping his brandy, listening to a Bach fugue while calculating the most efficient way to gas human beings is the reductio ad absurdum to all such assumptions. The century has taught us yet again that religious and ideological professions of love and justice are no guarantee against barbarism. That lesson colors all interfaith discussions and surely all exchanges between Jews and non-Jews.

Part II. Jews Talk with Christians

> *There cannot be an honest exchange of ideas between Judaism and Christianity or a sincere "Jewish-Christian dialogue." A dialogue between Judaism and Christianity (as distinct from a dialogue between Jews and Christians)—to which certain liberal Jewish circles aspire—is possible only for Jews who have lost any appreciation of what abrogation of the Torah and its Mitzvoth signifies and for Christians who are no longer sensitive to what the image of Jesus connotes.*
>
> *Yeshayahu Leibowitz*

> *Jews who for the sake of the pleasantries of Jewish-Christian dialogue are ready to overlook almost two millennia of Jewish suffering at Christian hands agree that an act of dishonesty may well be the basis for an encounter between Jew and Christian in search of better understanding. They are bound to be disappointed. The crime against the Jewish people is the cancer at the very heart of Christianity.*
>
> *Rabbi Eliezer Berkovitz*

Jews and Christians have been talking to one another for millennia, but for most of those years, these exchanges could hardly be called a meeting of the minds.

"You ask me, it's a waste of time." Everett Dulchin is a window-shade salesman in Pittsburgh, and most of his business colleagues are non-Jews. "I used to talk a lot more about our different religions, or at least what we knew about them, which isn't too much, but these discussions never got anywhere, so I don't bother anymore. One of the people I work with, James, is 'born again' and always asking me about Jewish things. He's also always trying to sell me his Christianity. I think that especially turned me off from these conversations.''

Dulchin alludes to two crucial asymmetries that underlie discussions between Jews and Christians at both the organizational and the individual levels—ignore these imbalances and you will never understand the reality behind Jewish-Christian exchange. The first asymmetry: Without Judaism, there is no Christianity. To understand Jesus, one must understand the faith and fate of Judaism, the religion to which he belonged. Judaism, on the other hand, precedes Christianity and proceeds without it. That is, traditionally, Jews cared about Christianity not for reasons of theology, but only insofar as it affected their temporal well-being. The second asymmetry is that Christianity, but not Judaism, is a universal religion. Most contemporary committed Christians respect the integrity of other religious persuasions and don't seek to impose their views on others, but they also believe that they have the truth and want to share that good news with the rest of humanity. (''I am the way, and the truth, and the life; no one comes to the Father, but by me''—John 14:6. *''Nulla salus extra ecclesiam''*—salvation must come through the church.) Christians are confident that the world would be a better place if everyone—including the Jew across the table—were also true Christians. Judaism, on the other hand, posits a distinct covenant between God and the people of Israel, and while anyone who wishes can join the tribe, no one is the worse for remaining a gentile. Jews have no religious directive to persuade anyone to become Jewish.

These classical asymmetries are not obscure, ancient theological fine points, but underlie even the casual conversations between contemporary American Jews and Christians. Yet these different religious agendas don't tell the whole story of current interreligious exchange in America. American Jews feel more confident, more secure, and more curious than ever before, and many are now willing to risk a more honest dialogue. But to understand the texture and mood of these ongoing personal and theological exchanges, we need to briefly highlight their historical background in America.

American Jews and Christian religious leaders began talking to one another in earnest a half century ago. For the most part, these discussions were initiated by the Jews, the party that saw itself with the most to gain. But before long, Christian organizations began to incorporate ecumenical programs into their calendar of events. (When used by Christian organizations, the term "ecumenical" refers to intra-Christian dialogue as well as interreligious dialogue. When Jewish organizations use the term, they mean interchanges with Christians.) A new phrase entered the national vocabulary—"Brotherhood Week." Ministers and rabbis traipsed across the country promoting this new spirit of mutual respect, and every Sunday morning, local television stations dutifully met their FCC public interest mandates by broadcasting interfaith panel discussions. Rabbis joined their fellow Christian clergymen in opening legislative sessions and in closing the day's programming on radio. The National Conference of Christian and Jews became a permanent fixture in the American expressions of pluralism and religious liberty. By the 1950s Christian Americans were beginning to see themselves as belonging to a "Judeo-Christian heritage," and although many Jews and Christians thought the description diluted the uniqueness of each religion, all agreed that it reflected Judaism's official parity with America's dominant Christian religions, Protestantism and Catholicism.

This was a heady and unfamiliar achievement for Jews. Why this burst of understanding? Certainly, the Shoah was a significant factor, for here was a stark and fresh lesson about the dangers of unrestrained anti-Semitism. But the Shoah and the subsequent religiously laden creation of the State of Israel couldn't be the whole story behind this interreligious enthusiasm—nothing comparable was going on in Christian Europe. What made America fertile soil for the interfaith movement was the country's ongoing history of immigration and its tradition of religious freedom. A changing sociological profile of American Jews also contributed to the spirit of acceptance. By the second half of this century, American Jews were highly visible in almost all sectors of American life: in politics, arts, entertainment, the sciences, and sports. Jews were mixing relatively easily with Christians at golf courses, in boardrooms, Ivy League schools, and under the canopy. The Jews had arrived in America and with them so had Judaism.

I'm in Sharon, Massachusetts, a suburb of Boston and home to many middle-to-upscale professional Jews. The discussion turns to how Jews should "talk to the *goyim*," a phrase otherwise translated as "ecumenical dialogue." One man, Robert, a professor, offers some insightful context:

"For fifty years we American Jews have been conducting something of a charade. Ostensibly, we talked about theology, but we never cared a fig about the substance of those discussions. Throughout history and in this country too, we talked to 'official'

Christians for one reason only: We figured, if they are talking to you, they aren't hitting you. The Christians talked God, we pushed civil liberties.''

Should things change now? I ask. ''Absolutely,'' says Robert. ''The fact is that whatever the motives, the results of these years of ecumenism have been dramatic. Judaism is far better known and respected, and Jews are safer than ever before in modern history. Christianity has undergone major changes. They have reached out to the Jews; they—I'm talking about the mainline Christian churches—are no longer interested in persecuting us anymore. I think the time has come to reconsider the Jewish approach to these exchanges. I think the time has come to really talk—find out what we have in common, what divides us, what we can learn from each other.''

Others in the room disagree, some vociferously. Pauline, a lawyer at a large Boston law firm, thinks Robert's call for a new approach is just wishful thinking. According to Pauline, ''It's still too early, way too early, to focus on anything but Jewish security and respect above all.

''Look, forget these pronouncements of mutual respect and shared beliefs by establishment religious organizations, both Jewish and Christian. They're just slogans, and have so little to do with where Jews and Christians really live. They're also irrelevant. I mean who cares what a group of priests and rabbis have to say. Especially rabbis. I remind you that most American Jews aren't observant. When Jewish theologians discuss Judaism with their Christian colleagues, they represent not *the* Jewish tradition, but only one sliver of a strain of that tradition, the thread to which the particular theologian happens to adhere. If this rabbi or some scholar wants to discuss the fine points of ancient Jewish cosmology, let him enjoy himself. But he shouldn't imagine that he represents the beliefs of most contemporary American Jews."

This is true: America, unlike Israel or England, has no chief rabbi. There is no "official" Jewish view on abortion, euthanasia, the West Bank, or affirmative action, as there might be an "official" Lutheran or Catholic view. American Jewish ideology is a mosaic all its own: Orthodox, Reform, Reconstructionist, Conservative, affiliated and nonaffiliated Jews, Chassidic and secular, Zionist and non-Zionist, socialist and politically conservative, and the intricate subdivisions within each of these groups. The American Jewish community rallies around political and social issues, not religious matters. Pauline winds up her analysis: "Can there be productive exchanges between Jews and Christians? Sure, on political and social issues like Israel, the separation of church and state, affirmative action, but not on Judaism and Christianity."

Many Jewish theologians are themselves wary of ecumenical programs but for different reasons. One fear is that as a result of these meetings, religious differences between Jews and Christians will be further blurred, which, in turn, will accelerate an already speeding rate of assimilation and intermarriage. Other Jewish religious leaders worry—more so in private—that in their eagerness for discussion, Jews become too quick to avoid the difficult issue of Christian anti-Semitism. No real discourse is possible, they insist, until the toxin of anti-Semitism is thoroughly drained from Christianity. Discussions of creed must await discussions of history.

Rabbi Eliezer Berkovitz, an influential Orthodox theologian, was one of the few religious thinkers who made this demand publicly and explicitly, excoriating those who sidestep this grievance in order to get on to more agreeable matters. Berkovitz traces Christian anti-Jewishness directly to the Gospels: "The first truth to note is the realization that in its effect upon the life of the Jews and the Jewish people, Christianity's New Testament has been the most dangerous tract in history. . . . Without Christianity's New Testament, Hitler's *Mein Kampf* could never have been written."

But many Jews, establishment and laypersons, think that harping on Christian anti-Semitism when they talk to Christians about their respective religions is simply unfair. Fred Arrow, a member of his synagogue's interfaith group in Memphis, thinks it's dishonest for Jews to minimize the major changes the Christian churches have adopted in their relations with Jews. "There is no one single attitude of Christianity. Sure, you can find anti-Jewish sentiments in the New Testament, but you can as easily find pro-Jewish sentiments. But look at the general trend. A history of persecution clouds Jewish-Christian relations, but you can't ignore the rays of change that come filtering through. These "rays of change" to which Arrow refers are easy to trace.

Modern-day Christian theologians are moving away from the Hellenistic depiction of Jesus and rediscovering his Jewishness. When in 1965 Vatican II issued the document *Nostra Aetate* and rescinded the canard that Jews were forever responsible for the killing of Jesus, the theological basis for anti-Semitism collapsed. American Christian churches are steadily confronting their past anti-Jewish "teaching of contempt." Martin Luther advocated burning synagogues and recommended the expulsion of the Jews, saying "we must drive them out like mad dogs"; Adolf Hitler quoted Luther as a justification for his persecution of the Jews. But in 1994 Bishop Sherman Hicks of the Lutheran Church expressed his forthright sorrow over his church's demonization of the Jews, saying "We confess our sins. We repent for the wrong that has been done. We ask for forgiveness. As a bishop of the church, it is with humility and gratitude that I present this declaration to the Jewish community."

"What more do you want these Christians to say and do?" Arrow asks.

Robert, the professor, agrees. "We Jews need to be more forthright about our own theological convictions. We have no right to a place at the ecumenical table unless we are willing to show our own cards. When I as an individual talk to my Christian friends about religious matters, we manage to get beyond this past history. We need to do the same as a community."

Pauline, as expected, will have little of this outreach. "I know it's the pretty thing to say—let's reach out, bury the hatchet, just be friends from now on. And I agree that as individuals, between my non-Jewish friends and myself, that makes sense. But as a community? Absolutely not. Jewish dignity is at stake. No burying of hatchets. We have a big moral score to settle first before we proclaim genuine brotherhood."

Judging from the intensity of the conversation that evening in Sharon, it would seem that Jews might have an easier time talking to the Christians than to each other. But this much is clear: as Jews and Christians become more intimate with one another, the American Jewish private conversation about the *goyim* has undergone radical change. Nevertheless, it is also clear that the specter of anti-Semitism still hovers in the American Jewish psyche. Indeed, just as American Jews began to relax in the expectation of a waning of anti-Semitism, anti-Jewish sentiment reemerged with surprising intensity in the most surprising of places—the African American community.

239

S c h m o o z i n g

Jews on Blacks on Jews: The Private Conversation

> *I think of the African problem: only a Jew can understand it in its full profundity.*   *Theodore Herzl*

> *But just as a society must have a scapegoat, so hatred must have a symbol. Georgia has the Negro and Harlem has the Jew.*   *James Baldwin*

> *I rejoice. There are white Jews too.*
>   *Ethiopian Jew on his arrival to Israel*

Jews are furious with the African American community.

This anger is but one emotion in a throng of others that include fear, frustration, alienation, a sense of betrayal, disdain, and utter bewilderment. Especially bewilderment. "Where," Jews wonder, "did all their venom come from?"

Rarely do these Jewish sentiments, particularly the bitterness—and the strands of Jewish racism that sometimes accompany that bitterness—get played out in the soft light of the public press. Books on the black-Jewish rift are all the rage, but do not express the outrage. On the media stage, politeness rules. Contributors to the op-ed pages and television talk show guests regularly and righteously intone the reflexive rhetoric of symmetry: We are all at fault, each community needs to accept responsibility, let's look for compromise, it's time to reach out to one another, and so on. But this is not how the talk proceeds in private, neither among blacks nor among Jews.

Stuart Cantor identifies himself as a "centrist liberal on Monday, Wednesday, and Friday, and a liberal centrist on Sunday, Tuesday, and Thursday." Saturday, presumably, is a day of political rest. Cantor is a businessman, a partner in an advertising firm in Manhattan. He regularly votes Democratic. He is also, he says, "fed up" with the black anti-Semitic discourse, but even more upset with Jews who continue to reach out for reconciliation despite all the bigotry. "Do you ever wonder why the blacks don't attack the Italians the same way they attack Jews? After all, the Mafia is Italian, and they're the ones who sell drugs to black children. Or why African Americans don't harangue the Irish, another ethnic group not particularly known for its sympathy toward blacks? Of course you don't wonder, because the answer is obvious. They'd get their asses kicked in if they tried that shit with these ethnic groups. But accuse Jews of infecting African Americans with the AIDS virus, call Jews bloodsuckers, beat up on Zionism, or stand by as other 'leaders' make these outrageous claims and what do you get? A request for a panel discussion. It's pathetic. It's time we Jews learned from everyone else to mind our own business. Maybe then we'll be left alone too."

Cantor's rancor might be extreme, but his assumptions about black anti-Semitism are not uncommon among Jews. American Jews now almost *expect* blacks to be anti-Semitic, to hear anti-Jewish venom on black radio programs, and to read anti-Jewish diatribes in black newspapers. They don't expect this of all blacks, of course, and they are aware that the media is much to blame for keeping the fires going—after all, here was a story begging to be paraded through the curving streets of the new multiculturalism—but whatever the cause of the ill will, the effect is unmistakable: Antagonism is presumed even in everyday meetings between individual Jews and blacks. The pervasiveness of black anti-Semitism is borne out by the research. In a 1992 Anti-Defamation League study that charted degrees of anti-Jewish feeling, 37 percent of blacks were at the level of "most anti-Semitic," more than twice that of whites. Only 14 percent of blacks gave responses that qualified as non-anti-Semitic. The study also showed that anti-Semitism was declining among all groups but blacks. A Louis Harris poll of 1994 found that a majority of African Americans, 54 percent, agreed with the comment "When it comes to choosing between people and money, Jews will choose money," while 27 percent of non-Jewish whites supported that assertion. Most worrisome, while higher levels of education usually result in reduced bigotry, some of the worst pockets of anti-Semitism were found among college students and the better educated.

Another growing sentiment among American Jews is indifference. The hot story of the war between blacks and Jews is becoming old news, cold news. And here we find the beginnings of a significant shift from the intimacy of anger to the distance of detachment; more and more American Jews are becoming indifferent to the protests and complaints of African Americans. Increasingly, American Jews ask themselves, why bother?

"Because I'm Jewish, that's why we should bother," says Tracey Weber. Southern Californian, Weber has a political profile that reads very much like Stuart Cantor's—a young entrepreneur, she too labels herself a moderate Democrat—but she differs sharply with him on this issue.

"I'm not going to let Farrakhan, Jeffries, or some other two-bit demagogue dictate my attitude to all African Americans," says Weber. "Jews don't have to take the bait of the Jew-baiters. I admit that at times my control is sorely tested—with all these headlines screaming at you, it takes effort to remind yourself that most blacks aren't anti-Semitic and most anti-Semites aren't black.'' Weber also thinks black leaders face a double standard when Jews ask them to respond to anti-Semitic outbursts of others in their community. ''It is unfair. We don't expect that kind of purity and accountability from other ethnic groups.'' What about the argument of those like Cantor who don't see why Jews should be more involved with the black community than anyone else? ''Because Jews are supposed to be different, that's why,'' says Weber. ''This isn't just some mealymouthed piety. I truly take my heritage as directing me not to desert people in trouble. Black anti-Semitism, like Jewish racism, is a problem to solve, not accept as a permanent reality.''

Black-Jewish discord has been going on for decades, but never has the depth and breath of the antagonism grown so blatant as in the past few years. Why this hostility? American Jews weigh in with their theories.

To listen to Joe Spiegel, now of Miami, is to take a trip back to the Bronx neighborhood of his youth. Speigel still speaks with classic Bronxian inflection, waving his cigar to underline his hard-ass analysis. ''I'm a believer in *Realpolitik,''* he says. ''Lovely sentiments had nothing to do with it. The Jews were never aligned to blacks because of any deep-seated sympathy, but only because they saw themselves on the same side of the fence, fighting for the same goals. We were fellow outsiders and joint targets of discrimination, and battling prejudice was in our mutual interests. The same fair-housing laws that allowed a black access to a modest apartment in Flatbush, Brooklyn, admitted the Jew to a posh condominium on the Upper East Side of Manhattan.''

Speigel believes that black anti-Semitism began when the paths of the two communities diverged. Jews merged with society's winners and became insiders, while the blacks remain huddled on the poor side of the fence, clamoring for their fair share of the pie, which inevitably included Jewish jobs and Jewish political power. Conflict was bound to ensue. Envy too. "Envy, pure and simple. But what do you expect? Both communities start out in the same boat, oppressed. The blacks are still the boat and the Jews are in the penthouse apartment on the shore. Jews are 2 percent of the population and more than 20 percent of the Forbes 400, while blacks are 12 percent of the population and have a grand total of one person on the list. I'm not discussing why this is so—it's certainly not the fault of the Jew—but whatever the reasons, the disparity has to rankle."

Eva Gross thinks this sort of approach just doesn't square with the facts. "For all the bravado about realism, it's ludicrous, besides being cynical, to talk about the Jewish relationship to blacks without talking about values. I appreciate the power of economics—I'm a real estate lawyer, aren't I?—but I also appreciate the impact of the prophetic tradition which exhorts Jews to fight for justice. We forget just how extraordinary was the Jewish participation in the black struggle in the sixties and seventies."

Jewish involvement in the civil rights movement was indeed extraordinary. Jews were there with their bodies: Two-thirds of the whites who went south in Freedom Summer of 1964 were Jews. Jews were there with their talent: Half the civil rights lawyers in the South were Jewish. Jews were there with their money: Between 50 and 75 percent of all donations to major civil rights organizations came from Jews. Jews were there with their votes:

Jews voted for black candidates at significantly higher rates than
other groups did. Gross doesn't think that this commitment has
entirely disappeared. "The rupture isn't as massive as the media
implies. Jews still support black candidates more than any other
white group—the adage is still true: 'Jews make money like Episcopalians, but vote like Puerto Ricans.' I take this as a compliment, not an indictment."

Gross is also upset by what she sees as the one-sided self-
righteousness of so many American Jews when it comes to their
relationship with blacks. "Even forgetting our own racism for the
moment, we American Jews should thank the African American
community for making it important and socially legitimate to be
interested in one's roots, for setting up academic disciplines of
ethnic studies, for making it okay to proclaim ethnic pride in
America. The truth is that because of their effort, we Jews, too,
became more self-conscious, which, in turn, prevented even more
American Jews from drifting into white-bread anonymous America. We owe African Americans a debt of gratitude."

There are other explanations for the rise of black anti-
Semitism. Many Jews believe, for example, that we underestimate
the extent to which blacks, as Christians, have inherited classical
Christian anti-Semitism along with the rest of the religious pack-
age. (One hears much about the Nation of Islam, but less than 1
percent of blacks are Muslim, and of these the majority are followers of Wallace D. Muhammad, who is not a segregationist,
supported Bush for the presidency, and backed the Gulf War.)
By attacking the Jews, blacks enter the American Christian mainstream. "Nonsense," reply other Jews. "The very opposite is the
case." In their view, the appeal of anti-Semitism is that it keeps
blacks apart from whites. Louis Farrakhan, they suggest, needs

to paint all whites as irredeemably antiblack, but the Jews, who also happen to be white folk, pose an annoying counterexample to this sweeping indictment with their record of extensive support for civil rights and justice for African Americans. Consequently, the Jews must be demonized to show that they, too, are white racists.

Academics and historians will have much to say in the years ahead about how the antagonism between American Jews and African Americans blossomed in the latter part of this century. But American Jews have to deal with the issue now. How should they respond to black anti-Semitism?

Squawk

Suri Klingberg, a freelance writer, lives in Forest Hills, Queens. She is in her forties, and her conservative politics contrast sharply with the activist liberal views she held in her twenties. She believes that American Jews must be adamant in their response to each and every outburst of anti-Semitism. "No discussions, no symposia, but the back of the hand. If there is one lesson we Jews should have learned from this century, it is to give anti-Semites no quarter. We should be screaming at the top of our lungs, using every piece of political clout at our disposal, leaning on everyone we can to make a clean break with the demagogues. You allow the disease to decay and you pay in the end."

Klingberg also insists that Jews have to get over their mistaken liberal presumptions. "First, we need to get over this insidious notion that our anger is driven by racism. Judging people inferior or superior because of their skin color is obviously stupid and unacceptable. But that's not what's going on here. Jews are physically afraid of blacks. Do you think my mother is bigoted because she'll cross the street if she sees a bunch of young black men congregating on the corner? She'd be stupid not to—it's a perfectly rational response, and elderly black persons do the same. I'm sick and tired of hearing bleeding-heart Jews living in the suburbs lecture us urban Jews on how we should be more understanding of our black neighbors. People complained about the bigotry of the Lubavitcher Chassidim in Crown Heights. Here is one of the few truly integrated neighborhoods in the country. Everyone—the Italians, the Irish, these same liberal Jews—fled when blacks moved next door except for these Lubavitcher Jews who stayed put. And they get branded as racists.''

Klingberg's fury is not atypical. Nor is it abated. ''I'm also sick and tired of hearing how the Jews were so involved in the civil rights movement. What was 'Jewish' about these people anyway? Yes, agreed, noteworthy Jewish theologians had a visible presence in the movement, and Jewish organizations were actively involved. But most of the Jewish activists were neither publicly nor privately Jewishly identified. Those famous murder victims, Goodman and Schwerner, for example, didn't even have Jewish funerals. Few of these great Jewish freedom fighters ever participated in Jewish struggles such as freedom for Soviet Jewry.''

Talk

''What's the point of just screaming back?'' counters Elaine Feder, voicing outrage. Feder, also in her forties, teaches fifth grade in a Manhattan public school. ''It makes you feel good for the moment, but that's no long-term solution.'' Feder argues that amid all the charges and countercharges we are losing perspective. "Condemnation isn't enough; Jews must initiate widespread educational programs to counter the hatred."

Feder emphasizes that even American Jews have good reason to be angry, but not to panic. The hateful harangues that occasionally emanate from some quarters of the African American community are disturbing, but they pose no imminent, direct threat to American Jews. Even if they sought to harm Jews—and assuredly, most do not—African Americans do not have anything approaching that sort of power in the United States. They have enough problems just trying to survive and achieve social and economic parity with the rest of the country. True, Jews fear violence on the street, and the rampage in Crown Heights is a frightening example of just how ugly that violence can be. Nevertheless, continued outbursts of that kind would surely be quickly contained. It is also true that the debased language of these anti-Semitic diatribes pollutes the civility of the society in general and makes anti-Semitism more respectable in particular. "But if Jews want to worry about the potential of serious harm to their well-being," says Feder, "their attention needs to be directed to those who do have power in the country, and their complexions are white."

Feder does worry that American Jews can lose something vital to them in this controversy—their moral standards. "Sure, we can become part of the rest of the white population flitting between benign neglect and outright hatred of blacks. I now hear Jews talk about blacks in a way that would have been impossible just a few years ago; I'm talking about sophisticated, liberal Jews. What happened to compassion?"

Dr. Larry Lowenthal, Northeast Regional Director of the

American Jewish Committee, is sympathetic to Feder's view and also notes a decline of interest among Jews in black-Jewish dialogue. Lowenthal has devoted much of his professional energies these past years in exploring ways to keep that relationship going. He cautions, however, against underestimating the depth of black anti-Semitism by describing it as merely fringe. "Anyone who thinks so is making a serious mistake. I've been to Farrakhan rallies, and let me tell you, it's a truly frightening experience, especially after the media people leave and Farrakhan really lets loose. We have a great deal of ongoing research which indicates that a substantial majority of blacks consider Farrakhan a positive force in the African American community. There's definitely a problem here." But, Lowenthal insists that there is still a powerful residue of liberal commitment within the Jewish community to help a highly disadvantaged community. "It's the only way out of the morass."

Walk

The time has come to just walk away. In this third view, an approach gaining increasing acceptance, American Jews should declare, if only in their own minds, a separation between themselves and the African American community and go off to focus on their own concerns. This is the view of Jacob Mann. Mann works at a temporary employment agency in Chicago, and values his relationships with his African-American colleagues. But public communal exchanges, he believes, are another matter.

"In the first place, I'm not persuaded of the virtue of making loud public rebuttals every time some black anti-Semite delivers one of his bigoted speeches. The only result is that because of the publicity, the guy commands a larger speaking fee. Why make rich heroes of these bastards? But more importantly, I think it's time for Jews to say to blacks: 'Okay, guys, you want to dump on Israel. You want to pick on Jews here in this country. Carry on. It's your problem. Beating up on your best past ally and most likely future ally is sheer political stupidity. But it's your problem. We're out of here.' "

Mann, and any who agree with him, believe that nothing truly helpful can be achieved at the moment—the rhetoric is too raw, the enmity too exposed. Says Mann, "The whole array of institutional handshakes proclaiming the need for mutual understanding, the procession of official pronouncements, the academic conferences, the symposia, the cheerful newspaper stories is shrugged off by most Jews—and most African Americans, I believe—as self-important mechanical drills. Harmless, perhaps, but meaningless—no one pays attention, few take it seriously. The tension between the two communities is too deep to be washed away by these exchanges of platitudes."

Where does he think this separation will lead? "Who knows? Perhaps to reconciliation, perhaps to permanent divorce. But right now we need to go our separate ways."

This is not the complete story. The discussion above, and indeed, most of the books and articles written on the subject of blacks and Jews, describe the interaction of the two *communities,* or the interaction of individuals as members of their respective communities. But while Jews *qua* Jews may be having a hard time with blacks *qua* blacks, the situation is not nearly as tense between Jews and blacks when their ethnic identities are not in play.

This distinction is at once subtle but essential in understanding the attitude of American Jews toward blacks, other ethnic groups, and more generally, the limits and obligations of "communal thinking" in a diverse America.

CHAPTER EIGHT

The Virtual Jewish Community:
A Concluding Essay About Beginnings

> *. . . How, by the way, do we recognize the parochial? It is the point of view that invented the ugly and intolerable term "ethnic." It is the point of view that dismisses as parochial a civilization not one's own. And it is, sometimes, the point of view that characterizes Jews who, for whatever reasons, personal or political, are not much interested in Jewish ideas. Such persons (unlike most gentiles who have severed any serious connection with Christianity) call themselves "universalists." It is striking to observe that universalism of this sort is, however, the ultimate Jewish parochialism.*
>
> > Cynthia Ozick

> *Hansen's Law: What the son wishes to forget, the grandson wishes to remember.*

> *The mark between Jewish and American is a hyphen, not an equal sign.* Leonard Fine

> *I think of the remnants, the pitifully few remnants, of the once vibrant and creative Jewish culture in America. In some ways, tracing Jewish life in America is like walking through a bombed-out city, where skeletons of buildings mutely bear witness to the lives that once thrived there. In a way, the tragedy is greater for the destruction is self-inflicted, and those who deserted it do not lament the eradication of that rich cultural world.* Eddy Zemach

> *American history seems to show that a group cannot achieve "integration"—that is, equality—without first developing institutions which express and create a sense of its own distinctiveness.* Christopher Lasch

When in 1994 a lawyer in Phoenix advertised his legal practice on the Internet, net users reacted with immediate outrage followed by the most traditional of communal punishments: They banished him. This restoration of exile sparked some thoughts about the development of communities in cyberspace. And thoughts about Jews.

The association between the Jews, our oldest thriving community, and the information highway, home to our newest communities, may seem a stretch at first. But, upon reflection, one can see many strands tying the two together.

The medium may not be the entire message, but how we talk certainly informs what we talk about; modern communications technology is already shaping not just the means but also the content of current discourse. Jewish forums devoted to a vast array of Jewish topics already populate the Web, and, unquestionably, a twenty-first-century book on the private conversations of American Jews will read very differently than the one before you now. (Indeed, the future "book" on Jewish discussions may not be a book at all; what counts as a "private" conversation will mean something else as well.) Much more needs to be said, but much has already been said, about how the information age will change the American Jewish community. More intriguing, though less often noticed, is the connection going the other way: how Jews serve as a model for the communities of the future, both on and off the electronic highway.

Cyberspace neighborhoods are based on an affinity of interests, not local geography. People from all over the world cluster around electronic forums, newsgroups, and bulletin boards to talk about their common agenda, to trade information, intentions, and inevitably their irritations. Jews have been a community of global interests for nearly three thousand years, and throughout those millennia, with varying success, they have managed to keep their international conversation going while attending to their immediate demands. For all these years, the Jews have been practitioners of the modern slogan "think globally, act locally."

Our world now features a constant tug between the national and the international, the determined push toward one world and the opposite pull to the smaller units of nation, tribe, and clan. The persistence of nationalism is, indeed, *the* political surprise of the twentieth century. Despite the repeated predictions of its imminent demise, we have entered an era in which national movements blossomed all over the globe and nations that were supposed to have vanished, such as the Estonians, Corsicans, and Latvians, have reappeared after long slumbers. For better and worse, human beings, it is now clear, are driven to belong to distinct groups. At the same time, the world really *has* become a global village, of shared economies and shared tastes for movies, music, and McDonald's.

Managing the local-yet-global paradox isn't easy, and contemporary American Jews are particularly uncomfortable with this "international tribalism." The unease is, in fact, that old American Jewish bugaboo—the battle between universalism and particularism. If there is one central theme to all the private conversations of American Jews, it is this dilemma.

It was all much easier a generation or two ago. Back then, the devotion to bettering "humanity in general," the campaigns against prejudice, the fight for better labor conditions, human rights, and justice, support for the developing nations, all these wonderful universalist causes happened to coincide with the particularistic agenda of American Jews. No political dissonance here—you could be on the side of all these progressive movements and promote your self-interest at the same time. But now the conflict has set in. American Jews are no longer among the downtrodden, they don't have to fight their way into the universities, they have achieved their fair share of the economy, attained the social acceptance, and Israel is no longer the military underdog.

Working for the needs of others now often entails undercutting your own needs. Faced with this dilemma, American Jews have gone off in both directions. Some have opted for the "universal," convinced that national, tribal loyalties are reactionary and divisive at root. Enough of the hyphenations here in the United States too, they argue: The time has come for all to cast off their ethnic pasts and become "just Americans" of the future. Other Jews have chosen the other route and become "particularists" with a vengeance. With an unabashed chauvinism, they believe that society has moved, as it were, from the *me* generation to the *us* generation, and now it is each group out for itself. This is the reality, they say, and it's high time for Jews, too, to shed their savior role and start worrying about themselves.

American Jews realize that they have to get beyond this predicament. Neither approach makes any sense; one road leads to the disappearance of American Jewry in favor of some a-morphous larger culture, while the other road leads to a narrowing of Judaism that utterly distorts its essential spirit. In the introduction to this book I referred to the signature motto of the Jewish people, to be "a light to the nations." In fact, I suggest, a proper understanding of this maxim goes some way in solving this unnecessary dilemma. Here (if only in outline) is how we might better understand the future Jewish communal role among other communities. Let me begin with what Judaism is not about.

Judaism is not about teaching ethics to the world. Of course, Judaism offers a rich ethical tradition, a sophisticated sense of justice, and an inspiring commitment to compassion. But a cultivated code of ethics is not unique to Judaism—all venerable religions have their sustaining ethical insights. Traditional Judaism, as do all other religions, also poses principles that offend modern ethical sensibilities. The observant say too bad for modern sensibilities; the nonobservant say too bad for traditional Judaism; and the ubiquitous apologists scramble to reinterpret those principles to make them fit just fine with contemporary morality. The upshot is that while our moral values are grounded in our religious traditions, they are not, and, as philosophers since Plato have shown, cannot, be reduced to purely religious terms. Ethics and religion are not identical.

The same is true for Jewish spirituality. Judaism teaches profound lessons to the willing soul, and Jews have no need to go elsewhere for their spiritual sustenance. Indeed, the spiritual possibilities in Judaism have been undergoing an exciting renewal these past years as both new and ancient spiritual techniques are (re)discovered by Jews of all persuasions. But again, Judaism neither has sole possession of the spiritual life nor claims it; all religions teach a spirituality, for if not, they would have long withered away. Judaism has always recognized that people can reach spiritual heights by pursuing their own religious paths.

"Light unto nations" means, I suggest, just what it says: unto *nations,* not individuals. The exhortation is made not to individual Jews, but to the Jewish nation, which is told to be an illumination not to individuals, but to other nations. Jews are asked to be examples in the business of building community.

What's involved in building community? The first task is recognizing that you have responsibilities to fellow members of your group that you don't to those on the outside. These special loyalties do not shrink one's humanity but enlarge it. It's lovely to say all people are your brothers, but then where does that leave your "real" brother? To love someone is to make that individual singular in your life, distinct from the rest; by definition, one cannot love everyone. Our familial responsibilities and personal attachments, however, enrich our lives without demoting one's obligations to everyone else. That's true of communal associations as well. Consider the case of usury.

The Bible says that Jews who lend money or goods may not charge interest. The rabbis interpret that ruling as extending only to other Jews; non-Jews may be charged interest. Discriminatory? Hardly. Unlike Islam and many versions of Christianity, Judaism does not deem usury immoral. Jews are forbidden to take interest from one another because of communal concerns, not ethical ones. The Korean grocer on my corner understands this perfectly. He was able to obtain an interest-free loan from a communal lending service devoted to helping immigrant Korean entrepreneurs. Plainly, I have no right to feel snubbed if denied a similar interest-free loan from this organization. More generally: Jewish law requires Jews to go further to help fellow Jews than others—

when it comes to your own community, you need to do more. These social rules are therefore not immutable. Once the Jewish economy was up and running, the rabbis devised legal niceties to permit the taking of interest from other Jews as well as from non-Jews. Nor do these strictures vitiate obligations to all human beings—charity begins at home but doesn't end there. This two-tiered responsibility is not prejudice, not clannishness, but demonstrates an understanding of how community is sustained.

For reasons of history or theology or both, Judaism has never been triumphalist at its core. It does not seek to convert the world. It has its own communal agenda—the injunction to be a holy people—and allows other communities to define their own goals. In the cyber world ahead, we will develop new kinds of communities with radically new goals. What will remain is the need for inter-communal respect for each other's purposes.

Cyberspace will also alter the grounds of the current debate between American Jews who see Israel as the center of world Jewry and those who see an ongoing self-sustained American Judaism. The distance between Israel and American Jewish life will become increasingly blurred as technology shrinks space and time. The Jewish community of a Jew in Los Angeles will as easily include a Jew in Haifa as a Jew in San Francisco. A Jew in Skokie, Illinois, can have an interactive study session in Talmud on his computer and it matters little whether the lesson originates in New York or Jerusalem. Rapid transportation will allow more Jews to have homes in both countries. American Jews and Israeli Jews who want to live rich Jewish lives can see themselves in real terms as citizens of both cultures.

Turf, therefore, will be conceptual, not just material, and so will the ensuing borders. All communities will need to rethink tolerance, how to live and let live, how to allow others the full range of their expression without destroying one's own group's interest. Here, in the United States, the complexity is greater still. Most of us belong to several communities at once, and all American Jews are Americans too, full participants in the culture of the country. A supreme value of this culture is the right to personal choice. Any discussion of the future of the American Jewish community must include the ramifications of this ethos, for as sociologists repeatedly remind us, all Jews are now Jews by choice. No one has to be Jewish anymore. Indeed, no one has to belong to any ethnic group anymore.

Two opposing metaphors dominate America's self-image this century—the unicultural America of the melting pot, versus the multicultural America of the salad bowl. But these descriptions are not mutually exclusive. Both dishes are on the American plate. Americans can choose to live their lives as part of a subset community or in cultural anonymity. You can define yourself, say, as a Greek American, actively preserve your ethnic and religious identity and at the same time flourish professionally and socially. Most Americans can shun their community of origin (racial barriers, unfortunately, continue to be much more enduring) and join the great wash of other Americans who have also chosen to repudiate their respective ethnic origins.

The choice is not as easy, morally or personally, as it may seem. We cannot glibly assume, as so many do, that we are only obligated to do that which we agree to do. It is by no means obvious that Jews are only responsible to care for their Jewish heritage if they so choose. Some obligations are thrust on us,

259

whether we like it or not. Such responsibilities might include the "duties of kinship"; we have, for example, a greater prima facie duty to care for our sick parents than a stranger does. Perhaps American Jews—especially Jews, with their precarious history—must see themselves as the custodians of American Jewish culture and, as inheritors of that culture, have a duty to preserve it. Perhaps not. These are not easy questions.

This is also the primary challenge to all communities in the United States. Philosophical arguments aside, if you want people to stay within your community, you must persuade them that they should. American Jews have been dealing with this assignment for years, and the dwindling number of American Jews does not suggest that they have done very well. Each defection (and there are exceptions) is a loss both for the individual who leaves and for the Jewish people.

My immediate concern here has been the conversations of Jews who identify themselves as Jews. And here, too, there has been a decline—the American Jewish conversation is losing its edge, its substance. Too many American Jews, it must be said, are simply too Jewishly ignorant to contribute meaningfully to the dialogue. Membership has its privileges, but also its dues. The bicultural American Jew must be at home in two worlds, two histories, two politics. She can be inspired by Jefferson and master the Federalist Papers, but she also must know the history of Spanish Jewry and be familiar with Maimonides. This is the first time in the several thousand years of Jewish history that a majority of a Jewish community cannot read a Hebrew sentence, let alone speak a communal language. (As the importance of Israel for Jewry looms ever more central, and as communication and transportation between the two countries becomes ever more swift, the need for fluency in Hebrew will become even more vital for commited American Jews.)

Yet one remains optimistic about American Judaism, and for good reason. For all the ignorance at large, never has Jewish scholarship been as active and thriving. The number and quality of published monographs, articles, and scholarly books in Judaica are astounding. Jewish studies are taught in leading campuses across the country. American Jewish life is itself a focus of much research: There are almost one hundred local Jewish historical societies in North America. At the time of this writing, sixty-three professors at American universities consider American Jewish history their area of specialty. It is still too early to determine what the significant contribution of American Judaism has been to the story of the Jewish people. Some propose egalitarianism, the religious enfranchisement of women, others the respect for personal choice, still others the mass learning of Torah. Jewish history is very old, but American Jewish history is still very young, and only time will tell.

In his famous essay "Israel, the Ever-Dying People" Simon Rawidowicz wrote that "he who studies history will readily discover that there was hardly a generation in the Diaspora period which did not consider itself the final link in Israel's chain. Each always saw before it the abyss ready to swallow it up. . . . Each generation grieved not only for itself but also for the great past which was going to disappear forever, as well as for the future of unborn generations who would never see the light of day." Jews consistently manage to bury their undertakers. Listen in on the private conversations of American Jews, and you will hear the voices of a community in flux but confident. They asked Mae West for the secret of long life. ''Keep breathing,'' she said. The secret for the long life of the American Jewish community? Keep talking to one another.

Annotated Bibliography

American Jews are a self-conscious group, as attested by the constant flow of books, journals, and magazines devoted to its history, demography, politics, and beliefs. Keeping up is a full-time pursuit. The following are just some of the many books and scholarly studies that provided helpful background information for *Schmoozing*.

General Surveys of Contemporary American Judaism

The United States Census does not include a separate category for religious affiliation, so statistical and demographic data about Jews must come from other sources. These sources provide particularly pertinent information:

The American Jewish Yearbook. American Jewish Committee and Jewish Publication Society.
Kosmin, Barry, and S. P. Lachman. *One Nation Under God:*

Religion in Contemporary American Society. Rowan
& Littlefield, 1991.

Roberts, Sam. *Who We Are: A Portrait of America Based on
the Latest U.S. Census*. Times Books, 1993.

Excellent first stops for books on contemporary American Judaism include:

Holtz, Barry W., ed. *The Schocken Guide to Jewish Books*.
Schocken, 1992.

Sarna, Jonathan D., ed. *The American Jewish Experience*.
Holmes & Meier, 1986.

Wertheimer, Jack, ed. *The Modern Jewish Experience: A
Reader's Guide*. New York University Press, 1993.

Among the many first-rate histories of recent American Judaism, the following were invaluable:

Bershte, Sarah, and Allen Graubard. *Saving Remnants*. Free
Press, 1992.

Cohen, Steven M., and Charles Leibman. *Two Worlds of Judaism: The Israeli and American Experience*. Yale
University Press, 1990.

Dershowitz, Alan. *Chutzpah*. Little, Brown, 1991.

Fein, Leonard. *Where Are We Now? The Inner Life of American Jews*. Harper & Row, 1992.

Goldshieder, Calvin, ed. *The American Jewish Community:
Social Science Research and Policy Implications*.
Scholars Press, 1986.

Lipset, Seymour Martin, and Earl Raab, eds. *Jews and the New American Scene*. Harvard University Press, 1995.

Raab, Earl, ed. *American Jews in the 21st Century*. Scholars Press, 1991.

Shapiro, Edward S. *A Time for Healing: American Jewry Since World War II*. Johns Hopkins University Press, 1992.

Silberman, Charles. *A Certain People: American Jews and Their Lives Today*. Summit, 1985.

Sklare, Marshall. *Observing America's Jews*. Brandeis University Press, 1993.

Teutsch, David. *Imagining the Jewish Future*. State University of New York Press, 1992.

Wertheimer, Jack. *A People Divided: Judaism in Contemporary America*. Basic Books, 1993.

Whitfield, Stephen. *American Space, Jewish Time*. Archon Books, 1988.

Woocher, Jonathan S. *Sacred Survival : The Religion of American Jews*. Indiana University Press, 1986.

Jews and Money

Baron, Salo. In *Economic History of the Jews*, edited by Nachum Gross. Keter Publishing, 1985. Baron is one of the century's preeminent Jewish historians.

Birmingham, Stephen. *Our Crowd*. Harper & Row, 1971.

Christopher, Robert C. *Crashing the Gates: The DeWasping of America's Power*. Simon & Schuster, 1989.

Ehrlich, Judith Ramsey, and Barry J. Reinfeld. *The New Crowd: The Changing of the Jewish Guard on Wall Street*. Little, Brown, 1989.

Korman, Abraham. *The Outsiders: Jews and Corporate America*. Lexington Books, 1988.

Kosman, Barry, and Paul Ritterbrand, eds. *Contemporary Jewish Philanthropy in America*. Rowman & Littlefield, 1991.

Kotkin, Joel. *Tribes: How Race, Religion and Identity Determine Success in the New Global Economy*. Random House, 1993.

Krefetz, Gerald. *Jews and Money: The Myths and the Reality*. Ticknor & Fields, 1982.

Levine, Aaron. *Economic Public Policy and Jewish Law*. Ktav, 1993.

Lipset, Seymour Martin, ed. *American Pluralism and the Jewish Community*. Transaction Publishers, 1990.

Novak, David. *Jewish Social Ethics*. Oxford University Press, 1993.

Jews and Their Smarts

Feuer, Louis W. *The Scientific Intellectual: The Psychological & Sociological Origins of Modern Science*. Basic Books, 1963.

MacDonald, Kevin. *A People That Shall Dwell Alone: Judaism as Group Evolutionary Strategy*. Praeger, 1994.

This book suggests an intriguing sociobiological analysis of Jewish intelligence.

Patai, Raphael. *The Jewish Mind*. Charles Scribner, 1977. An often cited survey of the Jewish intellectual presence.

Ritterband, Paul, and H. S. Wechsler. *Jewish Learning in American Universities: The First Century*. Indiana University Press, 1994.

Roth, Cecil. *The Jewish Contribution to Civilization*. Harper & Brothers, 1940.

Simonton, Dean Keith. *Greatness: Who Makes History and Why*. Guilford Press, 1994.

Whitfield, Stephen. "The Jew as Wisdom Figure." *Modern Judaism* 13, no. 1, (1993).

Jews and Their Bodies

Biale, David. *Power and Powerlessness in Jewish History*. Schocken Books, 1986.

Diamond, Jared. "Who Are the Jews?" *Natural History,* Nov. 1993. Provocative articles on the genetic ties of Jews have also recently appeared in such scholarly journals as *Human Biology*.

Eilberg-Schwartz, Howard, ed. *People of the Body: Jews and Judaism from an Embodied Perspective*. State University of New York Press, 1992. The body has reemerged as a topic of major interest in contemporary Jewish scholarship—this is a pioneering work in this reinvestigation.

Gilman, Sandor. *The Jew's Body*. Routledge, 1991. Gilman's series of books on the "Jew as other" is indispensable reading for understanding contemporary Jewish self-image.

Levine, Peter. *Ellis Island to Ebbets Field: Sport and the American Jewish Experience*. Oxford University Press, 1993.

Slater, Robert. *Great Jews in Sports*. Jonathan David, 1992.

Wisse, Ruth R. *The Schlemiel as Modern Hero*. University of Chicago Press, 1971.

Jews and the Battle of the Sexes

Bayme, Steven, and Gladys Rosen, eds. *The Jewish Family and Jewish Continuity*. Ktav, 1994.

Biale, David. *Eros and the Jews: From Biblical Israel to Contemporary America*. Basic Books, 1992. An important and balanced historical survey of the attitude of Jews toward sex.

Biale, Rachel. *Women and Jewish Law: The Essential Texts, Their History, and Their Relevance for Today*. Schocken, 1995.

Booker, Janice. *The Jewish American Princess and Other Myths*. Shapolsky, 1991.

Boyarin, Daniel. *Carnal Israel: Reading Sex in Talmudic Culture*. University of California Press, 1993.

Cohen, Steven M., and Paula E. Hyman, eds. *The Jewish Family: Myths and Reality*. Holmes & Meier, 1986.

Harrowitz, Nancy, and Barbara Hyams, eds. *Jews and Gender: Responses to Otto Weininger.* Temple University Press, 1995.

Kraemer, David. *The Jewish Family: Metaphor and Memory.* Oxford University Press, 1989.

Mayer, Egon. *Love & Tradition: Marriage Between Jews and Christians.* Plenum Press, 1985.

Prell, Riv-Ellen. "Why Jewish Women Don't Sweat: Desire and Consumption in Postwar American Jewish Culture." In Eilberg-Schwartz.

The *Journal of Jewish Communal Service* (New York, National Conference of Jewish Communal Service) and the *Journal of Jewish Sociology* (London, W. Heinemann) are two of several journals that regularly contain articles on the changing Jewish family.

Traditional Jewish sources have much to say about the rules of sexual behavior—illuminating loci include Talmud Nedarim 20.b, Mainonidees *hilchot issurey biah,* 221.9, and Tosefot, Yevamot 34.b.

From Self-Criticism to Self-Loathing

Gay, Peter. *A Godless Jew: Freud, Atheism and the Making of Psychoanalysis.* Yale University Press, 1987.

Gilman, Sandor. *Jewish Self-hatred: Antisemitism and the Hidden Language of the Jews.* Johns Hopkins, 1986.

Gresser, Moshe. *Dual Allegiance: Freud as a Modern Jew.* State University of New York Press, 1994.

Leibowitz, Yeshayahu. In *Judaism, Human Values and the Jewish State,* edited by Eliezer Goldman. Harvard University Press, 1992.

Ostow, Mortimor. *Judaism and Psychoanalysis.* Ktav, 1982.

Siegel, R. J., and E. Cole, eds. *Jewish Women in Therapy: Seen but not Heard.* Harrington Park Press, 1990.

Wechsler, Harlan. *What's So Bad About Guilt?* Simon & Schuster, 1990.

Yerulsham, Yosef Hayim. *Freud's Moses: Judaism Terminable and Interminable.* Yale University Press, 1991.

Traitors

Each of the central topics of this chapter—the Holocaust, Israel, and apostasy—has, by now, its own library. The following list, therefore, can hardly be called representative. These particular books, however, were especially helpful for the specific aims of this chapter:

Alexander, Edward. *The Jewish Idea and Its Enemies: Personalities, Issues and Events.* Transaction Books, 1988.

Golan, Matti. *Kesef temurat dam: Yahadut Amerikah neged medinat Yisrael.* Israel: Kineret, 1992. A provocative Israeli attitude of an Israeli toward American Judaism.

Goldberg, J. J. *Jewish Power: Inside the American Jewish Establishment.* Addison-Wesley, 1996.

Roskies, David, ed. *The Literature of Destruction: Jewish Responses to Catastrophe.* Jewish Publishing Society, 1988.

Vital, David. *The Future of the Jews: A People at the Cross-roads*. Harvard University Press, 1990.

Jews on Non-Jews

Berkowitz, William. *Contemporary Christologies: A Jewish Response*. Paulist Press, 1980.

Berman, Paul, ed. *Blacks and Jews: Alliances and Arguments*. Delacorte, 1994.

Chanes, Jerome A., ed. *Antisemitism in America Today: Outspoken Experts Explode the Myths*. Carol Pub. Group, 1995.

Dinnerstein, Leonard. *Antisemitism in America*. Oxford University Press, 1994.

Ginsberg, Benjamin. *The Fatal Embrace: Jews and the State*. University of Chicago Press, 1993. There are many accounts of recent black-Jewish relationships—this book contains one of the more comprehensive narratives.

Jacobs, Steven L., ed. *Contemporary Christian Religious Responses to the Shoah*. University Press of America, 1993.

Lipstadt, Deborah E. *Denying the Holocaust: The Growing Assault on Truth and Memory*. Free Press, 1993. A classic of the genre and important for the present discussion.

Manuel, Frank. *The Broken Staff: Judaism Through Christian Eyes*. Harvard University Press, 1992.

Annotated Bibliography

Novak, David. *Jewish-Christian Dialogue: A Jewish Justification*. Oxford University Press, 1989.

Shahak, Israel. *Jewish History, Jewish Religion*. Pluto Press, 1994. This is a highly tendentious but provocative "exposé" of the Jewish attitude toward non-Jews.

Tobin, Gary. *Jewish Perceptions of Anti Semitism*. Plenum Press, 1988.

Weisbord, Robert, and Wallace Sillanpoa. *The Chief Rabbi, the Pope and the Holocaust: An Era in Vatican-Jewish Relationship*. Transaction Publishers, 1992.

Virtual Jews

With regard to the philosophical issues of Jewish identity in the century ahead, one anthology that deserves special notice is *Jewish Identity*, edited by David Theo Goldberg and Michael Krausz (Temple University Press, 1993). I'm indebted here to two articles in particular: "Custodians," by Eddy Zemach, and "Universalism and Particularism in Jewish Law: Making Sense of Political Loyalties," by Gordon Lafer.